Eastcliff

Eastcliff
HISTORY OF A HOME

Karen Fults Kaler

University of Minnesota Press
Minneapolis · London

Floor plans were drawn by Karen Kaler. Additional floor plans, photographs, and stories about Eastcliff are available at https://www.Karen-Kaler.com.

Published by the University of Minnesota Press
111 Third Avenue South, Suite 290
Minneapolis, MN 55401-2520
http://www.upress.umn.edu

ISBN 978-1-5179-1376-2 (hc)
ISBN 978-1-5179-1524-7 (pb)

Library of Congress record available at https://lccn.loc.gov/2022052452.

Printed in Canada on acid-free paper

The University of Minnesota is an equal-opportunity educator and employer.

30 29 28 27 26 25 24 23   10 9 8 7 6 5 4 3 2 1

Contents

Author's Note

Dedicated to Eric, the love of my life, and to all of those who have called Eastcliff home. Thank you for sharing your stories.

THIS BOOK IS A MEMOIR OF EASTCLIFF, and you may wonder if it is appropriate to consider the story of a home a "memoir." As of the one-hundredth anniversary of the house in 2022, ten families have lived in Eastcliff, each prominent enough in the Twin Cities to have their private lives covered by the press. Eastcliff is registered with the National Register of Historic Places (NRHP) for its architectural significance, but I believe a stronger case could be made for other NRHP criteria: the significance of related people and events in American history. *Eastcliff: History of a Home* is about the *life* of Eastcliff.

During the eight years I lived there, Eastcliff slowly revealed her secrets. Some architectural details demanded both love and attention (such as the perfect little acorn carved in the mantel), while others begged to be investigated. Guests to the house provided snippets of information, and long-told stories featured conflicting facts that I wanted to resolve and document.

As I listened to these stories, it sometimes seemed the house was telling her own tale. Meanwhile, I came to treasure the friendships and the stories of people who had previously lived in the house, and I was honored to share the same home. This book is about all the families who have lived in Eastcliff. It is also an inside look at what it is like to be the spouse of a university president, and I am grateful to the other presidential partners and family members who shared their experiences.

The Edward and Markell Brooks family members, who first donated the house to the University of Minnesota, deserve a full book of their own, and fortunately they already have one. *Turning the Leaves* was written in the early 1990s by Edward and Markell's daughters-in-law, Marney Brooks and Ginny Brooks, with some chapters written by each of the four Brooks children who grew up in the house: Conley, Edward (Ted), Anna Markell (Binky), and Dwight. That book was an invaluable source of information for me, as were conversations with Conley Brooks Jr. I am also appreciative of the

University of Minnesota Archives, the University Engineering Records archive, and the library of the Minnesota Historical Society (where there is a wing named for ancestors of the Eastcliff Brooks family). I utilized countless online resources, chief among them the University of Minnesota Libraries' digital conservancy. The articles about the many Eastcliff families in the local newspapers of the time may have been a burden to the residents but they were a benefit to my research.

I am grateful for the stories from and about the Brooks family. Foremost among these stories are those from Binky Brooks, who grew up in the house, and Barbara Bentson, who grew up in the neighborhood. Each shared her vivid recollections, and each became my dear friend. My curiosity about the stories, and concern about documenting them, led Binky to tell me that I was the one to write Eastcliff's story. I am honored to do so.

Preface

THE WOBBLY FOUNDATION OF MEMORIES

Every home has a story.

Your home has a story. If you live in an apartment, you may be one of many chapters in your home's story. If you live in a new house, you are chapter 1. Most houses have been homes to previous residents and will be homes to others after the current residents move on. Some people hire house historians to research the history of their homes, while others buy a house and are not even interested in meeting the previous owners at closing. Being more inclined to the former than the latter, I wonder . . . is imagining someone else living in your home too intimate for some? Is it akin to meeting your partner's former love?

For most houses, you can discover who previously made the house a home, but you can't learn much about their lives. Eastcliff is an exception. In her century of existence, Eastcliff has been home to ten prominent families. I will introduce you to each of them.

I have become intrigued by memories. For all of us, some life events remain vivid while others disappear entirely. Even people suffering from dementia will remember surprising bits from the past.

But even the most vivid memories are tricky. What people seem to misremember the most are details about dates, or their own age when an event occurred. (This reinforces my belief that age is relative.) I've noticed that someone will tell me a story remembered in great detail, but then struggle when I ask *when* it happened. Multiple people may agree on the details of a story but disagree about the date. Remembering the order of events in a repeated sequence seems problematic, as does remembering how many times an event occurred.

I have, rightly and wrongly, been credited with an exceptional memory. My dear husband vividly remembers events from our sons' childhoods that happened when he wasn't present. (I like to think it's because I'm such a good storyteller.) Telling a story reinforces a memory, and that memory remains while others fade.

I remember many events of my life in detail, and from a very early age, but then I have no recollection of some events that my sister remembers clearly. My sister, brother, and I may all have different memories of the same event. I have asked my mother to be arbiter of some stories, but so far she hasn't had any definitive rulings as she remembers things differently from each of us. My mother enjoys telling stories; she insists I was speaking in full sentences and having conversations with imaginary friends at eight months old. The essence of this story is true: I was an imaginative and loquacious child. (To the surprise of . . . well, no one. Some things don't change.) Nonetheless, eight-month-old babies don't speak in sentences. I did the research. I found my baby book that she kept contemporaneously. (I trust what was written when it happened more than tricky memories.) There it was: I spoke in full sentences at *eighteen* months, not eight. Yes, that's still early to talk in sentences. The essence remains true; the devil is in the details.

This book relies heavily on memories. The stories are all true, but the details are sometimes elusive. Accuracy is very important to me, and I have researched factual data to verify stories, but I must accept that my best is all I can do. My procedure for story verification has been to seek contemporaneous written corroboration—or rebuttal. If, in my opinion, discrepancies remain, I will tell you what they are. While I have discovered a few "myth-busting" stories, they are really just corrections of the details.

I was five years into writing this book when the University of Minnesota Foundation located a videotape I had been hoping to find for several years. In 1998, then presidential partner Judy Yudof and Sally Wheaton Huscha, the interior designer who designed the Eastcliff renovation in 1997, interviewed Conley, Ted, and Binky Brooks (the three remaining of the four Brooks siblings who grew up in Eastcliff and donated the house to the University of Minnesota), along with Conley's wife and eldest son, Marney and Conley Jr., and Ted's wife, Ginny. Hearing the Brookses' memories of growing up in Eastcliff, I recognized the same patterns I see in my own family. The same stories are remembered again and again, with more or less detail, so those stories have remained and others have faded or disappeared. The three siblings would all remember each story but might remember details differently. When asked about the date, or their ages at the time of a story, all three had different guesses.

The close relationship between the three Brooks siblings was heartwarming to see. Although I already knew from their writing and Binky's stories that they were close, I had never met Ted, so this was my first experience with three of the siblings together. The youngest, Dwight, had passed away two years before the video, and they all felt his loss. While telling a story about Dwight, they each remembered details differently.

They recalled that Dwight rebuilt a Lysander airplane, which was a major feat. Binky explained that the original manufacturer of the Lysander tires remade tires for him. Conley gently corrected that he recalled that they couldn't find any tires that fit, but then found that a certain British motorcycle had the same size tires. That motorcycle manufacturer custom-made the tires for the plane. The essence was there; the detail was remembered differently.

You'll read a marvelous story in this book that Binky told me about "Bridget." Later, her nephew, Conley Jr., relayed an additional unlikely detail of this story to me. I later asked Binky about it, and she agreeably suggested the new detail might be true, even though she didn't know anything about it herself.

The participants in the 1998 interview retold stories that appeared in the book about Brooks family history, *Turning the Leaves*, which reinforced my belief that telling a story keeps it alive in memory. Conley and Ted were eager for Binky to tell the stories about Helen Keller and Katharine Hepburn, and they had nothing to add to those stories. I had already heard the stories from Binky, fifteen years after the videotape was created. The stories had different and additional details in the videotape; the dates were still unclear. Ted added a story about Hall-of-Fame Yankees catcher Bill Dickey that Binky had not shared with me. Ted and Binky both clearly recalled the people who were more meaningful to each of them.

So it goes with memories.

Eastcliff from the front lawn. Photograph by Patrick O'Leary. Courtesy of University Photographer records, University of Minnesota Archives.

1
Welcome to Eastcliff

WHEN WE LIVED AT EASTCLIFF, visitors were curious about the house and its history, and they often asked me questions.

GUEST: *What's it like living here? It must be wonderful!*
ME (smiling): *It is wonderful! It's such an honor to live here.*
GUEST: *What's it like living here? It must be awful having to entertain all the time.*
ME (smiling): *We actually love to entertain here. It's such a beautiful, welcoming home and we enjoy sharing it. Since we really* live *upstairs (over the store, so to speak), I never have to worry about picking up my shoes from under the living room sofa.*
GUEST: *Did you know a previous president lost his job over fixing this house?*
ME (trying to hide my grimace with a smile): *Um . . . Well . . . Yes, that is quite a story.*
GUEST: *What's it* really *like living here?*
ME (conspiratorially): *We love it, but it can be complicated.*
GUEST (sheepishly): *Thank you for inviting me. I have been driving/riding my bicycle/walking by here for years and I've always wanted to see inside.*
ME: *We're so glad you are here! Let me give you a mini tour:*

> *The house was designed by Clarence Johnston Jr. in 1921 and built in 1921 and 1922 for the Edward Brooks family. They raised their four children here. In 1958, four years after Mr. Brooks passed away, Mrs. Brooks donated the house to the University of Minnesota.*
>
> *In the foyer are photographs of all the presidential families who have lived here. The elevator was added during the Yudof administration—I agree, people often don't know it's an elevator when we use it as an overflow coat room.*
>
> *The first room to the right as you enter through the foyer is the walnut den. It is one of the few rooms with the original finishes. Isn't the paneling beautiful? Mr. Brooks was in the lumber business and chose to use a variety of woods throughout the house.*
>
> *Through the den is the restroom I call the "Tracy Moos powder room." Tracy has shared many delightful stories about the house.*
>
> *To the left after the foyer is the dining room. It was originally much smaller but was remodeled during the Keller administration and now seats around forty people. Through the far door at the back of the dining room is a family kitchen, then a large catering kitchen and an office. In 1922, there was an attached garage. In 1930, the garage was converted into maids' quarters, two guest rooms were added upstairs, and a detached carriage house was built as a five-stall garage with an apartment on the second floor. In the 1980s, the maids' quarters were remodeled into a catering kitchen and a small office.*
>
> *Next on the right is my favorite room. The peacock room is exquisite. See the door and ceiling paintings of peacock feathers? Step inside to appreciate*

the large peacock painted in gold on the back of the mirrored walls. The room is used as a bar. The house was built during Prohibition, and there are some interesting stories about that.

Walking forward, to the right is the beautiful grand staircase. In the entry to the right is a small telephone room. See how the door is curved to match the curve of the wall? Of course, back in the Brookses' time there was just one telephone in the house. Marney Brown Brooks, the wife of eldest son Conley, charmingly recalled calling her parents from there to tell them she was engaged.

Straight ahead under the stair landing is the front door. To the left of that door are stairs that descend to the basement space that the Brooks family called the amusement room.

Now we are in the living room. These photographs on the piano are of the Brooks family in front of the fireplace. Most of the art in this room is on loan from the University's Weisman Art Museum.

Finally, the garden room. It was originally a screened porch but now is glassed in and used year-round. Binky Brooks told me that Helen Keller sat in a hanging sofa swing right over there. Binky also talked about Katharine Hepburn's visit.

There's a beautiful Tiffany lamp from the museum in the corner. We turn it off and on with a remote control, as we aren't allowed to touch it.

Here to the left in the garden room is the reason I told you I would give you this "mini" tour. It's Eastcliff in miniature! Around 1940, Mrs. Brooks worked with a local miniaturist to make replicas of Eastcliff furnishings. Barbara Bentson, who had watched them work on the tiny furniture when she was a young girl, worked with family members and coordinated the creation of a new dollhouse, which was made from 2008 to 2010. See the gorgeous staircase? And the peacock room? The second floor shows the top of the stairs, on one side are the master bedroom and sitting room. One the other side is Binky's room. Eastcliff is L-shaped, with the bedrooms for the three sons, Conley, Ted, and Dwight down the hall from Binky's room in the west to east wing. And at the end of that hall are two guest rooms now called the Waller Suite. However, because the dollhouse doesn't include the other wing, the furniture in the miniature attic represents the boys' rooms.

See the dining room chairs? Mrs. Brooks needlepointed chair covers with the initials of each family member. The originals are still with the Brooks family. That tiny rug has eighty thousand stitches. The two paintings in the dining room are copies of family paintings made in the 1940s. Almost every item in the dollhouse has a story.

Do you see the miniature dog? If you look through the window behind the miniature house, the graves of three of the Brooks dogs are on the other side of the raspberry bushes. Rusty is the most famous—you may have heard his story. In the back corner of the yard is a sculpture garden where the Brooks family had a tennis court. Next to that is the swimming pool, with more wonderful stories . . .

THE FRONT FAÇADE

Houses, like people, change over time. Eastcliff has been renovated during her one hundred years, but the feature that has changed the least is the front façade. Its grand presence along Mississippi River Boulevard looks much as it did in 1922.

The house is colonial revival, a popular architectural style in the United States in the early twentieth century, which revived the Georgian colonial style. Georgian architecture was popular in Great Britain during the reigns of Kings George I, II, III, and IV (1714 to 1830) and was the most prevalent architecture style in the British colonies during the eighteenth century. Hallmarks of the style are symmetry and proportion based on classical architecture and formal, classical details.

Eastcliff displays elements of that style, with a prominent main entrance and four sets of shuttered double-hung windows, eight-over-eight on the first floor and shorter six-over-six on the second floor. The paneled front door is framed by sidelights and topped with a carved fan panel. Above the door is a projecting two-story bay window and above that a peaked roof extends well above the dentilled cornice and the roof shingled with cedar shakes. Two chimneys extend higher still.

In an unexpected and delightful variation on the symmetry associated with the style, the entrance of the house is well off-center with one set of windows to the left of the front door and three sets on the right. The result is both elegant and distinctive. The façade further extends to the left (north) with a porte cochére (a covered entry large enough that vehicles could formerly pass through and discharge passengers under cover) and to the right (south) with sunrooms on both floors. Another wing extends back from the left side of the house, resulting in an L-shaped footprint.

The front door and shutters on the white wooden clapboard house are dark green. Both the upper and lower shutters are louvered, and each of the taller lower shutters includes an oval cutout of a parrot silhouette.

Since 1922, the driveway has been rerouted; the screens in the south sunroom have been replaced with casement windows; trees have come and gone. Yet so few changes have occurred that visitors from nearly a century ago could look at the house today and know that it is Eastcliff.

Front entrance, circa 1925. Courtesy of the Brooks family; Eastcliff records, University of Minnesota Archives.

The Brooks Family and the Building of Eastcliff

In March 1915, Markell Conley wrote in her diary about her imagined future home:

> I want it to be on a hill, overlooking meadows, a lake, and other hills, it must have large windows on three sides, East and West particularly, so that I will be able to see the sun rise and set. And a grand piano will be in one corner, near a window, so that I will be able to feel the beauty of the seasons more fully by seeing the great outdoors.[1]

That same year, sixteen-year-old Markell met twenty-six-year-old Edward Brooks in church. When Edward first saw Markell, he stated, "That's the girl I'm going to marry." He agreed with the popular assessment that she was "the embodiment of grace and loveliness."[2]

Five years later, after she had attended Smith College and he had served in World War I in France, Edward's prediction came true. Edward and Markell married in April 1920.

In 1921, the newlyweds decided they wanted their family home to be in the Georgian colonial style, inspired by the home of family friends in Upstate New York. According to daughter Binky's recollection, Edward hired his friend, Howie, to design their house. The two friends were both born in 1888 so were around thirty-three years old when Edward asked for help with a house for himself and his pregnant wife.

This description sounds like a rather ambitious undertaking for two young men, until you consider that Edward Brooks was already a successful businessman at Brooks-Scanlon, the lumber company established by his father. Edward was also well traveled, having visited Louisiana, British Columbia, Oregon, Chicago, and New York on business, and he had traveled to Hawaii, Japan, China, and the Philippines with his mother and brother. He served as a captain in the U.S. Army Corps of Engineers in France.

Edward's friend, Howard, had a similarly impressive pedigree. He was Clarence Howard Johnston Jr., already a successful architect working in the firm of his father, prominent Minnesota architect Clarence Howard Johnston Sr.

Clarence Johnston Sr. was a nineteen-year-old draughtsman in a St. Paul architectural firm when he and a friend and coworker, Cass Gilbert, enrolled at the Massachusetts Institute of Technology to study architecture.

The Brooks family in the 1930s. Courtesy of the Brooks family.

Johnston dropped out before graduating because of financial concerns and went straight to work as an architect. By the time of his son's birth, he was established in his own firm in St. Paul. He served as Minnesota State Architect from 1901 until 1931, while continuing his own private architectural business. He designed dozens of buildings for the University of Minnesota, most notably Northrop Auditorium, Walter Library, and Williams Arena. Cass Gilbert also had a very successful career, including creating the master design for the Minneapolis location of the University of Minnesota campus, the Minnesota State Capitol, and the United States Supreme Court building.

Johnston Sr. also designed many houses, beginning with his first commission at age twenty-four: a mansion for William Merriam, who was later elected governor of Minnesota. He designed numerous stately homes along St. Paul's Summit Avenue. His most famous residential design was Glensheen, a thirty-nine-room mansion overlooking Lake Superior in Duluth. Glensheen, like Eastcliff, was also donated to the University of Minnesota.[3]

Clarence Howard Johnston Jr., known to his friends as Howie, joined his father's firm, Clarence Johnston Architects.[4] He was designing much of the firm's residential work in the 1920s. In the late 1930s, shortly after his father's death, Clarence Johnston Jr. designed many buildings for the

EASTCLIFF FAMILIES (1922–2022)

Names in parentheses are presidents' children who did not live at Eastcliff. Many of the maids, cooks, and caretakers who lived at Eastcliff are included in the text but not in this list.

Edward Brooks (lived at Eastcliff 1922–54)
Markell Conley Brooks (lived at Eastcliff 1922–60)
  Conley Brooks (born 1921; lived at Eastcliff 1922–40, 1945–46)
    Margaret "Marney" Brown Brooks (married Conley 1944; lived at Eastcliff 1945–46)
    Conley Brooks Jr. (born 1945; lived at Eastcliff 1945–46)
  Edward "Ted" Brooks Jr. (born 1922; lived at Eastcliff 1922–40)
  Anna Markell "Binky" Brooks (born 1926; lived at Eastcliff 1926–45)
  Dwight Frederick Brooks II (born 1929; lived at Eastcliff 1929–48)

O. Meredith "Met" Wilson (lived at Eastcliff 1961–67)
Marian Wilson Wilson (lived at Eastcliff 1961–67)
  (Owen Meredith Wilson Jr.)
  Constance "Connie" Wilson (lived part-time at Eastcliff, 1961–65)
  Mary Ann Wilson (lived at Eastcliff 1961–67)
  John Wilson (lived at Eastcliff 1961–67)
  David Wilson (lived at Eastcliff 1961–67)
  Margaret Wilson (lived at Eastcliff 1961–67)

Malcolm C. Moos (lived at Eastcliff 1967–74)
Margaret "Tracy" Gager Moos (lived at Eastcliff 1967–74)
  Malcolm Moos Jr. (lived at Eastcliff 1967–70)
  Katherine "Kathy" Moos (lived at Eastcliff 1967–74)
  Grant Moos (lived at Eastcliff 1967–74)
  Ann "Simmy" Moos (lived at Eastcliff 1967–74)
  Margaret "Margie" Moos (lived at Eastcliff 1967–74)

C. Peter Magrath (lived at Eastcliff 1974–84)
Sandra Hughes Magrath (lived at Eastcliff 1974–76)
  (Valerie Magrath)
Diane Skomars Magrath (lived at Eastcliff 1978–84)
  Monette Magrath (lived at Eastcliff 1978–84)

Kenneth H. Keller (lived at Eastcliff 1985–88)
Bonita Sindelir (lived at Eastcliff 1985–88)
    (Andrew "Drew" Keller)
    (Paul Keller)
    Jesse Keller (lived at Eastcliff 1985–88)
    (Alexandra Amelie Keller)

Nils Hasselmo (lived at Eastcliff 1988–97)
Patricia "Pat" Tillberg Hasselmo (lived at Eastcliff 1989–97)
    (Michael Hasselmo)
    (Peter Hasselmo)
    Anna Hasselmo (lived part-time at Eastcliff 1989–93,
        full-time 1993–96)

Mark G. Yudof (lived at Eastcliff 1997–2002)
Judith "Judy" Gomel Yudof (lived at Eastcliff 1997–2002)
    (Seth Yudof)
    (Samara Yudof)

Robert H. Bruininks (lived at Eastcliff 2002–11)
Susan Hagstrum (lived at Eastcliff 2002–11)
    (Robert "Todd" Bruininks)
    (Brian Bruininks)
    (Brett Bruininks)

Eric W. Kaler (lived at Eastcliff 2011–19)
Karen Fults Kaler (lived at Eastcliff 2011–19)
    (Charles "Charlie" Kaler)
    Samuel "Sam" Kaler (lived at Eastcliff 2014–16)

Joan T. A. Gabel (lived at Eastcliff since 2019)
Gary Gabel (lived at Eastcliff since 2020)
    (Grace Gabel)
    Jack Gabel (lived at Eastcliff 2020–21)
    Luke Gabel (lived at Eastcliff 2020–21)

Architectural drawing of Eastcliff, 1921. Courtesy of the Northwest Architectural Archives.

University of Minnesota, including Coffman Memorial Union and the James Ford Bell Museum of Natural History.

Johnston's 1921 drawings of Eastcliff are stored in the engineering records archives at the University. Although I had seen scans, viewing the actual ink on linen paper was a revelation. The drawings are in excellent condition and absolutely beautiful.[5] All the details are included, down to the leaded glass pattern in the sidelight windows by the front door, the wrought iron holdbacks for the shutters, and the sawed patterns on the shutters.

Edward and Markell had purchased land at 176 North River Boulevard for ninety dollars per frontage foot (for a total of $20,700) on May 20, 1921. The firm Lindstrom and Anderson began construction on the house in 1921 and finished in 1922. The cost of construction was about thirty thousand dollars.

In September 1921, a month after the architectural plans were drawn, Edward and Markell welcomed their first son and named him Conley, Markell's maiden name. A second son, Edward Jr. (always known as Ted), was born in November 1922, shortly after the family moved into the house.

Daughter Anna Markell (always called Binky) arrived in October 1926 and was followed by the youngest son, Dwight Frederick II (named for his paternal grandfather) in April 1929.

The young family was growing quickly. Edward and Markell hired Johnston a second time in the mid-1920s to design an addition to the house. The porches on the first and second floors at the south end of the house were extended to the east, enlarging the porch on the first floor and adding a den above it on the second floor. In 1930, they hired Johnston the third time for a major addition to accommodate their larger family and guests. A detached carriage house was built, including a five-stall garage, a second-floor apartment, and a full basement. The former garage space in the main house was remodeled into maids' quarters, with the two rooms above (the previous maids' quarters) enlarged and remodeled for guests. A new pool was built farther back on the lot with a bathhouse behind the pool. Even accounting for inflation, the 1930 addition cost more than the original structure.[6]

As with most homes, there were continual improvements through the years, including

Preparing the site, 1921. Page from Markell's scrapbook; courtesy of the Brooks family.

Eastcliff completed, 1922. Page from Markell's scrapbook; courtesy of the Brooks family.

decorating and bedroom renovations. Improvement costs were recorded in a handwritten ledger in Edward's careful penmanship.

St. Paul's Architecture: A History describes Eastcliff as "designed in the piece-by-piece manner of incessantly remodeled English country houses,"[7] which explains the off-center entry and asymmetry of the original design and why the design retained its grace when it was remodeled. The book calls

Eastcliff "one of the most complex renditions" of the colonial American revival style in St. Paul:

> Although the main façade of the Edward and Markell Brooks House is built up with proper Colonial detail, the building sprawls out onto its lot in a manner befitting the picturesque tradition. Every bay and wing of the house is infused with the classical proportions and refined vocabulary of the style's New England origins, and yet each of these appears as a separate pavilion joined almost haphazardly to the main mass.[8]

A Gift to the University of Minnesota

Edward Brooks died in 1954. The four Brooks children were adults with homes of their own in December 1958 when the family signed the agreement to donate Eastcliff to the University of Minnesota. At the time of the gift, Mrs. Brooks stated, "We have always had a high regard for the University of Minnesota, and we feel the house to be eminently suitable as a residence for the President and an appropriate setting for entertaining the visitors who come to Minnesota as guests of the University." Ever generous, the Brooks family has continued to contribute to the preservation of Eastcliff for more than sixty years. Expressing the appreciation of the University's Board of Regents for "this magnificent gift to the University from the Brooks family," Ray J. Quinlivan, chairman of the Board of Regents, commented, "This will be a distinguished home for University presidents for many years to come."[9]

Markell remained living in Eastcliff while her new home was being built. She hired another renowned Minnesota architect, Ralph Rapson, to design her house on Long Lake in Orono, Minnesota, near the home of son Conley and his family. Markell convinced Rapson to design the house based on Japanese architecture. He named the 6,119-square-foot home Longshadows. Although the midcentury modern, glass-walled house is completely different from Eastcliff, the homes have a few commonalities: Longshadows also has wood built-ins in most rooms, multiple (five) wood-burning fireplaces, a sunroom, wood flooring, and a basement recreation room with a fireplace. Rapson was quoted in the Brooks family history *Turning the Leaves* as saying, "Of all the houses I have ever designed, fifty or sixty in all, this was the most complete marriage of an architect and a client that I have ever experienced." Markell moved into Longshadows in 1960 and lived there the remainder of her life.[10]

Ninety Years Later

As we walked through the door, three dogs greeted us. I immediately felt welcomed.

It was November 2010 and my husband had just been elected the sixteenth president of the University of Minnesota. Robert (Bob) Bruininks, the fifteenth president, and his wife, Susan Hagstrum, had graciously invited us to Eastcliff, their home and the University's official residence. I had looked at photos of the house online and, when we arrived, I saw it was as beautiful as those photographs, but it was also comfortable—a real home.

I knew our lives would be changing completely. We had been associated with universities for all of our then thirty-two-year marriage. I had enjoyed the academic life and hosting associated dinners and receptions when Eric was a professor, department chair, dean, and provost. I had paid attention to presidents and their spouses; Louise Roselle at the University of Delaware was a role model for me, as was President David Roselle for Eric. I knew the demands on Eric would be enormous, but I also knew that he was as perfect for the job as a person could be. I wasn't worried about serving in the role of presidential partner.

Eric and I had met in the summer of 1979 while he was a chemical engineering graduate student at the University of Minnesota. I was studying art in graduate school at the University of Tennessee and worked in the residence hall where he stayed during a summer internship. Six months later, we married and I joined him in Minnesota. In the years before his graduation, I always said that Minnesota was cold but the people were warm. I felt that

At home on the terrace at Eastcliff. Courtesy of A & M Photography.

Minnesotans were my kind of people. Between leaving in 1982 and returning in 2011, when people asked me how I tolerated Minnesota's infamous
winters, I would say I would be happy to return to Minnesota—if we had a
garage. I could afford appropriate clothing this time around. And when we
visited Eastcliff that first time, I made note that it was warm, literally as well
as figuratively. I wasn't worried about living in Minnesota.

Our two sons were born in Seattle but grew up during our eighteen years
in Delaware. They were both in college when we moved to Long Island. As
we planned our return to Minnesota, one was finishing law school and the
other was finishing his undergraduate degree. This was a good time for a
transition for our family. I wasn't worried about Charlie and Sam.

What did worry me were our two Spanish water dogs. Mo and Lida were
part of our family. Could they be accommodated in such an elegant home?
When three large dogs bounded up to us as we first entered Eastcliff, I
was relieved. All three were flat-coated retrievers. One belonged to the Bru-
ininks/Hagstrum family and the other two were the house manager's dogs.
Dogs are part of the history of the house as well. Graves of three dogs are
in the yard, complete with markers. I heard that it was a stipulation in the
donation of the house that the graves were not to be disturbed.[11]

The Brooks family, whom I had heard called "lumber barons," were impressive people. They had built this gracious home, raised four children here,
and had live-in servants. Mrs. Brooks wore evening gowns for dinner. The
seven previous presidents and their families were also impressive. Living in
this historic house seemed a bit intimidating, but the home was warm and
welcoming, built on a human scale. The little pet cemetery made the Brooks
family seem more approachable.

Our first event as hosts at Eastcliff came two months before we moved
in. Bob Bruininks was giving the commencement address at the University
of Minnesota Crookston campus. He and Susan would therefore be out of
town on May 6, 2011, when the Dalai Lama would visit Eastcliff—*when the
Dalai Lama would visit Eastcliff!* When I heard that, my first thought was
to be heartbroken for Bob and Susan. How could they stand to miss it?
Then I learned that they had previously met His Holiness the Dalai Lama.
The strong Tibetan community in the Twin Cities, his doctors at the
Mayo Clinic, and the Nobel Peace Prize Forum Minneapolis, among other
Minnesota assets, kept him coming back to the state. This would be the
Dalai Lama's second visit to Eastcliff. For his earlier visit in 2001, during
the Yudof administration, strings of prayer flags were extended from the

roof of the home to the fence and gates. The Dalai Lama had rested in the walnut den before speaking in front of the fireplace. The second visit in 2011, called "One Heart, One Mind, One Universe," would be cohosted by the Center for Spirituality and Healing at the University of Minnesota and the Tibetan American Foundation of Minnesota.[12] Bob and Susan would attend a luncheon with the Dalai Lama the day after the Eastcliff event.

When I arrived at Eastcliff, Tibetans in national costumes were already lining the street in front of the residence. I met some of the other guests as we waited for His Holiness to arrive, and among the most special guests to me were members of the Brooks family. I met Binky Brooks for the first time that day, as well as Conley Brook's wife, Marney. Marney was accompanied by daughter Marlow and Marlow's daughter, Markell Kiefer.

In a foreshadowing of our life to come, Eric's schedule was so packed that day that the guest of honor arrived on the Eastcliff terrace before Eric did. Provost Tom Sullivan gave welcoming remarks, and then Eric gave brief remarks, mentioning how pleased the University of Minnesota was to offer His Holiness an honorary degree. The Dalai Lama then took off the *khata* (a ceremonial scarf common in Tibetan Buddhism) that he was wearing and placed it around Eric's neck. The director of the Center for Spirituality and Healing spoke briefly. The Center had provided more *khatas* for the guests, and His Holiness put them on each of us with a brief blessing. Then he spoke. While I don't remember his exact words, he spoke about compassion and forgiveness. I recall thinking that in spite of all the suffering he had seen in the world, he embodied joy. What I most recall was that when he laughed, he giggled.

I was in awe that even before I moved in, Eastcliff had given me the opportunity to meet the Dalai Lama.

176 MISSISSIPPI RIVER BOULEVARD NORTH

Eastcliff, on the eastern bluff of the Mississippi River, sits on a 1.6-acre lot, which is the equivalent of ten city lots. The property is bordered by Dayton Avenue to the north, Otis Avenue to the east, and a neighboring residence to the south. A white open-picket fence surrounds the entire property. The front yard was more heavily wooded when the house was built, with high-canopy oak and elm trees. Today, there is a rolling expanse of lawn, rimmed with a variety of trees, bushes, and flowering plants. Large oak trees are near the north and south edges of the property. A tall steel sculpture by Katherine E. Nash adds a modern touch.

Eastcliff. Photograph by Patrick O'Leary. Courtesy of University Photographer records, University of Minnesota Archives.

The house is L-shaped; looking at the building from the front left corner could give you the mistaken impression that it is gargantuan. While it is quite large, at nearly 10,000 square feet including the basement, it's not as big as it may seem. A two-story carriage house that includes a five-bay garage sits on the back left corner of the lot, and a pool and bathhouse are at the back center of the lot.

The street address is 176 Mississippi River Boulevard North. The North here is important: guests, and packages, sometimes arrive at 176 South Mississippi River Boulevard. (One guest angrily suggested that I should have put a sign in the yard of the wrong house. I gently replied that the map enclosed with her invitation might have been helpful.) The house is a bit difficult to find as it sits on an offshoot of the boulevard. In 1990, work on the new Lake Street/Marshall Avenue bridge required rerouting Mississippi River Boulevard immediately south of the bridge. The main boulevard now goes under the bridge, with a fork (going diagonally south to northeast in front of Eastcliff) that connects to Dayton Avenue. This rerouting resulted in the removal of the original Eastcliff driveway from the boulevard, and a circular driveway was added off Dayton Avenue.

In mid-June 2011, Eric, the dogs, and I drove from Long Island, New York, to Minnesota. (Actually, Eric drove. I navigated. The dogs slept.) We arrived at Eastcliff on Father's Day. The Bruininks/Hagstrums had moved out weeks earlier to allow for construction projects to proceed. Eric, true to form, began working without pay two weeks before his official start day. During those two weeks, although I unpacked and Eric worked, we had more free time in the evenings than we would have for the rest of the year.

We were sitting by the pool one evening, facing west through the pool gate arbor covered with roses. A vine-covered stone wall is to the right, and the house is across an expanse of green lawn. It was breathtakingly beautiful. Eric said to me, "Can you believe we are required to live here?" We looked at each other, and in unison described our situation with the sentiment we use when we revel in our good fortune: "This does not suck."

A few days later, we sat in the front yard looking up the river. Eric said how nice it was that Minneapolis had built the skyline for our enjoyment. The bank (or east "cliff") of the river is too high for the river to be really visible from the house or yard (just a sliver can be seen from a master bedroom window), but river and skyline views are available all along the boulevard and we never tired of those views.

The mighty Mississippi is one of the world's greatest rivers and the fourth longest. It begins in my adopted state of Minnesota and forms the western boundary of my home state of Tennessee. I loved living by the Mississippi River. Shortly before we moved out of Eastcliff, I took our then two-year-old granddaughter, who calls me "Amma," down along the river, where we threw rocks into the water. As we walked back, she spotted Eastcliff and called out, "Hi, Amma's house. We went to the river. I love you, Amma's house!" I shared her sentiment and enthusiasm.

Marian Wilson, the first presidential spouse to live in Eastcliff, described the house as "about the most beautiful home that I know, in its setting on the river. And the wonderful warmth of the house as both a family home and an official residence are things that were very, very gratifying."[13]

The Moos family were the second presidential family to live in the house. Tracy Moos grew up in Washington, D.C., near the Potomac. When her family moved into Eastcliff, Tracy said the first thing they did was discover the Mississippi River, as they had lived along a river in Tarrytown, New York. The river helped them feel at home. Tracy enjoyed the Mississippi River so much that when she couldn't find any passenger trips on the river, she convinced a sand and gravel barge operator to take her and some University guests for a ride—an event the barge company was then happy to continue for many years.

From the Brooks family album. Courtesy of the Brooks family.

The west side of Mississippi River Boulevard is parkland, with heavily used walking trails, bike paths, and magnificent river views. Eagles and hawks occasionally soar overhead. Coyote sightings concern owners of small dogs; the wild turkeys wobbling along are more comical visitors. The east side of the boulevard showcases a variety of stately homes, from unique mid-sized homes to grand mansions. I was surprised to discover that the oldest homes along the river were built decades after other houses in the neighborhood. Why wasn't the real estate along the river always the most prized location? Why was Eastcliff's ideal setting still undeveloped in 1921?

While Mississippi River Boulevard had its beginning in 1887,[14] when the St. Paul Board of Park Commissioners began plans to purchase the bluff land by the river to preserve it, the first portion of the boulevard wasn't built until 1900. High sale prices, dam construction, and a depression delayed the full purchase of the land for the road until 1907. The boulevard was fully in use in 1909, with a watchman to guard against vandalism.

The other streets bordering the Eastcliff property had been in use long before the boulevard. Dayton Avenue[15] became a residential street in 1854, although our end near the river was still an uninhabited dirt road in 1921 when Edward and Markell Brooks began building their home. Their property, and all the properties along the boulevard at that time, extended back to Otis Avenue.[16]

Edward and Markell were said to have considered the property to be out in the boondocks, even though Edward had been born and raised only a mile and a half away at 455 Lynnhurst Avenue in St. Paul. Markell's first home, from her birth in 1899, was at 438 Laurel Avenue in St. Paul. Two and a half years earlier, F. Scott Fitzgerald had been born on the same block in his parents' apartment at 481 Laurel Avenue. The Fitzgeralds moved before Markell was born.

Edward and Markell's son Ted wrote that, during his childhood, the whistle of a tugboat towing barges upriver was a sign that the ice on the river had melted; spring was arriving and school would be out soon. Another favorite sound of his childhood was of the early morning streetcars coming across the old Lake Street bridge and climbing uphill on Marshall Avenue.[17]

When Eastcliff was built there was already a golf course just across Marshall Avenue. The Town and Country Club also considered its location to be "out in the country," between the "towns" of Minneapolis and St. Paul. The club had moved to its Marshall Avenue location in 1890 and built the golf course in 1893. It is one of the nation's oldest golf courses.

The Town and Country Club was the site of bobsledding, sleigh rides, and dancing in its early years. F. Scott Fitzgerald would visit the club for hot chocolate and bobsledding parties nearly a decade before Eastcliff was

View from the front lawn. Photograph by Patrick O'Leary. Courtesy of
University Photographer records, University of Minnesota Archives.

built. Fitzgerald famously met his first great love, Ginevra King, at the club
in 1915. In 1919, Fitzgerald was living at 599 Summit Avenue, four miles from
the Eastcliff property, while he wrote *This Side of Paradise,* his first published
novel. The Fitzgeralds continued living in St. Paul and White Bear Lake,
Minnesota, through 1922, but I don't know of any occasion when they would
have met the Brooks family.

Eastcliff is located below St. Anthony Falls on the stretch of the river
known as the gorge—the only gorge along the Mississippi River. Bluffs crowd
in against the river, allowing little room for a floodplain. The Brooks family
named their home Eastcliff because of its location on the bluff. Nearby,
Shadow Falls is in a small tributary valley that necessitates a sharp bend in
the boulevard.

When Eastcliff was built, the river wasn't the beautiful attraction that
it is today. There were no eagles flying above looking for fish, for there were
very few fish in the river. The Twin Cities had grown rapidly and, beginning
in 1880, sewer lines emptied directly into the river. When locks and dams
were built at St. Anthony Falls and at Ford Parkway in 1917, the sewage no
longer "disappeared." In 1938, St. Paul opened the first wastewater treatment
plant in a major city on the Mississippi River. Within two years fish had
returned to the river. By 1960, the growing Twin Cities population necessi-
tated secondary water treatment and multiple plants. The Clean Water Act
of 1972 called for the river to be swimmable and fishable. As a consequence,
the eagle population rebounded remarkably. In 1963, there were only 417

nesting pairs of bald eagles in the lower forty-eight states; in 2007, there were 11,000. That year, Minnesota had 1,300 nesting pairs, more than any other state except Alaska.

In June 2014, at the annual Friends of Eastcliff Garden Party, a University of Minnesota Raptor Center eagle, Maxine, was on display in the backyard at Eastcliff. Maxine had arrived at the Raptor Center with a shoulder injury that could not be rehabilitated, but she had the personality and temperament to become an iconic education bird for the center. As Maxine sat on her perch in the sculpture garden, two guests at the event (Linda and David Felker) noticed Max was staring intently at the sky. As they watched, another eagle eventually came close enough to be in human view, soaring high over Eastcliff.

The Eastcliff property is now part of a national park. In 1988, Congress established a seventy-two-mile corridor along the river as the Mississippi National River and Recreation Area (MNRRA), a unit of the National Park System. Unlike a typical park, the park service owns only sixty-seven acres of the 54,000 acres within the borders. The park includes visitor centers and museums that highlight the history and science of the Mississippi River, city parks, regional parks, a state park, a national wildlife refuge, state scientific and natural areas, as well as many private homes and businesses.

When establishing the park, Congress stated:

1. The Mississippi River Corridor within the Saint Paul–Minneapolis Metropolitan Area represents a nationally significant historical, recreational, scenic, cultural, natural, economic, and scientific resource.
2. There is a national interest in the preservation, protection, and enhancement of these resources for the benefit of the people of the United States.

It is a popular misconception that pollution and crime only get worse over time. The Mississippi River is cleaner and healthier today than it was a hundred years ago, and St. Paul is safer now than the city was in the 1930s. I regularly see eagles flying along the Mississippi River: the sight never fails to fill me with wonder and optimism that humans can repair the damages we have caused.

THE SIDE ENTRY AND FOYER

Official Residence of Presidents

When we lived at Eastcliff, we entered the house through the back service door, but nearly all guests enter through the porte cochère door. Only a few enter through the front door. After Mississippi River Boulevard was rerouted in 1990, a circular driveway and pedestrian gate were added off Dayton Avenue, so the only approach to the house is from the side. Even during the years when the Brooks family lived at Eastcliff, the porte cochère door was used much more frequently than the one in the front. At the time, cars could drive up to it to let passengers out. It is still called the porte cochère door, even though the area under the roof was turned into a brick patio in 1991. At that time the entryway was also made accessible per the ADA (Americans with Disabilities Act).

Entering the home through the side entry, you may notice a brass plaque to the right of the door certifying Eastcliff's inclusion in the National Register of Historic Places. Coming inside, you first enter a small vestibule. Originally there was a door on the left opening to an interior hallway. That space became an open coat room in a 1980s renovation, and then part of the shaft for an elevator that was added in 2001.

On the wall surrounding the elevator door, there are photographs of each of the University families who have lived in the house. While Peter Magrath was president, his wife Diane Skomars Magrath wanted to honor the house's history as a family home. She framed a photograph of the Brooks family and displayed it in the walnut den, along with photographs of the next three families to live in Eastcliff. During the Hasselmo administration, photographs of the Brooks family and the four previous presidential families were displayed in the living room. As the number of presidential families increased (we were the eighth), presidential photographs were moved to the foyer, and the Brooks family photograph was displayed on the piano.

The first photograph is of Owen Meredith "Met" Wilson, the ninth president of the University of Minnesota, his wife Marian, and their family. The Wilson family moved into Eastcliff in 1961, just one month after John F. Kennedy's inauguration as U.S. president. There is a hint of Minnesota's own Camelot in the newspaper coverage of Marian Wilson moving into the

Side entry, circa 1925. Courtesy of the Brooks family; Eastcliff records, University of Minnesota Archives.

The O. Meredith Wilson family in 1964. The Wilsons were the first University of Minnesota presidential family to reside in Eastcliff. Eastcliff records, University of Minnesota Archives.

big white house on Mississippi River Boulevard. With four well-behaved Wilson children living at home (two more were away at college), the family appeared to have stepped out of the television set from the popular show *Father Knows Best*. The Wilson photograph, from 1964, shows the full family, including the first grandchild, posed in front of the Eastcliff fireplace.

The next photograph is of Malcolm and Tracy Moos and their five children. The Moos family moved into Eastcliff in 1967, during the turbulent years of the Vietnam War and a year before the assassination of Martin Luther King Jr. The photograph of the family, taken early in the presidency, portrays attitudes typical of children ages seven to fourteen who were made to dress up and pose for a family portrait. They had many adventures at Eastcliff.

A photograph of Peter and Diane Magrath with their young daughter on the front lawn follows. Peter Magrath moved into Eastcliff the month before Richard Nixon resigned the U.S. presidency in 1974. He remained through the Ford and Carter years, and through most of Ronald Reagan's first term. Peter and Diane were married in front of the Eastcliff fireplace.

The photograph of Ken Keller and Bonita Sindelir shows them in a quiet moment with their young son. The Keller tenure at Eastcliff, which began in 1985, was contained within Reagan's second term and was dominated by house construction.

Peter, Diane, and Monette Magrath at Eastcliff. Eastcliff records, University of Minnesota Archives.

Nils Hasselmo moved into Eastcliff in 1988, the year that George H. W. Bush called for "a kinder, gentler nation." President Bush later said he wanted to make American families "more like the Waltons and less like the Simpsons." The photograph of the Hasselmo family portrays the close ties exemplified by the television Waltons, with Nils and Pat, their three children, spouses, and grandchildren on the Eastcliff lawn.

Mark and Judy Yudof are pictured on campus after their arrival in 1997. Mark and Judy were living at Eastcliff on September 11, 2001, during the terrorist attacks on America at the World Trade Center Towers in New York and the Pentagon. Judy was in New York City that day, visiting their daughter.

Bob Bruininks and Susan Hagstrum moved into Eastcliff in 2002, during George W. Bush's first term, and Bob was at the helm of the University during the Great Recession. The University continued to struggle with the state legislature's disinvestment in the University long after the U.S. economy had recovered. The Bruininks/Hagstrum photograph, taken in front of Eastcliff, includes their dog, Dunbar.

Eric and I are shown in a photograph with beloved University mascot Goldy Gopher. The photograph was taken at an event at the McNamara Alumni Center. Barack Obama was president of the United States during most of the Kaler tenure at Eastcliff, which began in 2011.

Joan Gabel became the University's seventeenth president in 2019, during the polarization of the Trump presidency. Two nationwide crises arrived early in her presidency: the worldwide coronavirus pandemic and the sorrow and outrage over the horrific murder of George Floyd in Minneapolis. The Gabel family portrait was taken at their daughter's wedding in Washington State, within a few weeks of Joan becoming president. It shows Joan and Gary Gabel and their three children, as well as Joan's father and Gary's mother.

The Pillsbury Mansion

Since President Wilson was the ninth president of the University and the first to live at Eastcliff, I wondered where the first eight had lived. I knew that the University of Minnesota was founded as a preparatory school in 1851, seven years before Minnesota became a state, but its first president, William Watts Folwell, wasn't inaugurated until 1869. The school had closed for a time during the Civil War due to financial difficulties, and it reopened in 1867 largely as a result of the Morrill Land-Grant Act of 1862 and the work of John Sargent Pillsbury. Pillsbury, not Folwell, is known as the "Father of the University": John Sargent Pillsbury was a Regent of the University from 1863 (before there was a president) until 1901. In 1877, shortly after being elected governor of Minnesota, John Sargent Pillsbury and his wife, Mahala, built a four-story, yellow-brick house near the University of Minnesota campus at 1005 Fifth Street Southeast, Minneapolis (at the corner of Fifth Street and Tenth Avenue Southeast). The Pillsburys' daughter Susan May Pillsbury married Fred Snyder in the home. Fred Snyder later became the longest serving Regent at the University, serving from 1912 until 1951.

When President Folwell and his wife, Sarah Heywood Folwell, arrived in 1869, they were offered a wing of a campus building, Old Main, as a home.[18] The quarters were already occupied—with "turkeys in one room, hay in

The Pillsbury mansion. Courtesy of University of Minnesota Archives Photograph Collection.

another, and wood in a third."[19] The Folwells chose to rent elsewhere. In the summer of 1878, they bought what was known as the Moulton at 1020 Fifth Street Southeast in Minneapolis. This house was built the year before the Pillsbury house and was right across the street. The Folwells entertained at the Moulton during his presidency and lived there the rest of their lives until she died in 1921 and he in 1929.

When Cyrus Northrop became the University's second president in 1884, he and his wife, Anna Elizabeth Warren Northrop, along with their two children, moved into a house around the corner from the Folwells and the Pillsburys, at 519 Tenth Avenue Southeast, Minneapolis. The Northrops lived in that house throughout his twenty-seven-year presidency and afterward, until both passed away in 1922.

In 1901, John Sargent Pillsbury died. His family continued to live in the Pillsbury mansion for ten years. In 1911, they leased the house for a dollar a year to the University to serve as the official residence for the University president, just in time for the arrival of the University's third president. For eleven years, the first three presidents of the University lived on the same block near the campus.

George Edgar Vincent, his wife, Louisa Palmer Vincent, and their children were the first University of Minnesota presidential family to live in the official residence. The house became the center of University activity. Mrs. Vincent used the third floor during the day as a gymnasium for faculty wives.

The gymnasium became a ballroom in the evening, when undergraduates were invited over to dance to piano music. Mrs. Vincent later converted the gymnasium/ballroom into a theater. She was active in the new University of Minnesota Faculty Women's Club (now University of Minnesota Women's Club) and wrote a play that was performed at the Shubert Theatre for the club's fundraiser to support female students.

When Marion Burton, a former Congregational pastor, became president in 1917, the first two presidents still lived a few steps away. All three former presidents were at his inauguration ceremony. President Burton and his wife, Nina Moses Burton, served the University and lived in the official residence until 1920, when he became the president of the University of Michigan. Like Mrs. Vincent, Mrs. Burton had been active in the University of Minnesota Faculty Women's Club, and she encouraged the formation of a similar club at Michigan.

Lotus D. Coffman was dean of education at the University when he was elected the fifth president in 1920. He and his wife, Mary Farrell Coffman, moved into the official residence and entertained there regularly, including annual faculty receptions inside the residence and receptions on the lawn for graduating seniors. The Coffmans' daughter, Catherine, was married in the house. Coffman died in the residence in September 1938, while serving in his eighteenth year as president.

Guy Stanton Ford had been dean of the graduate school at Minnesota for twenty-five years when he was elected president in 1938. He had known all five previous presidents and served as acting president in 1931 when President Coffman traveled to Australia and New Zealand, and again in 1937–38 when Coffman was ill. The Board of Regents set President Ford's salary at fifteen thousand dollars per year "plus pay for a caretaker at the large residence which the University maintained for its president at 1005 Fifth Street S.E." Among the events Ford and his wife, Grace Ellis Ford, hosted at the official residence was a reception for all seniors on Cap and Gown Day. Ford served as president only three years before he reached the University retirement age of sixty-eight.

Walter Coffey was dean of agriculture at the University when he was asked to serve as acting president after a failed national search for Ford's successor. He was elected president a few months later as the nation and the University became involved in World War II. War Department courses brought five thousand trainees to campus. President Coffey's wife, Jennie Lardner Coffey, like her predecessors in the role, was active in the University of Minnesota Faculty Women's Club, hosting the annual meeting at the official residence. The club was heavily involved in war-related assistance projects, including bandage preparation and work with the Red Cross.

In 1945, the Pillsbury mansion was deeded to the University outright by the Pillsbury heirs. The University had been leasing the president's official residence for thirty-two years and, since it wasn't owned by the University, there had been no renovation. James Lewis Morrill was elected the eighth president of the University in 1945, and the house was remodeled before President Morrill and his wife, Freda Rhodes Morrill, fully moved in. The yellow brick was repainted off-white as the house was updated inside and out. The house was transformed from its original modern gothic to nineteenth-century New Orleans style. Events at the mansion during the Morrill time included an annual Alumnae Club fall tea. During Morrill's fifteen-year tenure, the enrollment grew so that many of the large faculty and student receptions no longer fit in the residence and those events were discontinued or moved elsewhere.

When Eastcliff was donated to the University, an article in the *Minneapolis Star* stated:

> It is to the credit of the state and the university that so many Minnesotans have had the interests of the university at heart. The gift of the Brooks house, following by thirteen years the gift of the Pillsbury heirs, is another testimony to the high regard in which Minnesotans hold their university. It is a regard that has not been misplaced.[20]

Mrs. Brooks continued to live in Eastcliff until her house on Long Lake was finished. When O. Meredith Wilson became president in July 1960, the Wilson family moved into the former Pillsbury mansion. They entertained there, including a dinner party for Sir Tyrone and Lady Judith Guthrie to encourage them to locate the Guthrie Theater in Minnesota. (The University theater department has been closely connected to the Guthrie Theater since its beginning.)

After about eight months, the Wilson family moved into Eastcliff—and Eastcliff became the official residence of University of Minnesota presidents. The Pillsbury mansion stood empty. It was razed in 1964 so the site could be used for the Pillsbury Court Apartments, which provide housing for University faculty. A dining room table and two chandeliers from the Pillsbury mansion were moved to Eastcliff.

As I sought to learn more about University of Minnesota presidents' spouses, I couldn't find even the names of all the spouses documented together. While I planned to include them in this book, I mentioned the lack of information to University historian Ann Pflaum. She took on the project and published an article in *Minnesota Alumni* magazine.

PRESIDENTS OF THE UNIVERSITY OF MINNESOTA AND THEIR PARTNERS

1869–1884	William Watts Folwell and Sarah H. Folwell
1884–1911	Cyrus Northrop and Elizabeth Warren Northrop
1911–1917	George Edgar Vincent and Louise Palmer Vincent
1917–1920	Marion Burton and Nina Moses Burton
1920–1938	Lotus D. Coffman and Mary Emma Farrell Coffman
1938–1941	Guy Stanton Ford and Grace V. Ellis Ford
1941–1945	Walter Coffey and Jennie Crisler Lardner Coffey
1945–1960	James Lewis Morrill and Freda Rhodes Morrill
1960–1967	O. Meredith Wilson and Marian Wilson
1967–1974	Malcolm Moos and Margaret Tracy Moos
1974–1984	C. Peter Magrath and Sandra Magrath (1974–76); and Diane Skomars Magrath (1978–84)
1985–88	Kenneth H. Keller and Bonita F. Sindelir
1988–97	Nils Hasselmo and Patricia Tillberg Hasselmo
1997–2002	Mark G. Yudof and Judy Yudof
2002–2011	Robert H. Bruininks and Susan Hagstrum
2011–2019	Eric W. Kaler and Karen Fults Kaler
2019–	Joan T. A. Gabel and Gary Gabel

Looking toward the living room from the side entry.
Photograph by Patrick O'Leary. Courtesy of University
Photographer records, University of Minnesota Archives.

2

Gangsters, Weddings, and Celebrities

WALKING INTO EASTCLIFF FROM THE SIDE DOOR through the foyer, you can see straight ahead past two doorways and a front hall (to the right), through double doors straight ahead into the living room. The dining room is on the left. The first door to the right is the walnut den, and there is a small half bath at the back of the walnut den. Next to the walnut den is another door to the right, leading to the peacock room. The hall then opens to the right to the front entry and grand staircase. Straight ahead is the living room, followed by the garden room.

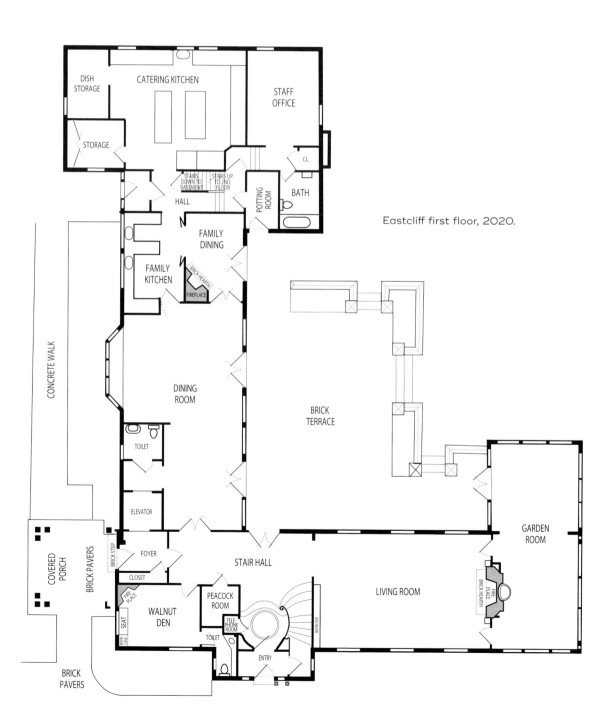

Eastcliff first floor, 2020.

THE WALNUT DEN

The walnut den remains little changed since the paneling was added early in the life of the house. The walls are completely covered in dark walnut and cherry in a double-raised square pattern, and the ceiling is beamed with walnut. The 1921 architectural drawings for the house indicate oak flooring; the floor is now terra cotta tile. Between the original drawing and construction, the brick fireplace was moved to the corner. Mr. Brooks used this room as a private library and filled it with books, maps, and trophies.

I always told visitors that the handsome paneling in the den "reflects the Brooks family lumber heritage." Edward Brooks's paternal grandparents, Sheldon (1811–1883) and Jeannette (1814–1894), with their sons, George, Lester, Dwight, and Anson, moved from Redfield, New York, to the Minnesota territory in 1856, two years before statehood. Sheldon helped plat and settle the town of Beaver in Winona County in southeastern Minnesota and was elected to the second state legislature of Minnesota in 1859. Sheldon bought and sold wheat and then entered the grain elevator business in Minneiska in late 1861. Son George died of typhoid that year. In 1873, Sheldon's three remaining sons formed the Brooks Brothers partnership to carry on the businesses of their father. These businesses included lumber, banking, a flour mill, and the Brooks Elevator Company, which owned thirty-three grain elevators.[1]

Dwight F. Brooks (1849–1930) married Anna Keys in Winona in 1875, obtained his medical degree in 1876, and practiced medicine in Minneiska while continuing in the family businesses. It has been noted that he neither had hobbies nor took vacations—and little wonder, as he excelled at two demanding professions concurrently.

Around 1900, the Brooks Brothers sold the grain elevators and focused on lumber. The brother known as "Dr. Dwight" related later that he was at a lumber auction in Brainerd, Minnesota, and one man kept outbidding everyone else. Dwight Brooks met the high bidder, M. J. "Joe" Scanlon, after the auction. In 1901, the Brooks brothers and Scanlon collaborated to form Brooks–Scanlon Lumber Company.[2] The Brooks–Scanlon mill near Cloquet, Minnesota, was considered the largest white pine mill in the world. Dr. Dwight and Joe Scanlon expanded the business into Louisiana; Florida; Oregon; the Bahamas; Cuba; and British Columbia, Canada.

The walnut den, during the Bruininks administration. Photograph by Patrick O'Leary. Courtesy of University Photographer records, University of Minnesota Archives.

Dr. Dwight and Anna Brooks had three sons, Harry, Sheldon "Sam," and Edward, and all three joined the family businesses. Harry ran the Brooks–Scanlon lumber manufacturing firm in Bend, Oregon. Sam managed the Powell River Company Limited, owner of the largest single newsprint mill in the world, in Vancouver, British Columbia. Edward oversaw all operations from the Minneapolis headquarters. Edward later became president of Brooks-Scanlon Incorporated, and senior director of the Powell River Company.

Dr. Dwight was a member of the Masonic Fraternity and Past Master of the Minneiska Lodge. He was a member of the Urban League of Chicago and the Minneapolis Club. He was known to be intelligent, honest, and unassuming. His grandchildren remembered him as a quiet man who always wore a black fedora hat. He was also known to be quite frugal. When he and Joe Scanlon traveled together, Dwight would take a single berth on the train while Joe traveled in the spacious private accommodations known as a drawing room. Joe would stay in the best hotel, while Dwight would choose a modest hotel nearby. Dwight had only one known extravagance, but it was major one. In 1923, he purchased the Gates mansion in Minneapolis.

The Gates mansion was built by Charles Gilbert Gates, who was the son of John Warne Gates, an industrialist who first made his fortune promoting and manufacturing barbed wire. Charles Gates commissioned the home for his bride, Florence. It was the largest private residence ever built in Minneapolis. The 1913 construction costs were said to be more than the then astronomical amount of one million dollars (nearly $30 million in 2022). The 38,000-square-foot Italian renaissance style home, at 2501 Lake of the Isles Parkway East, was built of the finest materials, imported from around the world. There was an elevator. There were eighteen telephones. The mansion was particularly notable as it was said to be the first private home to have air conditioning installed.

Dwight Brooks bought the Gates mansion for $150,000. He called it his Italian villa and had his daughter-in-law Markell furnish the house lavishly and beautifully. He gave her carte blanche to buy whatever she wanted, including sending a buyer to Europe to purchase Aubusson rugs and furniture. Dr. Dwight maintained a staff, who lived in a corner of the third floor, to keep the house in perfect condition. Charitable organizations were given use of the mansion for fundraising events.[3] Dwight never spent a night in the house, remaining in the home in Merriam Park, St. Paul, where he had lived with Anna. (She had died in 1920, before he bought the mansion.) Dr. Dwight died in 1930, leaving an estate of over six million dollars.

Gates Mansion. Photograph courtesy of the Minnesota Historical Society.

In 1933, Edward Brooks tried to sell the Gates mansion, but couldn't find a buyer; the upkeep and taxes were too costly. (It was estimated that the annual maintenance cost was $60,000.) Several charitable organizations considered accepting it as a donation, but then refused. The Brooks estate couldn't *give* the house away. Edward, as executor, had to have the mansion razed. Smaller houses were built on the site.

Did seeing that grand house torn down haunt Edward and Markell? It's impossible to say for certain, but twenty-five years later Markell Brooks commented to her family that she knew she could readily sell Eastcliff to a developer who would tear down the house to build on the site. Instead, she donated Eastcliff to the University of Minnesota.

THE PEACOCK ROOM

Gangsters in the Neighborhood

The peacock room, approximately four by six feet, was designed in 1921 as a telephone booth. In 1930 the room was remodeled as a "ladies' room." During that remodel, artist Frank Post designed the peacock decoration, for which he was paid $350. E. Henricke was paid $104 to paint the ceiling. Costs also included $329.80 to Pittsburg Glass and $424.50 to Nelson Lundblad Company for gold-leaf mirrors and silver for the eglomise (reverse painted) walls. Nelson Lundblad was a painting contractor, and it seems that company created the specialized mirror painting based on Frank Post's design.[4]

Next to the walnut den is the peacock room, my favorite room in the house. It's very small: standing in the center, I could reach out my hands and almost touch each wall (not that I would—I might leave fingerprints). When the door is closed, you would assume the room is a closet. But open the door and you will see what a magazine article in 1931 described as a "unique little modernistic powder room done by that local genius of modern art, Frank Post."[5]

The inside of the door features a peacock-tail design painted in teal greens, blues, and metallic gold with coral accents. The curved ceiling is similarly adorned. There are two art deco light fixtures accented with metal peacock feathers. On first glance, the smoked mirror walls appear to have abstract designs painted in gold leaf on the back of the glass prior to

Glimpse into the peacock room from the foyer. Photograph by Patrick O'Leary. Courtesy of University Photographer records, University of Minnesota Archives.

silvering. The walls are beautiful, but you must step inside to fully appreciate them.

On the right mirrored wall is a giant peacock. He is about five feet tall, shown standing on a hill so that his head is about seven feet above the floor. His wings are spread to cover the walls to his left and right. The right wall contains the door; the mirrored back wall is actually double doors that open to reveal shelves. On the wall opposite the peacock, peacock feathers outline a mirror. Below the mirror is a countertop of black onyx with gold veins. An octagonal sink is recessed into the countertop to the right of the mirror.

Like the presidential families before us, we used the peacock room as a bar. The shelves contain an ample assortment of glasses and bottles that are hidden when the doors are closed. In 2017, I hosted a reception at Eastcliff for artist Harriet Bart to promote donations to fund an exhibition catalogue of her retrospective at the University's art museum, and she displayed one of her exquisite pieces in a vitrine in the peacock room: it was fitting to display this work of art inside a work of art.

I was told that the peacock room was designed to be a powder room, with a sink and a mirror (no toilet). The original eighteenth-century powder rooms were used for powdering wigs. In the 1920s, powder rooms were where women touched up their makeup. The beautiful peacock room stimulates conversation, and guests shared anecdotes about it. One guest asked me when we took the toilet out. When I explained that there is a half bath behind this room, accessible through the walnut den, she insisted that she had used the toilet (that never existed) in the peacock room. Well, I hope not.

A woman with a deep knowledge of the history of Eastcliff told me that Mr. Brooks delighted in the peacock room and enjoyed showing it to guests. Another guest looked at the peacock bar and told me that St. Paul had an interesting history during Prohibition. He implied the room was a hidden bar. It seemed to me that the room was designed to look like a closet in order to remain hidden. The shelves were behind doors to further conceal its function, while its disguise as a powder room covered up the fact that the sink was for mixing drinks. Since Eastcliff was built during Prohibition, I became curious about the history of the neighborhood during that time.

Bank Robberies and Kidnappings

I discovered that in the 1930s, John Dillinger and his gang had a weapons depot in the Town and Country Apartments, just three blocks from Eastcliff and across Marshall Avenue from the site of F. Scott Fitzgerald's sledding parties in the 1920s. Ma Barker and her sons rented an apartment on Marshall Avenue, two blocks away from Eastcliff.

Three miles south of Eastcliff was the Hollyhocks Club, one of the oldest buildings on Mississippi River Boulevard. It is now a private residence, but during the early 1930s it was run by Jack Peifer as an elegant speakeasy. It was known to be a gangster hangout for members of the John Dillinger and Barker–Karpis gangs, among others.

Alvin "Creepy" Karpis, J. Edgar Hoover's Public Enemy Number One, declared:

> Of all the Midwest cities, the one I knew best was St. Paul, and it was a crooks' haven. Every criminal of importance in the 1930s made his home at one time or another in St. Paul. If you were looking for a guy you hadn't seen for a few months, you usually thought of two places—prison or St. Paul. If he wasn't locked up in one, he was probably hanging out in the other. St. Paul was a good spot for both pleasure and business. You could relax in its joints and speakeasies without any fear of arrest, and when you were planning a score, you could have your pick of all the top men at all the top crimes.[6]

What part did Prohibition play in this? The Eighteenth Amendment establishing Prohibition, which outlawed the manufacture and sale of alcoholic beverages, passed in 1919. The Volstead Act, named for its author, Congressman Andrew John Volstead of Granite Falls, Minnesota, was enacted in 1920 to enforce Prohibition. Ironically, Volstead's home state was well positioned to be a center of bootlegging. The 547 miles of unguarded border between northern Minnesota and Canada provided easy paths for illegal importation, and St. Paul's strong railroad system helped with distribution. German immigrants had established more than one hundred breweries in Minnesota and at least one, Schmidt Brewery, continued to make regular beer under the guise of nonalcoholic beer. The University of Minnesota's Northern Dent No. 13 corn was grown (and illegally distilled) in Stearns County. The grain was said to be of such high quality that the moonshine was branded Minnesota 13 and earned the reputation of being superior to the whiskey available prior to Prohibition.

Disregard for Prohibition during the Roaring Twenties may have led to a more general disrespect for laws among the public, and the lack of legal alcohol gave criminals a business opportunity. Yet the foundation for St. Paul's status as a sanctuary for criminals had been established many years prior to the passage of Prohibition. A later FBI memo explained succinctly why criminals had gravitated toward St. Paul:

> This city was a haven for criminals. The citizenry knew it, the hoodlums knew it, and every police officer in the city knew it. Hoodlums from the entire United States knew that they could come into St. Paul, make their presence known to the Chief of Police, and stay here with immunity, provided they committed no crimes in the city.[7]

This corruption, known as the O'Connor system, was decades in the making. The system was named for John J. O'Connor, St. Paul police chief from 1890 to 1912 and 1914 to 1920, and continued after his tenure. The widespread corruption begun under Chief O'Connor included police bribery, tolerance of gambling and money laundering, and police providing tips to criminals. The system allowed criminals to rob banks nearby as long as they didn't rob banks in St. Paul. In 1932, forty-three bank robberies (twenty-one percent of all bank robberies in the United States) occurred in Minnesota, with many additional robberies in North Dakota and Wisconsin. That year, the Barker–Karpis gang murdered three people in a Minneapolis bank robbery. They did not rob any banks in St. Paul.

Bootlegging, gambling, and money laundering were exceptions to the "no crimes in St. Paul" rule. Bootlegging was not a serious crime—until bootleggers Abe Wagner and Harry Davis were murdered in St. Paul. The hit was linked to notorious criminal Benjamin "Bugsy" Siegel and Mafia boss

Meyer Lansky. Siegel claimed the public had nothing to fear from organized crime and was widely quoted as saying "We only kill each other."

Then there were the kidnappings. In September 1931, powerful bootlegger and racketeer Leon Gleckman was kidnapped from his home at 2168 Sargent Avenue, just a mile from Eastcliff. The kidnapping ended with payment of a reduced ransom. One of Gleckman's daughters, Florence, an eighteen-year-old student at the University of Minnesota, was kidnapped on July 3, 1932, and released the next day.

The kidnapping and murder of Charles Lindbergh's son in New Jersey in 1932 was an international news sensation that ended any illusion that innocence equated to safety. The next year that realization came directly to St. Paul.

The O'Connor system was already starting to unravel when Jack Peifer, Fred Barker, and Alvin Karpis met at the Hollyhocks Club to plan the kidnapping of St. Paul's Theodore Hamm Brewing Company president and heir, William Hamm Jr. Hamm was kidnapped in St. Paul on June 15, 1933, held in Illinois, and released for $100,000 ransom. Later FBI investigations revealed that St. Paul Chief of Police Thomas Brown, called "Big Tom" (he was 6'5"), didn't just ignore criminals—he aided them. In the early 1930s, after suspicions that he had helped the Barker–Karpis gang escape capture as known bank robbers, Brown had been demoted from chief to detective and made, of all things, head of the kidnap squad. He was then in a prime position to assist the bank robbers in becoming kidnappers. He helped plan the Hamm kidnapping, fed the participants information, and helped them escape. He received one-quarter of the ransom money for his contributions. Emboldened by the successful kidnapping, in August the same group robbed the South St. Paul Post Office payroll, killing one police officer and wounding another.

That same summer, escaped convict Frank Nash was captured in Arkansas and brought to Kansas to be imprisoned in the U.S. Penitentiary at Leavenworth, Kansas. When Nash and his police escort arrived at the train station in Kansas City, Missouri, Vernon Miller and two other outlaws who knew Nash attempted to help him escape custody. However, they ended up shooting and killing Nash and six lawmen. It was dubbed the "Kansas City Massacre." This helped turn public sentiment: outlaws were no longer seen as glamorous, and public support to strengthen the FBI grew.

Closer to home, both literally and figuratively for the Brooks family and

Eastcliff, was the kidnapping of Edward Bremer on January 17, 1934. Bremer was president of the Commercial State Bank of St. Paul; his father, Adolf, was president of Jacob Schmidt Brewing Company. The Edward Bremer family lived three houses south of Eastcliff at 92 Mississippi River Boulevard North. Bremer had just taken his eight-year-old daughter, Betty, to Summit School, where she was a classmate of Binky Brooks, when he was kidnapped. Imagine Mr. Brooks reading the January 18 *Minneapolis Star*, emblazoned with the two-line headline, "St. Paul Bank President Is Kidnaped, Held for $200,000," and recognizing that his young daughter Binky was arriving at school at the same time as the horrific crime.

Great fear was felt by prominent families in the area. The Brooks children wrote about this time of intense stress: "Real fear now settled in the neighborhood. Edward, along with other residents in the area, decided to provide a good deal more illumination and installed powerful spotlights at the corners of the main house. Everyone wondered who would be next."[8] Binky recalled the Bremer kidnapping to me as the one dark time in her childhood.

After Edward Bremer was kidnapped, President Franklin Roosevelt (said to be a friend of Adolf Bremer), Minnesota Governor Floyd Anderson, and J. Edgar Hoover all issued statements decrying the situation and offering support in the return of Bremer. While people worried about which law-abiding citizen would be next, Bremer's kidnapping was not a random choice. Harry "Dutch" Sawyer, a business and underworld contact through Schmidt Brewing's relationship with the Green Lantern speakeasy, had selected Bremer. Both Adolf and Edward Bremer may have had contact with the underworld through the brewery and the bank.

Edward Bremer was bound and transported to Illinois. The kidnappers sent ransom notes along with notes from Bremer to prove he was alive. In a lexicon that I thought had been invented by Hollywood writers of gangster movies, the kidnappers wrote: "First of all, all coppers must be pulled off. Second the dough must be ready . . . the money must not be hot . . ."[9] As with the Hamm kidnapping, Big Tom Brown was feeding the criminals information before the kidnapping and throughout the ordeal. After twenty-one days and delivery of the $200,000 ransom, Edward Bremer was dropped off in Rochester, Minnesota. From there, traumatized, he made his way home to St. Paul by train and bus.

Merely a month after the kidnapping, St. Paul's Mayor William Mahoney declared, "There are no criminals here. They got Machine Gun Kelly in Memphis and Harvey Bailey in Oklahoma. These fellows just come here to visit our lakes. We have ten thousand lakes and a resort for every crook."[10] The public, however, had become less eager to welcome "these fellows." The Bremer kidnapping was the last straw. Police reformers, the FBI, and business leaders (who raised $100,000 for a team of investigators) joined in a campaign to clean up the police department. Extensive wiretaps uncovered widespread corruption. FBI director J. Edgar Hoover, who was particularly interested in capturing the Barker–Karpis gang, stated:

> Crime lives next door to you. Crime often plays bridge with you. Crime dances with your sons and daughters. It is ever present. But this veneer of social grace that our criminals have adopted in no way makes them less foul. . . . They are marauders, who murder for a headline, rats crawling from their hide-outs to gnaw at the vitals of our civilization.[11]

After the quick arrest and acquittal of the wrong people (the Touhy gang) in the Hamm kidnapping, the FBI spent two years carefully investigating the Bremer case. They were aided by Bremer's detailed recollection of the wallpaper in the house where he was held; FBI employees looked through sixty thousand wallpaper patterns to find that link. A gas can with Doc Barker's fingerprint was another important clue, but most helpful to capturing the criminals was that Tom Brown was under FBI investigation and no longer able to help the gangsters escape.

A few of those thought responsible never went to trial. Fred Goetz, a.k.a. George "Shotgun" Ziegler, thought to be the mastermind behind the Hamm and Bremer kidnappings, was shot and killed six weeks after Bremer's release, perhaps because he was bragging too much and implicating his accomplices in the kidnapping, or perhaps in a dispute over the ransom money. Ma Barker and son Fred were killed in a six-hour machine gun battle with the FBI in 1935. Legend claims that Ma died with a smoking machine gun by her side.

Of those arrested and convicted for the Bremer kidnapping, William Byron Bolton received the shortest sentence after pleading guilty and becoming a government witness. Jack Peifer, proprietor of the Hollyhocks Club (which closed shortly after the kidnapping in 1934), was sentenced to thirty years. Shortly after Peifer arrived at Leavenworth Prison, he died from ingesting a potassium cyanide pill. Arthur "Doc" Barker, Harry "Limpy" Campbell, Volney "Curley" Davis, William "Lapland Willie" Weaver, Alvin "Creepy" Karpis, and Harry "Dutch" Sawyer were each sentenced to life in prison. Jess Doyle and Edna "the Kissing Bandit" Murray were tried and found not guilty but were sent back to prison to finish sentences for other robberies. Murray returned to the Missouri prison from which she had previously escaped three times.

Tom Brown was discharged from the police force in October 1936, three months after the statute of limitations expired in the Hamm and Bremer kidnappings. He ran a liquor store in Ely, Minnesota, until his death in 1959.

John Dillinger was wounded but escaped during a March 1934 shootout with FBI agents in St. Paul. In July, he was shot and killed by FBI agents in Chicago.

By the fall of 1936 most members of the Barker–Karpis, Dillinger, Keating–Holden, Harvey Bailey, and Frank Nash gangs were imprisoned or dead. The St. Paul police department was swept clean.

Doc Barker was killed in January 1939 while attempting to escape from Alcatraz. Alvin Karpis, who served twenty-six years, was the longest-held prisoner at Alcatraz. After Alcatraz closed, Karpis was transferred to McNeil Island in Washington State to serve seven more years. There, he taught fellow inmate Charles Manson to play the guitar. Karpis was released on parole in 1969. He later claimed he was reunited with some of his bank robbery gains, plus interest, as he had deposited the stolen money in a bank.

Prohibition ended in 1933, prior to the Bremer kidnapping. By the end of the 1930s, St. Paul was once again a wonderful place to raise a family, and Edward Brooks had a beautiful bar decorated in silver leaf—and not hidden—in the basement amusement room of Eastcliff. But although Prohibition made Minnesota a center of bootlegging activity in the 1920s, crime and kidnapping had actually intensified with its repeal in 1933 as the gangsters sought new sources of income.

A guest at an Eastcliff open house in 1989 said he was glad to see the peacock room, as he learned to drink in that room during Prohibition.[12] Despite that anecdote, it is unlikely that the peacock room was ever intended to be a secret Prohibition bar. However, that era was the darkest cloud on the idyllic childhood of the Brooks children and an important part of the Eastcliff story.

That it might have been a Prohibition bar is not the only "maybe" associated with the peacock room. A booklet about Eastcliff from 1980 suggests that one might "imagine F. Scott Fitzgerald and Zelda holding hands in it [the peacock room], though [there is] nothing to substantiate that story." Fitzgerald lived in St. Paul intermittently from his birth in 1896 until 1922, when he, Zelda, and their daughter moved away for good. The peacock room dates don't work for Zelda to have visited—but Katharine Hepburn would have seen the room and perhaps she powdered her nose there.

THE BLACK BATHROOM

Off the den and behind the peacock room there is an actual powder room, known as the black bathroom. Eric and I affectionately called it the "Dean Martin bathroom" or the "Tracy Moos bathroom." Dean Martin refers to its Rat Pack 1960s style: the toilet is black, the countertop is honed black granite, and bronzed black tiles cover the walls. My dear friend Tracy Moos lived in the house from 1967 until 1974 and oversaw the bathroom's renovation. With five children living upstairs and hundreds of guests visiting, a nice powder room was a necessity. A second, larger half bath was added next to the dining room in 1987. It was made wheelchair accessible in 1991 and was remodeled in 1997.

If you study the floor plans, you can count six bathrooms (four full and two half baths) in the house in 1922. In 1930, there were eight baths in the house, plus two in the carriage house and two in the pool house, for a total of twelve. In 1990, there were a total of fourteen. In 2020, there were nine bathrooms in the main house and one in the pool house, for a total of ten.

To get to and from the black bathroom, you walk through the walnut den and down two steps. The Wilson family used this cozy den as a small television room. It was outfitted with a couch and easy chairs. During the Yudof years, the room contained reupholstered wing chairs and was decorated with President Yudof's antique maps from the British Isles, a nice connection to the maps that hung on the wall when the room was Edward Brooks's private library.

Bomb Threat from the SDS

Ann "Simmy" Moos was the first member of the Moos family I met. Simmy recalled the walnut den fondly, as that was where the Moos children regularly played games with a police officer. She said it was great fun to have the officer's attention, although she didn't recall why he was there. Later, her mother, Tracy, told me more of the story: the SDS (Students for a Democratic Society) had threatened to blow up the Moos family. "Every day they would call and say, 'Thirteen days, twelve days, eleven days,' like a countdown." Regarding the stress of the daily bomb threats, Tracy added cheerfully, "They said they would blow us up, but they didn't!" Tracy insisted on looking at the bright side and considered the security officers assigned to guard them day and night as free, and skilled, babysitters.

I recalled Simmy's memory of the fun of having an officer in the house when I read about Edward Bremer's kidnapping. Years after Bremer was kidnapped, his daughter Betty recalled how her childhood innocence helped to relieve the tense atmosphere three doors down: "We had an FBI man living on our second floor throughout the time my father was kidnapped. I thought FBI agents were nice to have around! I thought it was a lark and the agents would play with me." Betty remembered a particular incident when her grandfather brought cheese to the house: "I can still see the FBI agent, Brennan, drawing his gun at it and saying, 'If that cheese moves, it's a goner!'"[13]

The SDS was protesting the draft and the Vietnam war. The threat of bombing the Moos family was worth taking seriously. The Weather Underground, a violent offshoot of the SDS, had claimed responsibility for two bombings. The group's earlier name, the Weathermen, was taken from a song by Bob Dylan. (Dylan had been a student at the University a few years earlier.)

Beginning in 1967, the year Malcolm Moos became president, there were antiwar sit-ins at the University of Minnesota and on many campuses. A demonstration at the University of Wisconsin in Madison was violently dispersed by the Madison police and riot squad, resulting in many injuries. A mass rally and a student strike then closed that university for several days. President Moos was credited with helping keep Minnesota students safer and keeping protests from becoming more volatile. At one antiwar rally in front of the president's office in Morrill Hall, Moos joined the crowd. When they began chanting "Are you with us?" Moos responded, "I'm with you right now!" As son Grant Moos, who shared the story with me, pointed out, the response meant nothing but successfully diffused the situation.[14] When SDS protesters were picketing in front of Eastcliff on a winter night, Moos's daughter Kathy innocently invited a group of them in to talk with her father. The president met with them in front of the living room fireplace.

Widespread protests of the war in Vietnam that began on campuses in 1967 lasted until the war ended in 1973, and the Moos administration encompassed those years. Marian Wilson looked back with gratitude for having fewer such volatile issues: "We had a few unpleasant experiences during those years when someone burned a cross on the front lawn once, and when a Russian exhibit was at the Union building and they had a Russian flag and an American flag, and there was some burning of the flags. There was a fire in the ROTC building once, but there was never just a groundswell, terrible unrest."[15]

Peter Magrath followed Malcolm Moos as president. In his first fall as president, student demands that the University boycott lettuce and grapes and serve only produce picked by Cesar Chavez's United Farm Workers included picketing at Eastcliff.[16] Diane Skomars Magrath wrote their daughter, Monette, with a succinct description of her life as an introvert married to a university president, who had to deal with anxious situations:

> Although I was never suited for public life, your Dad, Peter, was. He was the consummate public servant. He was a populist and as polite to those who called him at midnight as he was to those who met him by daylight. He treated his staff the same way he treated the rich and famous. And he worked tirelessly for the university.
>
> Our public servants pay a terrific price for their positions. I have profound respect for Peter and those who choose such a path.
>
> I remember once when a disgruntled employee threatened to "Shoot the President!" I drove up to Eastcliff and saw the University police stationed in the driveway. "Where is the President?" I asked. "Out jogging" was the answer. Peter was unfazed by such threats.
>
> Another time when Peter was hung in effigy on campus, his mother, who was suffering from dementia then, pointed to her television and said with pride, "Look! It's my son Peter."[17]

THE ENTRY HALL

Guests who enter by the front door pass through a small, tiled vestibule, with a door to the right that opens to the basement stairs and a glass-paneled door straight ahead. That door opens into the front entry hall surrounded by a circular Georgian staircase with a banister of iron grillwork and wooden balustrade. Part way up that grand staircase is a landing over the vestibule and a beautiful oversized oriel window.

The entry hall walls are topped with denticulated molding, typical of Clarence Johnston's style. The vestibule and entry hall floors are tile. The entry hall floor has a circular inlay of hand-fired, iron-spot quarry tile with a green marble border. Two curvilinear steps lead to the hallway. Double French doors to the terrace are straight ahead.

When the house was built in 1922, a curved door to the left of the front entry hall led into a smaller hall where one could either continue into the den or access the half bath at the front of the house. During the 1930 renovation, this small hall was enclosed to be a telephone room, and the former telephone room became the peacock room. The new telephone room, designed by Frank Post, had a translucent glass ceiling that let light through, and its front wall was a blackboard, with a chalk trough at the bottom, for jotting down messages.

A Wedding of Importance

During the Brooks era, the steps leading from the tile entry floor were covered with a soft, prune-colored carpet, as was the hallway, the stairs, and the living room. Above the entry hall, in the center of the circular staircase, hung a wrought-iron light fixture. Straight ahead, the French doors to the terrace were curtained in a Chinese chintz. Nearby was a Korean chest with a red lacquer interior, and a lamp stood on a tall teakwood stand. Mrs. Brooks said of the lamp, "One of Mr. Brooks's aunts bought that lamp thirty years ago in Japan, and it had never been taken from its thirty-year-old Japanese newspaper wrappings until we moved it here."[18]

Eastcliff had its first major remodel with the Brooks family in 1930. They continued to change and redecorate the house through the years. In 1960, the house was spruced up for the first presidential family. At that time, the carpeting was changed to off-white, and a large crystal chandelier from the Pillsbury mansion was hung over the stairs. Beginning in 1986, Eastcliff had its second true remodel, with an expansion of the dining room, the addition of a catering kitchen, and an update to other parts of the house, but no "decorating."

Eastcliff was due for a major facelift in 1997. The University hired interior designer Sally Wheaton Huscha, who specialized in period residences, to work with Miller Dunwiddie Architects and the Eastcliff Technical Advisory Committee on the project. Mark Yudof had recently been hired as president and was still living in Texas, so Sally flew to Austin to begin working with Judy Yudof. They would spend many hours together on the project.

What they did with the grand staircase is my favorite part of the remodel. I love the Eastcliff staircase. Many steps have different shapes, as the curve causes each step at the bottom to widen. The tread of each step is honey-brown wood with a darker wood trim in a curvilinear pattern at each end of the step, so the pattern climbs the full staircase. The inlaid wood design reflects the curved design of each of the iron balusters holding the curved wood. The beautiful 1920s design is a wonderful complement to the other woodwork throughout the house.

It seems remarkable that the beautiful inlaid wood would survive all these years. In fact, it has not. The Brooks had carpeted stairs, and the carpet was replaced before the Wilson family moved in. Sally Wheaton Huscha told

Main staircase, circa 1922. Courtesy of the Brooks family.

me that their intention had also been to rejuvenate the stairs with new carpeting, but, with each custom step a different size, new carpet was cost-prohibitive. Sally explained that the beautiful pattern that looks like inlaid wood was actually painted on as a cost-saving measure.

Reproduction art wallpaper was used on the entry and stairway walls and in several other rooms. The original drapery hardware and chandelier had been removed prior to the donation of Eastcliff to the University. The curved wrought-iron curtain rod over the two-story oriel window was made in 1997 by a Wisconsin blacksmith. It is based on photographs of the original hardware, although the original featured a daisy and the replica has a lady slipper, the state flower of Minnesota. The crystal chandelier from the Pillsbury mansion remained for several years after the 1997 remodel, but by 2010 the glass arms had become dangerously brittle. That year, a new wrought-iron lantern-style chandelier was made based on photographs of the original fixture.

The telephone booth off the entry, behind a curved wooden door that had been custom made to exactly match the curve of the wall, was enhanced by wallpaper with a pattern of antique chairs. Guests were still using that telephone for calls when the room was remodeled.

When I first met Marney Brooks, the day the Dalai Lama visited Eastcliff, I mentioned to her that I had heard the charming story of how she called her mother from the Eastcliff telephone booth to share that she and Conley were engaged. She was curiously noncommittal. Seventeen years before I met Marney, and fifty years after her wedding to Conley Brooks, Marney described her vivid memories in *Turning the Leaves*. Ten years after that, in 2004, she wrote again about the wedding and titled the story "A Wedding of Importance." The story appears in "Marney's Memoirs," an unpublished collection of Marney's writing from 2004–7. My descriptions here are based on those memoirs.

Marney Brown grew up on Sargent Avenue, just a mile from Eastcliff. Marney and Binky Brooks were friends and classmates at Summit School. Marney's father, Montreville "Monte" Brown, met her mother, Minnie Stinchfield, in 1904 while they were both students at the University of Minnesota. Monte was captain of the University of Minnesota baseball team. He later practiced law and became assistant attorney general for the State of Minnesota (1917–25). Monte's father, Calvin Brown, was chief justice of the Supreme Court of Minnesota (1912–23).

Marney and Conley began dating when he was a freshman at Yale

University and she a senior at Summit School. They were dating steadily when she enrolled at Vassar College in 1941. Conley wrote, "It was all marvelous. By sophomore year, I had my own car and the 77.2 miles between Yale and Vassar were traversed many times."[19]

With concern over Hitler's aggression in Europe and the Japanese attack on Pearl Harbor, Conley joined the Army Air Corps in 1943. By then, the couple had fallen completely in love, so Marney, still in school in New York, visited Conley at bases in Atlantic City, Boston, Pennsylvania, and Georgia. She recalled selling her sweaters for train fare to visit him in camp, with her parents declaring that she should be engaged if she were going to visit him. Conley had written to his parents that he wanted to marry Marney, and Edward called the newspapers to announce his son's engagement (and Marney didn't know anything about it)! Marney wrote, "Con still jokes about how our mothers engineered the engagement, calling October 17, 1943, 'Mother's Day.'"[20] When Conley discovered that the engagement announcement had been released, he called Marney to apologize for his father's faux pas. Marney was too happy to complain, and they became properly engaged when they next saw each other. (I'm not sure how, or if, the story of Marney calling her mother regarding her engagement fits with Conley and Marney being on the East Coast when their parents arranged that very engagement, but researching this book has reinforced my observation that memories change over time and differ among the people involved.)

With the wedding planned for March 1944, Markell invited Marney to travel from the Vassar campus in Poughkeepsie to Tiffany's in New York City to shop for silver, china, crystal, and linens. Markell had "such exquisite taste" and was "a genuinely generous person, but she always had a penchant for seeing that things were done right."[21] Harold's in the Twin Cities was the next shopping spree, for a wedding dress and trousseau, including a bridal dinner gown—"a purple Hattie Carnegie with a gorgeous pale blue, beaded silk sash. Needless to say, this was all pretty heady stuff for a twenty-one-year-old Sargent Avenue girl who'd never heard of Hattie Carnegie."[22]

The bridal dinner was held the night before the wedding at Eastcliff on March 17, 1944. Marney wrote:

> One couple—my mother-in-law Markell's best friend and her husband [Frannie and Tom Underwood]—put on a skit, fastening a ball and chain around Con's ankle while they sang a song about how he was

Conley and Marney's wedding dinner. Courtesy of the Brooks family.

about to enter servitude. It was all very jolly and I was very nervous. I was to become more nervous as we entered the living room and saw the long U-shaped table gleaming with candlelight and what I learned later were Capo di Monte gold porcelain figures surrounded by maiden-hair fern and roses.[23]

In a photograph of the dinner, it's easy to see how the setting took Marney's breath away. The photograph shows more than a dozen candles, each about three feet tall, arranged on the tables so that all the glittering candlelight is reflected in the oval mirror above the fireplace. The tables are arranged in a U shape, with about a foot between tables so everyone is seated on the outside facing in, with Conley and Marney in front of the fireplace. The entire group isn't visible in the photograph, but with twelve people on the right side there appears to be seating for twenty-six. The dining room at the time could not have accommodated more than twelve; furniture was removed from the living room to provide space for the tables. As Marney wrote, "Markell was a master at creating an exquisite setting, whatever the occasion. She really went all out that night, even painting designs in gold on the place cards."[24]

Edward was known for speaking easily and thinking on his feet, but when he stood to give a toast that night he began, "I want very much to welcome Marney into our family. I want to welcome her with—I want to welcome her with—Markell, what do I want to welcome her with?" The answer was "affection." After toasts, and then dinner, Binky played a medley of love songs on the piano, including "The Man I Love" and "It Had to Be You."

The wedding was at Unity Church in St. Paul the next day, followed by a reception at the Browns' home. Marney wrote that she remembered much less about the wedding than about the dinner the night before.

Binky married at Unity Church nine years later, on April 18, 1954, and the reception was held at Eastcliff. When she described the wedding to me (in 2015), she most remembered two details. First she recalled, "My father had had a heart attack about four months before, so they said, 'You'll want to go down the aisle with one of your brothers, which one?' I said, 'I don't want to go down the aisle with my brothers, either one or all of them.' I went down alone, but they were sure I would have to have my arm on a man."[25]

For Binky, the highlight was the music in the Eastcliff living room at the reception. She said, "Mother was really wonderful, because she said, 'I wonder what kind of music you would like.' I said there was no doubt that I would like a string quartet, and I don't know how she found this group, but it was a wonderful quartet, something like the Budapest Quartet. And they were sitting in the living room all the reception. The whole reception had that music."

THE LIVING ROOM

Twin Cities Public Broadcasting System (TPT) produced a documentary in 2011 titled Glorious Spaces: Clarence H. Johnston, Minnesota Architect. *This feeling of glorious space is a comforting presence as you enter the Eastcliff living room. The balanced proportions and symmetry give me, and likely others, a feeling of enhanced well-being. The north wall, around the entrance, has built-in bookshelves. The east and west walls are symmetric, with light flowing through three double-hung windows on each side and room for paintings to be hung between the windows. At the south end of the room is a brick fireplace surrounded by painted*

The living room. Photograph by Patrick O'Leary. Courtesy of University Photographer records, University of Minnesota Archives.

columns topped with a mantel enhanced with dentil molding and small carved acorns on the corners.

In 1931, the Brooks living room had a grand piano in front of the bookcase, prune-colored carpeting, and "lustrous, soft gold draperies painted in dull lacquer red and green with gold tie-backs." The sofa and chairs were upholstered in English floral linen, and there was an antique Chippendale secretary between two windows.[26]

Eastcliff was redecorated throughout after Mrs. Brooks moved out in 1960 and Eastcliff became the official residence of the University president. Marian Wilson worked on the redesign with University designers, and particularly with color consultant Michael Hopkins. The beige and white color scheme in the living room and dining room was described as a monochromatic eggshell white. The woodwork was painted white, or off-white, upstairs and down. The carpeting throughout was variously described as creamy beige or off-white. The living room walls were covered with beige straw cloth (or grass cloth). Most of the furniture was covered in cream-colored fabric,

Living room, circa 1940. Courtesy of the Brooks family.

with a few occasional chairs and the dining room chairs covered in what was described as vivid strawberry red, raspberry pink, or American beauty red and pink. Color was also introduced in purple, turquoise, and bronze striped living room chairs as well as purple and turquoise sofa pillows. When the Moos family arrived seven years after the Wilson family, Tracy Moos mentioned the carpet color when explaining why her dogs now had to live outside: "Can you imagine what they'd do to this lovely white carpeting?"

Peter Magrath's first wife, Sandra Magrath, worked with a University designer to redecorate the house prior to their arrival in 1974, using University furniture on most of the first floor. Every piece of furniture had PROPERTY OF THE UNIVERSITY OF MINNESOTA on the bottom, and later Peter and Diane Magrath joked that if you turned their daughter, Monette, over, you would find the same tag on the bottoms of her feet.

During the Keller remodeling of the dining room, little to no decorating was done to the living room (the floor and ceiling were replaced, but that was functional, not decorative), nor was anything done during the Hasselmo administration, so the 1997 redecoration during the Yudof administration was sorely needed. The living room wall color is most interesting (a purple/brown called Fresco Urbain #1253). Its use was inspired by paint used for a Marsden Hartley exhibition at the Weisman Art Museum in 1997. The Weisman has the largest collections of works by Marsden Hartley, Alfred Maurer, and B. J. O. Nordfeldt of any museum in the world. Beginning during the Keller administration, Eastcliff has regularly displayed works by those artists as well as other fine art from the collection. The museum owns more art than can be displayed in its galleries, and Eastcliff has a robust security system, so more of the collection can be shared with the public by being displayed at Eastcliff. The wall color now in the living room serves as a pleasing complement to any painting I've displayed or seen there.

During the Bruininks administration, the loveseats added during the 1997 renovation were moved downstairs and replaced with reupholstered sofas discarded from the Wisconsin governor's mansion after Walter Koehler was in office (1951–57). After fifteen additional years of use at Eastcliff, these sofas looked—and sat—their age. Shortly before we moved out in 2019, Regent Emeritus Dallas Bohnsack and his wife Joannie gave a generous gift to Eastcliff that was used to purchase the current leather sofas.[27]

The Sound of Music

During our time in Eastcliff, three photographs of the Brooks family sat on a grand piano to your right as you enter the living room. All three photographs were taken in this room in front of the fireplace. Diane Skomars Magrath had the first one printed and framed in honor of the house's heritage. I added two more, to show the Brooks family over time and to include a photograph of their dog Rusty.

Music was very important to the Brooks family. Ted said, "Whatever there was of music in the house, and there was a lot of it, came from my mother. . . . My mother was, could have been, a very accomplished pianist. Very, very able. But she married early, twenty-one when she married, and immediately the children started to come along. There went any thoughts of conservatory training, although she certainly had the stuff for that, to qualify for that kind of training."[28] Markell's family all agreed that she was musically gifted. Markell herself was quoted as saying "with modest incredulity" that during her life she had sung "one perfect note"—and "clearly it had been a transcendental experience."[29]

Markell and her Chicago friend Frannie Underwood had played together through the years, with four hands on two pianos. They played variations by Brahms, Hayden, and Schumann, and the Rachmaninoff E Minor Symphony. Markell later played the same way with daughter Binky and daughter-in-law Marney, enjoying it so much that the family added a second piano to the Eastcliff living room.

Conley, the eldest son, recalled, "We were required to take piano lessons . . . I went to my mother after this one piano lesson and I said, 'Would you mind if I gave up the piano for a month?' She said, 'Why no, dear, but we

Left to right: Edward, Binky, Dwight, Ted, Markell, and Conley Brooks. Written on the reverse: "January 2, 1942, Con (20), Ted (19), Dwight (12), Binky (15), Parents (age unknown!)". Courtesy of the Brooks family.

think it's important for you to learn something.' I stopped; that was the last time. That's when I was seven."[30] Markell's musical influence was stronger in her next two children. Ted continued with his lessons, then studied music at Harvard University, receiving his degree in 1944. His obituary in 2004 stated that "Mr. Brooks was a great lover of music and, like his mother, a strong patron of the arts and education in the Twin Cities." Markell's obituary had suggested donations to the Minnesota Dance Theatre and School. Daughter Binky studied piano at Mills College in California, then majored in music at Smith College and studied music for two more years at Salzburg Mozarteum in Vienna, Austria. The youngest Brooks child, Dwight, like the eldest, followed more in the musical footsteps of his father. According to Ted, Edward "had no musical sense or appreciation at all"—but "he did love to dance."[31]

I don't know if University President O. Meredith Wilson was musical, but the Broadway musical *The Music Man* was written by Meredith Willson. The two men were sometimes mistaken for each other, and when they were introduced to each other by a mutual acquaintance they became friends.

Marian Wilson loved the opera. Beginning in 1945, New York's Metropolitan Opera included the University's Northrop Auditorium on its national tour. The company would perform four to seven different operas over two to five days each May. Mrs. Wilson said she never missed a performance. This continued until 1986, when the opera discontinued the tour.

The Moos family also appreciated music and opera. They moved their own baby grand piano into the Eastcliff living room in 1967, and daughter Kathy played it. Tracy recalled Arthur Rubenstein visiting Eastcliff and playing the piano. Malcolm and Tracy would invite the guests who were joining them at Northrop for the opera to come for dinner at Eastcliff prior to the performance. But after the big dinner, guests kept falling asleep at the opera. "Finally, I caught on!" Tracy said. She started having the Eastcliff gathering *after* the opera, which had the added benefit that the opera stars could join them; they were famished after their performances. Tracy particularly remembered Joan Sutherland visiting Eastcliff at an after-opera gathering. Kathy Moos recalled a particular guest invitation: Her mother had become friends with Dean Zimmerman, who was well-known for his counterculture views. Tracy gave him two tickets to the president's box at the opera. He responded that he planned to attend and would bring his dog as his plus-one. Moos family members don't recall if he actually did so.

Peter Magrath's grandfather, George Magrath, was a professional pianist and later a symphony orchestra conductor. He was born in Quebec but performed and studied music in Europe, particularly in Paris and Vienna, and he married an Austrian woman—a small, delightful Eastcliff connection, as Binky Brooks would study in Vienna and then live in Austria about fifty years later. Peter Magrath's father, Laurence, met his Italian wife, Giulia, the woman who would become Peter's mother, in Somalia (then Italian Somaliland) while he was teaching her to play the piano. It was reported by Peter's first wife, Sandra, that Peter could not sing or "play one note of music"[32]—nonetheless, one could say that he owed his existence to music. Sandra and Peter Magrath hosted a Minnesota Opera Association membership event at Eastcliff in September 1976. Opera stars performed in the Eastcliff backyard. The "price of admission" was bringing a new member to join the association.

After Peter married Diane Skomars, she kept her own baby grand piano upstairs directly above the living room in the room used by the Brookses as the master bedroom (the Magraths used it as a family living room). The School of Nursing Alumni Society and Foundation Board donated a baby grand piano from Powell Hall for the Eastcliff living room. The piano had been rebuilt by the School of Music and the music rack regularly held the score for "Eastcliff," a piece composed by Professor Reginald Buckner for the piano dedication on March 1, 1982.

The Magraths hosted mezzo soprano Risë Stevens of the Metropolitan Opera for tea at Eastcliff. Diane also fondly recalls hosting members of American Ballet Theatre (ABT) for a reception after their performance at Northrop Auditorium. Diane and daughter Monette remember seeing both Mikhail Baryshnikov and Alexander Godunov perform, and both are certain that Godunov visited Eastcliff with members of the American Ballet Theatre, but they are not sure whether Baryshnikov did.

Ken Keller and Bonita Sindelir hosted a dinner for Maestro Edo de Waart early in his tenure as director of music and conductor of the Minnesota Orchestra. They hosted two pre-opera dinners in 1985 and three dinners for the last touring season of the Metropolitan Opera in 1986.

The Hasselmos hosted a dinner before the Bolshoi Ballet. The menu was Russian salad, duck sukarov with smetana sauce, potatoes and wild mushrooms, and pear muscovite for dessert. Longtime University friends Stan and Karen Hubbard and John and Jane Mooty were among the twenty guests. A dinner before the Dance Theatre of Harlem performance included Conley and Marney Brooks as guests. The Hasselmos hired a string quartet or a harpist for most formal dinners, although Nils's true love was jazz.

The Yudofs had their own baby grand piano in the living room; Judy Yudof suggested that the Friends of Eastcliff purchase the current piano, a 1922 Steinway baby grand, to replace their piano when they moved out. The Yudofs hosted a reception for Finnish composer Einojuhani Rautavaara and renowned Minnesota conductor Phillip Brunelle in 1999, and a reception for Finnish conductor and composer Kari Tikka in 2001.

Bob Bruininks is a talented trumpet player with a great love of music. He majored in music, as well as in special education and sociology, as an undergraduate. Susan Hagstrum was on the board of the Minnesota Symphony. In 2003, she and President Bruininks hosted a dinner at Eastcliff to benefit the Minneapolis Symphony Orchestra Cirque du Symphony.

While we lived in Eastcliff, music students would occasionally be hired to play during events. Otherwise, the piano was played only by Tomas Hardy when he came bimonthly to tune it. I learned that pianos, particularly in Minnesota's dry winter weather, need to be "watered," and a special water pitcher for filling the humidifier tank in the piano is tucked away behind books in the bookshelf.

I remind you of the three Brooks family photographs on the piano. The family members are all beautifully dressed, and Markell is wearing an evening gown in each photograph.

Celebrity Guest Stars

Besides being known for her music, Markell Brooks, with her husband, Edward, was renowned for throwing wonderful parties and inviting interesting people to visit. Markell's friend Frannie Underwood described events at Eastcliff as "always exquisite . . . Markell would have dipped the grapes in gold, you know, candlelight and always very interesting people."[33] Frannie had introduced the Brookses to some of those interesting people, including her friend Katharine Hepburn. Ted Brooks wrote:

> Over the years Eastcliff has seen a number of persons of some fame or notoriety in various walks of life, as visitors or guests. Those who come to mind are the following: Helen Keller (with whom my Father developed a fast friendship), Katharine Hepburn, Clark Gable, Chester Morris, Noel Coward, Bill Dickey . . . , Joe Louis (I may be mistaken about this), and the Budapest String Quartet. Eugene Ormandy, Dimitri Mitropoulos, and (again I'm not certain about this) Serge Rachmaninoff have been guests at Eastcliff.[34]

Ted recalled Bill Dickey's visit in the 1998 video interview:

> It was especially thrilling for me, along in the earlier 1930s, I was very interested in athletics. Bill Dickey was a catcher for the New York Yankees back in the Lou Gehrig and Babe Ruth days. He was brought to the house by a man named Claire Long, a close friend of my parents. It was some social occasion at the house and the Longs were invited. They said, "May we bring Bill Dickey along? He's in town," for whatever reason.
>
> Gee, to have Bill Dickey in our home and to be able to touch him was such a thrill for an eleven- or twelve-year-old.
>
> Mr. Long was known as "Shorty" (Shorty Long) and was a University of Minnesota alumnus, very active in alumni affairs, especially in football back in the Bernie Bierman days. He used to procure season tickets for our family to Gopher games.

The New York Yankees were regular World Series champions during Ted's youth, and Bill Dickey played for the team from 1928 to 1943. During his playing days, he was named to eleven all-star games, including in the year Ted Brooks was twelve. Claire "Shorty" Long had been an All-American quarterback on the Gopher football team in 1916 while in law school.[35] Binky was less interested in sports and Mr. Dickey, but remembered Katharine Hepburn distinctly. The actress was well known for her progressive and unconventional attitudes and lifestyle, but after great success in the early 1930s, her career nearly came to an end in the mid-1930s. Dorothy Parker criticized, "She runs the gamut of emotions all the way from A to B." When Hepburn auditioned for the role of Scarlett O'Hara in *Gone with the Wind*, David O. Selznick rejected her with "I can't see Rhett Butler chasing you for twelve years." While she had successful performances throughout the 1930s, Andrew Britton wrote, "No other star has emerged with greater rapidity or with more ecstatic acclaim. No other star, either, has become so unpopular so quickly for so long a time." In 1939, Hepburn took her career into her own hands and left Hollywood to star in the stage production of *The Philadelphia Story*, and then starred in a national tour of the play. She performed at the Lyceum Theater in Minneapolis in 1940.

According to Binky Brooks, her mother's very close Chicago friend [Frannie Underwood] said, "My friend Katharine Hepburn is coming to Minneapolis to play in *The Philadelphia Story*. Why don't you invite her for tea?" Markell was happy to do that, and Hepburn visited several times.

Binky was twelve years old and was included in an afternoon gathering. Markell asked Binky to play a short piece on the piano. Binky described the actress as "very dynamic, a lovely person. I remember she had very red hair, and a totally unique voice. And she was interested in other people. I don't remember much of the conversation except her talking about creativity. She said her brother had written nineteen unsuccessful plays, which I thought was a wonderful comment—just because they weren't successful didn't stop him from creating them!"

The Brookses gave a party for the cast of the play. It was "a wonderful, harmonious time, a delightful evening with everyone," Binky said. "She and my Father just clicked. He called her Kate."

Binky further recalled that the actress treated the Brooks family as good friends. "Once I was home from school with a cold," Binky continued, "and apparently Katharine Hepburn also had a cold. She telephoned to see if my mother, who wasn't here at that moment, could go in the attic and find some warm boots belonging to my brothers because she wanted to take a long walk. 'Whenever I get a cold, I go for a three- or four-mile walk,' but she didn't have the right clothes."

On another evening, before dinner, Edward and Hepburn were talking, and he recognized the scent that she was wearing. According to Binky, he exclaimed, "'I have that!' He sent one of the family upstairs to his medicine cabinet to bring down a bottle of New Mown Hay, and she was thrilled."

Guerlin's perfume New Mown Hay (Foin Coupe) was created in 1896. It was popular in the early twentieth century and then discontinued. It was likely unavailable for purchase by 1940 when Katharine Hepburn visited

Eastcliff, which would explain why he was excited to give, and she was thrilled to receive, a bottle of it. As Binky told the story:

> Sometime after dinner it was time for her to leave. She had come in a car, with a driver, and she left. We were closing up the house, turning off lights and walking through the living room. When we came around to the front entrance where she had left, there was the bottle of New Mown Hay on a table by the front door. My father was very disappointed because it had been with such a sincere enthusiasm that she accepted it. We were sorry she had forgotten it, and everyone went to bed.
>
> The next morning (we always had breakfast at 7:30), I don't know who was the first one down, but the New Mown Hay was missing. Ellen, who was one of the girls working for us, said that sometime late in the evening, the doorbell had rung, and Katharine Hepburn had returned from the other side of Minneapolis where she had been driven. She came back to collect that bottle. It was a joy and relief—my father was just so pleased. It was like having a wound soothed.

After the success of the play, Hepburn starred in the film version of *The Philadelphia Story* with James Stewart and Cary Grant. She said of her character in the play, "I gave her life, and she gave me back my career." The rest, as they say, is history. Hepburn received an Academy Award nomination for Best Actress in 1941, and in total during her career received four Best Actress awards and eight nominations.

Dumbwaiter Drama

Eastcliff has nine fireplaces: three on the main floor (in the walnut den, the living room, and the breakfast room), one in the basement amusement room, four upstairs, and one on the front of the pool house. I had heard that the Brooks family, being in the lumber business, used scrap lumber in the fireplaces to heat the home. I mentioned this to Conley Brooks Jr., grandson of Edward and Markell. Conley, ever gracious, laughed and said that his grandparents had all the amenities of the time, including heating. The fireplaces were for enjoyment.

Several Brooks family portraits were taken in front of the living room fireplace. The fireplace is centered on the south wall of the living room and flanked by shallow square columns on each side and a French door on the outside of each column, one next to the east wall of the house and one next to the west wall of the house. During large receptions, we typically arranged a buffet table in the dining room and a bar in the garden room. For smaller gatherings, or for a short reception, we set up the bar in the peacock room. Guests frequently entered the garden room through the left door. The right door was rarely used. I wondered if the purpose of that door was symmetry, since it seemed unlikely it was useful in the Brooks home.

I had heard about a dumbwaiter filled with logs for the basement, first-, and second-floor fireplaces. The family said this was also a favorite place for the children to hide, or to imprison a sibling, most particularly Binky, as she was the smallest. Tracy, Kathy, and Grant Moos told me a great story involving a dumbwaiter in the living room.

Where was the dumbwaiter? I knew there was a locked, former dumbwaiter in the walnut den, but there was not one in the living room. This mystery was solved when Sally Wheaton Huscha visited me at Eastcliff. Sally told me that the door on the right of the fireplace was previously mirrored, and the dumbwaiter was behind that door. We looked behind the door and, now knowing what I was looking for, I could see in the garden room floor a slight difference in the brick in about a three-foot-square area that is evidence of where the dumbwaiter had been. Right below this area in the basement amusement room there is now a closet with a beautiful oak door with a semicircular top.

In the fall of 1968, Hubert H. Humphrey, vice president of the United States, was running against Richard Nixon for president. While campaigning, he arranged to visit Minnesota on a Saturday to watch the Gophers play football. Humphrey and University of Minnesota president Malcolm Moos had both studied political science at the University in the 1930s. Members of the Moos family fondly recall a favorite story the two men loved to share: while at the University, they were asked to debate on the radio. Moos, who would go on to become President Dwight Eisenhower's speechwriter, was to argue the Republican case; Humphrey, who would later be elected mayor of Minneapolis, a U.S. Senator, and vice president under Lyndon Johnson, had the Democratic Farm Labor side. The allotted time for the debate was thirty minutes. Humphrey went first and spoke without pause for twenty-seven minutes, leaving barely three minutes for Moos's remarks. The two remained great friends.

Malcolm and Tracy Moos had invited Humphrey to join them for the Gopher football game that fall Saturday, but they did not anticipate his arrival at Eastcliff, Secret Service in tow, early in the morning. The vice president entered with a hearty "Got anything to eat?" Tracy said that there was oyster stew left over from an event the night before, so the Secret Service agents helped themselves and heated it on the stove.

The Moos family, including Malcolm, Tracy, and all five children, went to the game with Vice President Humphrey. The University president and his spouse, then as now, were kept very busy entertaining guests at the football game. Son Grant Moos and his friend Alan Searle, both active adolescent boys, got bored and decided to walk back to Eastcliff. They were surprised to find the house locked when they returned—the family never locked the door. But no problem: they crawled in through the kitchen window, to the surprise of the Secret Service agents. This didn't bother Grant and Alan, who proceeded to the basement. Grant recalled that he was eager to show Alan how the dumbwaiter worked. The Moos children had discovered that, rather than using the pulley system to lift firewood, they could hoist themselves up and pop into the living room.

The Moos family in front of the living room fireplace. Courtesy of University of Minnesota Archives Photograph Collection.

Grant and Alan did just that. They didn't know that in the time it had taken them to walk home and occupy themselves downstairs, the football game had ended and there was now a crowd of about twenty people in the living room, including the rest of the family, guests who had attended the football game, the United States vice president, his aide, and Secret Service agents. Fifty years later, Tracy Moos and daughter Kathy still recalled their shock as the door by the fireplace sprung open and the Secret Service agents whipped out their guns, pointing them at the intruders. Grant recalled that the two boys "trotted through the room, oblivious" to the commotion they had caused, with the bravado that is a specialty of thirteen-year-old boys. Tracy, Kathy, and Grant all agreed that the vice president of the United States and the president of the University of Minnesota were both very amused with the entire episode.

Hubert Humphrey was probably the first sitting vice president to visit Eastcliff, but he was not the last. In December 1980, Vice President Walter Mondale visited Eastcliff to discuss his involvement with the University after his term as vice president and his plans to make his papers available to the Humphrey Institute at the University. After the meeting, he stayed for dinner. Diane Skomars Magrath recalled that two or three Secret Service agents arrived early to walk through the house and make sure it was secure. For safety, they taste-tested the food that was to be served. Diane remembered that their dog, Max, kept barking at the agents.

The dinner was intimate, just eight or ten people in the dining room. The menu was inspired by Norwegian cuisine, in honor of Mondale's heritage, and was prepared by Erica Juntunen, the Eastcliff cook at the time. For Diane, a memorable part of the event occurred the next morning. The phone rang, and it was the vice president calling from Air Force Two (calling from an airplane was an amazing feat at the time). Mr. Mondale asked President Magrath to get Mrs. Magrath. He had called to thank her for the lovely evening.

THE GARDEN ROOM

In the 1921 architectural plans, this room is called the "south porch," and it was a screened porch rather than a room. The wall between the garden room and the living room is still the white clapboard of the house exterior and includes a cement wall niche with a lion's head fountain that, at one time, poured water into a protruding concrete well. The niche is surrounded by brick. The walls that were once screens now have tall glass windows. When the room was screened, there were large ceiling fans for the summer and green canvas curtains to buckle down in inclement weather. The floor has always been terra cotta tile. The room was expanded in 1926.

The garden room was winterized during the Wilson administration. This was important because, from 1960 until the dining room was expanded in the 1980s, dinner guests were seated throughout the house, including in the garden room. The garden room is now furnished with Gustav Stickley reproduction wicker seating pieces, purchased during the 1997 renovation. These were chosen to recall the two stick-willow peacock-back chairs of the Brooks family that were upholstered in a Chinese lacquer red "leatherized" fabric.

The most distinctive furnishings in the garden room during the Brooks years were two large box-spring swings—swinging couches—heaped with

Garden room, circa 1922. Courtesy of the Brooks family.

colorful pillows. Binky described them as "deep red leather, not a bright red, and they were nice because you could see out everywhere from the swings." On an afternoon in the 1930s, Helen Keller sat on one of these swings.

Helen Keller at Eastcliff

Ted Brooks said his father "developed a fast friendship" with Helen Keller, and Binky Brooks had vivid memories of Helen Keller visiting Eastcliff, though she didn't remember the dates.[36] Hearing Binky speak of her personal connection with this remarkable woman, through the eyes of her childhood, filled me with awe. It is probable that the visit Binky recalled wasn't Miss Keller's first visit to Eastcliff, or at least not her first meeting with Edward Brooks.[37] Edward had many interesting friends, including doctors at the Mayo Clinic, and through these acquaintances he found out that Helen Keller would be in Rochester, Minnesota. A doctor friend suggested that Edward and Markell invite Miss Keller for tea or dinner.

Everyone was excited about the visit, even the dogs. "We had a very ferocious dachshund at the time, called Weenie," Binky recalled. "Very small, but ferocious. She bit the pants off the mailman once—tore them, is what I'm trying to say. So we decided Weenie needed to be put away for this event."

When Helen Keller arrived with her companion and interpreter Polly Thomson, they came into the garden room. Binky explained that at the west end of the room was a dark red leather swinging couch on four chains. Helen Keller sat on the couch, then Polly next to her, then Binky sat next to Polly. Suddenly, Weenie arrived. (I imagine that Weenie had been shut in one of the children's bedrooms, but went through the Jack-and-Jill bathroom into the adjoining bedroom and then out that bedroom door.) Weenie ran through the garden room door, cutting a wide curve for speed, and jumped into Miss Keller's lap.

"This wild little dachshund! We were all very nervous about it. Her hand stroked this little thing and the dog settled right down," Binky said. "She just calmly started to stroke the dog. She never expressed any kind of shock or wonder; I also didn't hear her laughing. She was perfectly comfortable with this dog on her lap."

In a tribute published by the American Foundation for the Blind, Helen Keller would write, "The charming relations I have had with a long succession of dogs result from their happy spontaneity. Usually, they are quick to discover that I cannot see or hear. Considerately, they rise as I come near, so that I may not stumble. It is not training but love which impels them to break the silence about me with the thud of a tail rippling against my chair, or gambols round the study, or news conveyed by an expressive ear, nose, and paw."

"After my dad put Weenie away again," Binky continued, "we went for a walk in the backyard into the garden. There were fuchsia bushes. When Helen came out there, Polly Thomson was guiding her and put her hands on the plants. She felt the blossom and said 'fuchsia.' How did she know? So amazing. She was so educated and so exposed to so many kinds of knowledge through her fingers."[38]

Binky often played the piano for guests, but for a deaf guest? Binky explained:

My parents had me play the piano for them, a little Beethoven. Helen stood with her hands on the piano. After I finished this short piece, she lifted her hands and said "Beethoven." She knew from the dynamics and the spaces.

When we had dinner, Helen sat next to my father, who was at the head of the table. Suddenly I saw him putting his hand out, palm up, near her plate. I thought, "How could he do that? Doesn't he know she's blind?"

Then it was like in tai chi when they follow the movement of somebody coming to them, and they take that energy and they just follow it around. My father held out his hand, and she just put her hand in his. There was no sound; there was no comment about it. It was in silence. It was amazing to see that. She could feel his energy.

Helen Keller was in Minnesota in the fall of 1937. She had gallbladder surgery in Rochester in September and was well enough to meet with a news reporter on October 9. A photograph accompanying the article shows her touching a bouquet of flowers and is captioned: "Through her fingertips, Miss Keller 'sees' the fragile beauty as a floral bouquet, and her appreciation is as keen as that of a seeing person."[39] She recovered and left Minnesota, with Polly Thomson, for her Long Island home on October 14.

Miss Keller returned to Minnesota a year later, on October 2, 1938, for a follow-up visit to the Mayo Clinic. On October 7, she visited thirty-five hearing-impaired students in Rochester and told them, "Like you, I know the trials of silence and it thrills me to find myself among you walking toward new victories."[40] She likely visited Eastcliff at that time, as she stayed in Minnesota several days, visited the University of Minnesota Twin Cities campus, and attended a Gopher football game.[41]

A front-page story by Jack Keefe in the October 9, 1938, *Minneapolis Sunday Tribune* was headlined "Helen Keller 'Sees' Game, Becomes Minnesota Grid Fan" with the second headline "Helen Keller Thrilled by Gopher Fans Roar." This was Keller's first football game since 1904, when she was a student at Radcliffe College, and her first in a big stadium. (It was Polly Thomson's first football game ever.) Miss Keller could follow the vibrations of the 52,000 fans cheering and was told of the game's progress by Miss Thomson and Dr. C. F. Dixon. When the Gophers scored (they won 7–0 over Purdue), she knew and was on her feet cheering without being told what had happened. After the game, she remarked that her greatest thrill was when Wilbur Moore returned a punt and, while being tackled, tossed a lateral pass to John Mariucci, who ran to the Purdue 15-yard line. Unlike other fans, she also commented that she appreciated how the sunshine and wind brought the smell of the grass on the field to her.

Eastcliff in Miniature

When the house was built in 1922, the width of the south porch (now called the garden room) was the same as the living room. The south porch width was extended from nineteen to thirty-four feet (into the backyard) in 1926, with a sleeping porch for Mr. Brooks added on the second floor off the master bedroom sitting room.

The garden room addition has tall windows over low walls, like the rest of the room. Double French doors open to the terrace on the north-facing wall. The room addition is currently furnished with a round oak table, a Stickley sideboard, and a rectangular oak table holding a large 1:12 scale miniature of Eastcliff.

Doors into and out of the garden room from both the living room and the terrace make it an excellent place to serve beverages during warm-weather events. The room is also the beverage area during large cold-weather events, to keep guests moving around the house rather than congregating near the food in the dining room.

Several people mentioned to me that the garden room would be a lovely place to enjoy my coffee in the sun each morning—if only I had had the time! Their suggestions did inspire me to have small meetings in that room, as well as visits with very special people.

During one of Binky Brooks's visits, I asked Barbara Baer Braman Bentson to join us. Barbara had been a classmate of Binky's younger brother, Dwight, and Barbara told Binky that she probably remembered her as a "little brat." I couldn't imagine that Barbara was a bratty child, as she was one of the kindest people I ever met. She became a very dear friend.

As we sat in the garden room, Barbara vividly recalled the first time she visited Eastcliff. She was in eighth grade (around 1940) and Dwight Brooks invited her and other classmates to a pool party. Barbara had told me previously that she could still remember the swimsuit she wore that day, with rickrack trim. Markell Brooks was inside sewing, and meeting the elegant and artistic Mrs. Brooks left a lasting impression on Barbara, who became a designer and art collector as an adult.

When I asked her to share the story with Binky, she said, "I was looking at all the girls and boys swimming, and I thought, 'I could see them any day,

I'm going in to talk to Mrs. Brooks. So I went in and spent the afternoon with your mother. We sat in front of the fireplace, and I had such a good time. Your mother showed me the needlepoint chairs she was doing; I'd never heard of needlepoint. She even took me upstairs and showed me where the safe was. I'll never forget it."

Shortly after that 1940 meeting, Barbara learned that Mrs. Brooks was working with miniaturist Elsa Mannheimer,[42] a friend of the Baer family, to furnish a dollhouse with miniature furniture and artwork that matched furnishings in Eastcliff. Many days after school, Barbara would ride her bicycle to Miss Mannheimer's house on Holly Avenue in St. Paul to watch the progress of the dollhouse. She thought the two women were an unlikely pair to be friends: Barbara recalls Mrs. Brooks looking elegant in a perfectly tailored brown crepe dress, while the very petite Miss Mannheimer always worked in a housecoat. The two women worked together furnishing the dollhouse as it sat on Miss Mannheimer's dining room table.[43]

In 2005, Barbara was back at Eastcliff. She had married longtime friend Larry Bentson. Larry and his late first wife, Nancy Rubin Bentson, had established the Bentson Scholarship at the University of Minnesota. During an Eastcliff event, Barbara asked President Bruininks what had happened to the Eastcliff dollhouse. Barbara and her first husband had been close friends of Ted and Ginny Brooks, so she knew their daughters, Kakie and Julie, had played with the dollhouse while growing up and had saved all the little pieces. Barbara knew Julie Brooks Zelle had donated the dollhouse to the University. Barbara, with her long-time interest in art and miniatures, was inspired to renovate and refurbish the original dollhouse, and over the next five years she spent countless hours on the project. She shared the detailed story with me in 2014.

According to Barbara, Markell Conley Brooks had a dollhouse when she was a child in the early 1900s. Around 1940, she purchased a similar dollhouse to furnish as a replica of Eastcliff. Many of the items made for that dollhouse were still intact over sixty years later. The furnishings that Markell and Elsa Mannheimer had made were works of art, but the structure was not. Barbara decided to re-create the re-creation, with the distinctive staircase, hand-painted peacock room, and many newly created pieces of furniture.[44] She hired artisan Patrick Kinney to build the house with working windows and doors, hard-wiring for lights and outlets, and the exquisite center staircase. The house includes hardwood flooring (made by Karen Halls), a peacock room (painted by Judy Harrigan), fireplace reproductions, and walnut paneling in the den.

Barbara worked closely with Marney and Ginny Brooks on the interior of the house. They used pieces from the original dollhouse and found a few

The new dollhouse. Photograph by Patrick O'Leary; courtesy of University Photographer records, University of Minnesota Archives.

perfect pieces in miniature shops in Minnesota and New York. Almost all of the new pieces in the house were custom-made by a team of artists and artisans who copied furnishings that were still with the Brooks children and grandchildren or were visible in photographs from the 1940s.

Among the many pieces that remain from the original dollhouse are glass figures and tiny glass bottles (the family's care of the dollhouse is exemplified by the fact that Kakie and Julie played with the house as children yet the vases still retain the original stoppers), and artwork on the walls including two paintings by Elsa Mannheimer, one a copy of a portrait of Mrs. Brooks's beloved aunt Lena Flower and the other a copy of a painting of Minneopa Falls from 1865.

The pieces created for the 2010 house include copies of Markell Brooks's needlepoint creations that are still in the family (including a rug and dining room chairs monogrammed with Brooks family members' initials that required 840 hours of work by miniaturist Peggy Meyers), a hand-painted Venetian secretary made by artist James Hastritch that is a faithful copy of the original (including hinged doors, a dropleaf, miniature drawer pulls, and tiny portraits painted on the working drawers), a grandfather clock that keeps time using a hearing aid battery, and a tiny Eastcliff dollhouse within the dollhouse.

The pieces purchased, but not commissioned for the house, include two needlepoint rugs made by Jo Crooks of the Shakopee Mdewakanton Sioux Community (one of the rugs has more than 87,000 tiny stitches), two sterling silver candelabras, two knife boxes with silver knives, and many books (including some whose pages turn and contain writing).

Barbara donated pieces from her own collection, including a miniature silver pot representing the coffee pot Edward Brooks kept next to his chair and a beautiful painted chest that holds the dollhouse within the dollhouse. Carl Drake Jr., former chairman of the St. Paul Companies, heard about the dollhouse restoration project and donated items from his mother's dollhouse. His parents, Carl B. Drake, MD, and Louise H. Drake, had been friends of the Brooks family, so the miniature Eastcliff was a fitting home for her pieces.

I had written text for a children's book titled *Weenie Meets Helen Keller*. Barbara and I collaborated on the concept of illustrating it with photographs of paper dolls in the Eastcliff dollhouse. Extensive details and photographs of the dollhouse are included in the book.

The miniature house remains a popular attraction for visitors to Eastcliff. It presents a visual history of the remarkable home and is a tribute both to the Brooks family legacy and to Barbara's vision. Barbara Baer Braman Bentson (1929–2017) was a very special woman and a wonderful friend to me and to Eastcliff.

The dining room, during the Bruininks administration. Photograph by Patrick O'Leary. Courtesy of University Photographer records, University of Minnesota Archives.

3
What's for Dinner?

THE BROOKS FAMILY DINING ROOM *could accommodate twelve diners. In the late 1980s, the room was enlarged into the space of the former kitchen.*

As a dinner guest in the Eastcliff dining room, if you face east, you will see a swinging door. Waitstaff go back and forth through that door to serve meals, just like they did in 1922, though in 1987 the door was moved twenty feet back and eight feet to the left. Currently, when waitstaff serving at Eastcliff events walk out of the dining room through the swinging door, they go through the family kitchen, past the service door going outside on the left and the door going down to the basement on the right, into the catering kitchen.

Looking at the 1921 and 1930 floor plans, I recognized that live-in help requires a lot of space. The east end of the house was used almost exclusively by people who were not members of the resident family. This changed, to a greater and lesser degree, as the house changed. The kitchen changed as well.

THE DINING ROOM

For the Brooks family dining room, Mrs. Brooks had stitched needlepoint cushion covers for twelve American Hepplewhite chairs. The individual monograms

of Edward and Markell and their four children were on two chairs each. The chair Edward regularly sat in was a large wing chair. The chairs remain with the Brooks family, and miniatures of some of these chairs are in the dollhouse. A small side table sat next to Edward's chair at the dining room table, holding a silver coffee pot. Next to Markell's chair was a button for summoning the maids.

A large crystal pendant chandelier hung in the room, as well as silver candelabrum wall fixtures with tall black candles. The carpet in the

Dining room before the murals, circa 1922. Courtesy of the Brooks family.

room was a soft green, and the French doors opening to the terrace were antiqued silver leaf.

Over a baseboard of dark olive green were silver-leaf walls painted with tropical foliage, flowers, and flowering trees, along with birds and butterflies. A graceful white crane emerged from the plants, and a peacock perched over a mirror, with his plumage trailing around the mirror's frame. A peahen sat on a tree. These gorgeous murals, painted in 1927, reportedly took six weeks of work from artist Gustav Krollmann.[1] When Mrs. Brooks moved out, she took the bird murals that were on the dining room walls. They remain with the Brooks family.

Elegant with a Capital E

When I imagine Markell Brooks entertaining, I picture her floating down Eastcliff's Georgian staircase in an evening gown. I heard that Markell always dressed for dinner. Family photographs often show her in evening gowns. The Minnesota Historical Society has one of Markell's dresses in its collection, a Delphos (finely pleated silk) rose-colored evening gown designed by Mariano Fortuny.

I never floated down the grand staircase for Eastcliff events. I went out of my way to go down the hall and down the back (formerly servants') stairs and emerge from the kitchen. I joked that I was attempting to create the illusion that I was in the kitchen cooking. (Everyone knew that we hired caterers to cook meals for events.) In truth, I would picture Markell and think that I couldn't make a Markell-quality entrance. Markell's daughter-in-law Marney wrote when she was a new bride, "Markell had a way of encouraging talent in others and, I must say, I learned a tremendous amount from her. But how was I ever going to follow in her footsteps? Today I wonder why I thought I had to."[2] I'm grateful that I was old enough when I "met" Markell to admire her without being intimidated. Marney wrote:

> I remember so well sitting at the dinner table at Eastcliff, my mother-in-law sitting regally at the end, pressing the button for the maids to clear or produce another course. The table, as usual, was beautifully appointed—Marshall linens, probably maiden hair fern and flowers in the winter. In other words, elegant with a capital E. The meal would begin with a cream soup, probably, and the second course I remember best was a veal dish called Veal Paprika. I think that was what it was called. I have the recipe in the old notebook full of her favorites. It was veal simmered in a tomato sauce, onions, and garlic cooked to just the right degree of succulence. There would be wide noodles to accompany

this dish and maybe her wonderful lima bean and green pea puree. All of this was delectable. Anna, the cook, was a pro as you could guess from the size of her. After the second helping had been passed and devoured, we waited in great anticipation for the piece de resistance, having had a whiff from the kitchen of what it might be. Eureka—out it came, a perfect chocolate soufflé and with it the yummy sauce that seemed to blend perfectly. I always wanted to try my hand at it but never had the courage.[3]

My impression of Markell's elegant entertaining was further reinforced by a neighbor. Ginna Kilpatrick was a young child in the late 1950s when her family moved to a house on Otis Avenue near Eastcliff; she moved back into the family home as an adult. She told me she remembered the kindness and

Dining room murals. Courtesy of the Brooks family.

grace of Markell Brooks who, then a widow, invited the new neighbors for eggnog in December. Ginna recalled that Mrs. Brooks welcomed them to Eastcliff wearing an elegant black velvet evening gown.

Family dinners were surely a different matter. Or maybe not. Small glass figurines were placed in fingerbowls at the dinner table to teach the Brooks children to delicately wash their fingers; some of these figurines have survived and are in the Eastcliff dollhouse. A child who misbehaved at dinner was sent by Mr. Brooks into the hallway to stand and finish dinner there. If the dinner wasn't finished, the child was served it again at breakfast.

> Children were brought up to observe rules and guidelines, and these were never questioned. The family met for breakfast by seven o'clock. They all knew they had better be there on time. The breakfast table was always set, and Alice and Alvina served. Markell sat at the west end of the table with an electric button close at hand, which she pushed to summon the servants.[4]

Complementing their sophistication, the Brookses were true Minnesotans who relished being outdoors. During pleasant weather, meals were served on the flagstone terrace. Their outdoor table had a large round top on a base made from a gigantic tree stump. They also had a lake home on Gull Lake. Many Minnesotans go to "the Lake," without specifying which of the 11,842 large Minnesota lakes, but unlike typical Minnesotans, the Brookses' lake entourage included their servants.

Conley Jr., as a grandchild, escaped the strict discipline, but he did recall the family's elegance and formality. He confirmed the rumor I had heard: his grandmother Markell did always "dress" for dinner. He also recalled that his grandparents always used Lawry's Seasoned Salt on their scrambled eggs, which he thought was quite elegant at the time.

Entertaining was part of Brooks family life long before Edward and Markell married. A 1902 newspaper article[5] (when Edward would have been thirteen, Markell barely three) described a party that Edward's parents held at their home on Lynnhurst Avenue in St. Paul. Three hundred invitations were sent, and guests visited all evening. According to the article, "Yellow roses enhanced the beautiful furnishings in the library, and an elaborate centerpiece of pink roses decked the table in the dining room." Long-stemmed white lilies were in the drawing room and American beauty roses were in the hall and living room. A stringed orchestra played throughout the evening.

Entertaining in style, as Dwight and Anna Brooks had, lasted throughout the years Edward and Markell Brooks lived at Eastcliff and was passed on to the next generation. Barbara Bentson told me that when she and her first husband, Eddie Braman, were a young married couple, Ted was one of the "last eligible bachelors" in their circle. Ted invited Barbara and Eddie, along with a few other couples, to a dinner party at Eastcliff. The dishes were Chinese porcelain painted with a dragon on an orange background, and the servants wore orange silk with white aprons. Barbara recalled the elegance many years later.

The last eligible bachelor married at the advanced age of thirty-two. Ted met Ginny Dahleen, a Northwest flight attendant, on a date arranged by mutual friends in November 1956, and they married five months later. Barbara said that Ted was so charming that she and Eddie considered Ted and Ginny their very special friends. Then they went to a party and discovered that one hundred other people there felt the same way. Ted had great charisma. I was reminded of this story at Barbara's memorial service—I felt Barbara was my very special friend, and more than one hundred people at her service felt the same way.

The Stemwinder

As you read of Markell Brooks's dinner parties, perhaps you wonder why I don't write more about Edward as the host of those parties. Even before I read their friend Frannie's description of Markell, I suspected that she was the "stemwinder for the parties." Their friend Barbara Foote said of Markell and Edward: "She had such sensitive, intuitive, almost mystical qualities, and he was very much down to earth and practical."[6] Ms. Foote told a story of a rather large dinner party at Eastcliff. As guests began to leave, they asked where Edward was. Markell deflected the questions with "he must have just slipped upstairs for a minute, but I'll tell him you said goodbye." Before Barbara left, Edward appeared looking over the banister in his pajamas and explained, "It gets sort of boring. At least two of the men wanted to marry you. I did get bored and just went off and polished up the car, then decided there

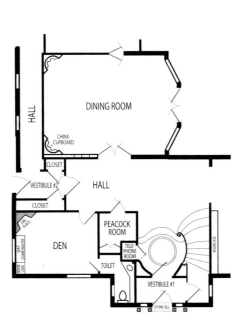

Dining room plan (unbuilt), circa 1937. Drawn by the author from an architectural drawing stored in the University's engineering archives.

was no point in going back, so I went up into the shower and I am here. Why don't you girls come up?"

Ms. Foote said that Markell had obviously seen this before, and she thought that Edward had once even returned to a party wearing his pajamas.

A Too-Small Dining Room

Although the original Eastcliff dining room was a large (sixteen by seventeen feet) elegant room for a family, its size limited sit-down dinner parties to twelve guests. In 1937, the Brookses hired the Clarence Johnston architectural firm to draw plans for a dining room expansion. The plan would expand the dining room nearly seven feet south into the terrace, increasing the width of the room from sixteen to nearly twenty-three feet. However, the expansion was never built.[7]

Presidential Entertaining

When Eastcliff was donated to the University, a reproduction Duncan Phyfe walnut table (now approximately one hundred years old and still used), ten chairs, and a crystal chandelier were moved from the Pillsbury mansion to the Eastcliff dining room. During the Wilson administration, the chairs were upholstered in red, matching occasional chairs in the living room. Marian Wilson explained to the interested newspapers that for large groups, meals would be served buffet style in the dining room, with seating all around the house.[8]

According to newspaper columnist Barbara Flanagan, who met with the Wilsons at Eastcliff in 1960, "I remember that it was the kitchen that stopped them. On a walk-through before they moved in, Marian looked at the old-fashioned room, smiled, and said, 'Something will have to be done with this.'"[9]

The Eastcliff kitchen was modernized before the Wilsons moved in, albeit with the same layout. The cabinets and appliances were replaced. The live-in cook helped design the kitchen she would use.

The Moos family ate dinner around their own large dining room table. The top was Cold Spring granite from quarries in Stearns County, Minnesota. Malcolm Moos had the granite slab cut and polished, and a stainless-steel base was custom-made to support the weight of the granite. It took eight men to move the table into the house.

The Moos family arrived in 1967. On September 13, 1968, the Board of

Regents voted to designate Brooks Cavin as architect for a proposed addition to Eastcliff. The plan he drew, like the 1937 plan, expanded into the terrace but was much more extensive. The original dining room remained almost unchanged as a family dining room. A gallery approximately forty feet long and twelve feet deep was added alongside the entry and living room. This gallery opened into a new, very large dining room (approximately sixteen by thirty-two feet) running parallel to the existing dining room and kitchen. In an extension of the basement below the dining room, there was a large activity room and a small wine cellar, as well as a large men's toilet. A women's toilet and powder room were planned in the existing space.

Planned expansion, 1967 (unbuilt). Drawn by the author from 1968 architectural drawings stored in the University's engineering archives.

At the next meeting of the Board of Regents on October 11, 1968, the Regents voted to approve the borrowing of up to $70,000 from the North-western National Bank for the expansion of Eastcliff. The loan was secured, but the expansion was never built.[10] This time we know why. Former Min-nesota governor and then Regent Elmer Andersen[11] said:

> I remember on the Board of Regents having a visit with Malcolm Moos that something needed to be done at Eastcliff, that it was a ceremonial center, and it wasn't properly equipped for what it was supposed to do, and it was deteriorating physically, and it just needed attention. We needed to have a committee to really set up a program and finance a proper rehabilitation of Eastcliff. So he agreed to the committee, and we set up the committee, and we got an appraisal and an estimate. It was going to cost quite a bit of money and I remember him saying, "Elmer, we can't. I can't in good conscience with all the disturbance there is and the concern of the students and the general society insta-bility." He said, "I can't go with an item to the legislature for Eastcliff; so, please, forget it." So we forgot it.

During the Magrath administration, the Pillsbury era table was again in use, and the dining chairs were covered with "Flame Point" Williamsburg fabric. (They still are.) The draperies (there are none now) were cranberry red and silver stripe.

The "new" kitchen appliances were twenty years old when the position of live-in cook was eliminated. The family continued to use the kitchen, but food for events was typically prepared on campus and transported to East-cliff. The dining room was as small as ever, and the house continued to age. In a letter in 1982 to staff associated with Eastcliff, Diane Skomars Magrath wrote: "Eastcliff has obviously withstood the problems of 1981/82 with open arms to all and with dignity. With the budgets at the University so severely cut, everyone associated with the residence has tried to be sensitive and less demanding on Physical Plant for repairs and maintenance, and even more careful about food costs, and cautious about any major changes and/or projects at Eastcliff. We will follow the same pattern in 1982/83."

Clearly the dining room wasn't being expanded in the early 1980s. In 1984, in response to the Board of Regents' suggestions that Eastcliff needed to be renovated, President Magrath appointed a committee to make recom-mendations. The minutes from a Board of Regents' meeting in September 1985 stated, regarding Eastcliff renovation: "The repairs and updating were suggested last year by a committee appointed by former university president C. Peter Magrath, but were delayed after his resignation. Repairs are needed in some parts of the 20-room house and a larger kitchen and dining room are necessary because of the many university functions that take place at Eastcliff."

In the interview quoted earlier, Elmer Andersen continued:

> Then, along came Peter Magrath and we went through the same thing with him. He said, "Elmer, when we can't do adequately first for salaries of the faculty . . . We're going past years now with no increase at all, so actually their real income is going down." He said, "I can't see us spending a lot of money on Eastcliff when I haven't the money for salaries; so, please, forget it." So we forgot it.
>
> Then Ken Keller came along. We said, "We just have to do something about this. It just cannot go on any longer. The place is just going to crumble." So Ken Keller bit the bullet and, of course, it became a big fracas.

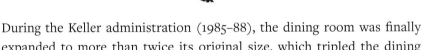

During the Keller administration (1985–88), the dining room was finally expanded to more than twice its original size, which tripled the dining capacity. Two crystal chandeliers similar to the chandelier from the Pillsbury mansion were added to the expanded dining room. The servants' bedroom area, no longer needed, was converted into a catering kitchen. This renovation has been the event most written about in the history of Eastcliff, with the controversy centered on the catering kitchen.

In the mid-1990s, during the Hasselmo administration, the ceiling of the lovely and now appropriately sized dining room was refurbished with sound-absorbing acoustic tiles. The restroom off the dining room was remodeled to be accessible to wheelchairs.

In 1997, during the Yudof administration, moss green on green medallion wallpaper was added to the dining room; the accessible restroom was remodeled to be more attractive; and a second rectangular table and chairs were purchased. In 2001, an elevator replaced the closet in the entry opposite the restroom.

During the Bruininks administration, a sideboard that had been in the Brooks family dining room was donated by the Brooks family and returned to the Eastcliff dining room.

In addition to describing the history of Eastcliff, this book is intended to give you an understanding of the life of the partner of a university president through the experiences of the nine University of Minnesota presidents' spouses who have lived at Eastcliff.

I delight in evocative collective nouns: a mob of kangaroos, a parade of elephants, a murder of crows, a prickle of porcupines. The Eastcliff carriage house previously contained so many boxes that I called them "a fire hazard of files." During the slower summer months of our tenure at Eastcliff, Pam Hudson, who worked in the Eastcliff office, went through the boxes and boxes of files. The winnowing of these files resulted in six large file boxes of event folders—nearly eight linear feet. The archived files begin in late 1984 and go through 2012 (although 2009 through 2011 are missing). Reading through those files, one event at a time, gave me a glimpse into the events of the past and the food that was served. I did not have files from the Wilson, Moos, or Magrath administrations, but I had wonderful conversations with Tracy Moos and Diane Skomars Magrath, and some of the Wilson and Moos events were covered in the newspaper. Diane wrote about her experiences both contemporaneously and later.

How many guests do you entertain in your home each year, not counting family members? How many people do you consider to be *a lot* of guests? Estimates for events held by presidential families at Eastcliff range from 50 to 150 annually. The numbers of guests entertained have been reported in different years as between 3,000 and 7,500. No matter who has lived in Eastcliff, we have all entertained *a lot.* Eastcliff is such a gracious home that it is a joy to entertain there, and the house seemed to have welcomed the guests and insisted on inviting people in.

People often asked me if we *had* to entertain every night, or if we had to entertain a lot. We certainly didn't entertain every night; some nights we were at events elsewhere. I would also respond that we didn't have to have events. Each event we were hosting was special, or we wouldn't be hosting it. That wasn't just a compliment to the group or honoree that was the reason for the event. We hosted many special events; at our great university there were many more causes for celebration than the hundreds of events we were able to host, and fortunately there are many event venues. The average frequency of events (not including meetings), when we were in town, seemed to be three times a week. Is that a little or a lot? I was often reminded of a scene from the movie *Annie Hall.* Annie's and Alvy's therapists, in separate locations, ask about "how often." She answers, "Constantly; I'd say . . ." He answers, "Hardly ever; maybe . . ." Then together they finish their thoughts: "Three times a week."

Markell Brooks was the first and the longest-tenured Eastcliff host, living in the home for thirty-eight years. She was said to be such a gracious hostess that I assumed she loved entertaining, but perhaps even for her it could be exhausting. I found one small anecdote to be telling: She was in the hospital after her first heart attack, and a friend was visiting her. She said to her friend, "Isn't it wonderful? I won't have to give any more big parties."[12]

Sandra Magrath was quoted as saying, "The social life connected with a university administration is very demanding. We attend so many dinners and we give many. I prefer to give small buffet or sit-down dinners for twelve to twenty rather than have large numbers. It is easier to get to know people in smaller groups."[13] Sandra wrote in a "Notes from Eastcliff" column that "Many times I am asked questions by curious, but interested, people how often we must entertain others, how busy our schedule must be or how we like our life here in Minnesota. 'Public people,' and I truly feel we have to describe ourselves as such, arouse curiosity about the lives they lead. The public wants to know how these people become prominent and why they should deserve public notice."[14]

I doubt there were many more painful times to be a public person than six months later in April 1977 when the *Minneapolis Star* and the *University Brief* published news that the Magraths had decided to separate after twenty-two years of marriage. Their public statement read: "After much thought and consideration, we have made the difficult decision to separate on an amicable basis. A divorce is possible, but that decision is left open. Since this is a personal matter affecting the two of us, we sincerely ask that our desire for privacy be respected."[15] The couple did divorce shortly thereafter in July 1977. Two years later a newspaper article mentioned that the pace of being the spouse of a university president is difficult and contributed to the divorce. President Magrath was quoted in an article in 1982 describing his early years in the presidency: "I focused everything on 'my work.' Maybe that's when you're a bit younger and trying to rise and achieve. I believe I slighted my family and personal considerations more than I should have. I don't do that now."[16]

For all of us, I expect that entertaining was interesting and at times exhilarating but often exhausting.

Guest Lists

Breakfasts, lunches, dinners, receptions, award ceremonies with buffets before or after—almost all events include food. However, the focus of each event was, quite obviously, the guests.

Names of some of Eastcliff's notable guests are listed at the end of this book, and categories of guests are described here. Each presidential couple has hosted events in all these categories, and they have each hosted many of the same events. Reading through many articles and files, I became aware that all the presidents entertained, not surprisingly, somewhat according to their own preferences and strengths. For example, in the history of the University there have been just three University-wide capital campaigns. President Keller started the Minnesota Campaign; President Yudof started the Campaign for Minnesota. President Kaler joked that there had been only two campaigns because we had run out of names, then he initiated the campaign *Driven*. These three presidents viewed fundraising as an important part of their responsibilities, and they held many donor events. President Hasselmo is credited with improving the undergraduate experience at the University, and it's no coincidence that commencement receptions at Eastcliff began during his tenure.

While President Moos and President Kaler are the only two University alumni to become president of the University of Minnesota (many University alums have led other institutions), President Keller and President Bruininks

President Nils Hasselmo, 1989. University of Minnesota Libraries, University Archives.

were both more *of* the University, having spent all of their pre-presidential careers at the institution. Both their wives are Minnesota natives and received degrees from the University, Bonita both her undergraduate and law degrees, and Susan her doctorate in education. These experiences may have subtly influenced their uses of Eastcliff: President Keller had monthly dinners with faculty, and President Bruininks opened Eastcliff to departments for meetings.

Eric and I rarely hosted events after music or dance performances. Eric served on the board of the Guthrie Theater, and while we are big fans of the University and Guthrie Theater BFA in Acting program, we went to very few performances. Eric was always up so early answering emails that he would often fall asleep as soon as the lights dimmed.

While faculty and staff are included in many types of events, there are a few annual events just for them. The President's Award for Outstanding Service "recognizes faculty and staff who have provided exceptional service . . . well beyond the regular duties . . . and demonstrate unusual commitment to the University community" across all campuses. These are fun events, as each award recipient invites ten guests and each guest is happy to be there supporting these remarkable people.

The Outstanding Service event requires a tent and chairs on the lawn, so it was typically planned to be within a day or two of another award presentation that Eric delighted in: a celebration of civil service and bargaining unit employees (those represented by labor unions) with twenty years of service and with each five-year increment over twenty. Recognition began in the Hasselmo administration in 1990, with a gift for every five years of service. President Hasselmo had a drawing for employees with more than twenty years of service, and the selected few joined him for lunch at Eastcliff. After a few years, the current plan was adopted. Employees with forty or more years are recognized on stage. Eric loved telling of their service, particularly those who served the University for forty-five and fifty years, of whom there were more than you might expect.

New faculty receptions are also a regular event. Each December we also hosted a winter open house for all faculty and staff (hundreds, but not the potential thousands, attended), and President Gabel has continued that new tradition. There are occasional retirement dinners, and the University of Minnesota Retirees Association (UMRA) and the Retiree Volunteer Center have had an annual reception at Eastcliff for twenty years. I spoke at the event each fall, as did Susan Hagstrum before me, and Judy Yudof before

Katherine E. Nash's stainless-steel sculpture *Continuum*, on the front lawn. Photograph by Patrick O'Leary. Courtesy of University Photographer records, University of Minnesota Archives.

her. The University of Minnesota Women's Club, which began as the Faculty Women's Club over one hundred years ago as a group for faculty wives and expanded to include anyone with an interest in the University, has had regular events at Eastcliff since the 1960s.

There are so many interesting and brilliant members of the University faculty, but only thirty at any one time can hold Regents Professorships. This group is the best of our best. Some of the receptions for new Regents Professors have been at Eastcliff, and those during our tenure left me in awe of the excellence of the faculty.

Students have visited Eastcliff throughout each presidency. One freshman honors student who attended a tea with President and Mrs. Moos was Baudette High School valedictorian Bonita Sindelir; a little more than twenty years later, Bonita would move in when her husband, Kenneth Keller, became president. Diane Skomars Magrath wrote, "Coming from a background in student affairs, I especially loved inviting the student government representatives to meet with the President for breakfast at the house." I remember our first reception for student leaders: Minnesota Student Association (MSA) President Lizzy Shay and Vice President Colin Burke attended, as did Graduate and Professional Student Association (GAPSA) President Abou Amara and Abdul Omari, who was a student representative to the Board of Regents.

Most governors of Minnesota since 1960 have been guests at Eastcliff, including our most famous governor, Jesse Ventura. Governors Elmer L. Andersen and Wendell R. Anderson became Regents and visited more regularly in that capacity. The first twenty-one Minnesota governors were all Regents, but that was before Eastcliff. All the University presidents have sought to further engage elected officials in learning about the University—Eric liked to call the legislators his 201 best friends. The University's Regents are elected in a joint session of the Minnesota House and Senate. Every presidential family has entertained University Regents regularly.

Many national and international leaders have visited Eastcliff, as well as leaders of tribal nations. Walter Mondale and Hubert Humphrey visited while they were sitting United States vice presidents, and Mr. Mondale visited many times after that as a wonderful, and humble, University citizen. Humphrey taught at the University after serving as vice president, so he likely was a regular guest as well. Ambassadors and ministers have been regular guests. Presidents or chancellors from Minnesota private colleges, Minnesota State Universities, and all Big Ten schools have visited. I started making a list of other university presidents, ambassadors, ministers, and so on, who have been guests, and the list became too long to include them all. It spans from A to Z, from the leader of the University of Amsterdam to the ambassador from Zambia.

University of Minnesota Alumni Association (UMAA) leadership events at Eastcliff are fun because everyone is enthusiastic about the University. They all feel like longtime friends even if you've just met them. Seeing a UMAA guest list from the 1980s, I was heartened to see the names of many people who are still good friends of the University—and good friends of ours. Alumni are also the honorees at one of our favorite events, the Outstanding Achievement Award (OAA) recognition. The University has around a half million living alumni, of which only a handful each year win this award. As Judy Yudof said, "It's a heartwarming event and one of the nicest uses of the house."[17] When the presentation is at Eastcliff, the awardee suggests a guest list and the guests are all delighted that someone they love has won the award. That makes for a great party. The procedure is similar for honorary degrees, which are even greater honors, and the recipients are not typically alumni.

While there are many events celebrating donors, reading through guest lists for dinner parties throughout the years I saw the names of many guests who *later* became major donors to the University. It was a reminder, if I ever needed one, that relationships are at the heart of philanthropy. Friends become donors; donors become friends. Events help potential donors learn more about something they may want to support or are held to thank donors for their support.

An event for University Art Museum donors during the Sauer interim presidency in 1988 took good advantage of Eastcliff being vacant. Paintings that had been donated to the University's art collection were hung on the Eastcliff walls, so the donors were welcomed and thanked in the presence of the artworks. A pivotal moment for the art museum occurred a few years later at Eastcliff. A museum board member, Billy Weisman, met Frederick R. Weisman, a former University of Minnesota student who owned Mid-Atlantic Toyota. The two Weismans discovered they weren't related, but one thing led to another and they talked about the University's art museum. Lyndel King, the museum's director, then talked to Nils Hasselmo, and Nils invited Frederick Weisman to lunch at Eastcliff. Weisman agreed to donate four and a half of the twelve million dollars needed to build a new museum, designed by Frank Gehry. Weisman's gift inspired further donations.

Beginning in 2005, and each fall for more than ten years (until the group became too large), a President's Club new member reception was held at Eastcliff, welcoming donors who had achieved a high level of lifetime giving. During our tenure, after a dinner in a large tent on the Eastcliff lawn, an always inspirational student speaker would tell the group how scholarship support had changed his or her life. Eric always said that he never wanted to follow the student speaker; they were always so good that anything else was superfluous.

Research has shown that giving money to a good cause is one of the few ways that money really can buy happiness. I enjoy helping people find work to support that will bring them joy. I created an event series called Women, Wine, and Wise Words (nicknamed W4) to introduce women thought leaders to University researchers (who also were women). The researchers were so generous with their time and the topics were fascinating. Rebecca Schlafer, for example, spoke about children of incarcerated parents and the prison doula project, and Judy Eckerle spoke about the adoption medicine clinic; both gained new advocates through the events. I hosted more than a dozen of these events to shine a needed spotlight on brilliant research.

Members of the broader community are also regular guests. I refer to the University of Minnesota as just "the University" throughout this book, and throughout Minnesota the University is widely known as just "the U." It is *the* major research university and economic driver of the state. Many different constituencies and community partners are stakeholders in the University, and they have gathered at Eastcliff throughout the years.

The house has also hosted its actual neighbors. It's important, but challenging, to feel a part of the neighborhood when you live in the big house with the big fence. Throughout the years, neighbors have been invited to open houses, the Friends of Eastcliff Garden Party, and National Night Out. We were very grateful that Eastcliff has such good neighbors who endure their streets being packed with parked cars on a regular basis.

It's always special when former residents visit the house. Members of the Brooks family have been on Eastcliff guest lists throughout the years, both as part of other events and at gatherings just for the family.

In 1996, O. Meredith and Marian Wilson attended a dinner in their honor with the Hasselmos. Peter Magrath, Ken Keller, and Bonita Sindelir joined the Yudofs at Eastcliff after the dedication of the Magrath Library in 1998. Tracy Moos and Diane Skomars visited me at Eastcliff. Tracy attended events throughout the years, particularly with the women's club (UMWC). Diane went on to work in university relations and development on the Duluth campus and helped plan events at Eastcliff in that role. At a Board of Regents' dinner in December 2013, Regent Patricia Simmons's husband, Les Wold, was out of town so Patty brought Bonita Sindelir as her guest. I had a delightful evening sitting between Patty and Bonita.

Future residents have also been invited, unaware. In 1983, the Magraths hosted a going away party for the Hasselmo family. Nils Hasselmo had been at the University for eighteen years. He was leaving his role as vice president for administration and planning under Magrath to become provost and vice president for academic affairs at the University of Arizona. Neither would have guessed that Nils would return a little over five years later as president. In 1991, the Hasselmos hosted a welcoming event for new College of Education Dean Robert Bruininks, who had been on faculty since 1958. The guests included his wife and in-laws, Mr. and Mrs. Vincent Hagstrum. Bob Bruininks later became provost. The last dinner the Yudofs held, in 2002, was "honoring Robert Bruininks for his outstanding leadership as Executive Vice President and Provost." Bruininks was never an official candidate for president and described himself as "stunned" when he was chosen for the position after serving three months as the interim president.

In 2015 it occurred to Dr. Gary Engstrand, secretary to the faculty, that for the first time in history there were six living presidents of the University, and it might be interesting to get them all together on stage. "A Conversation with Six Presidents" was held on the Carlson Family Stage in Northrop Auditorium. After the on-stage conversation among the presidents, C. Peter Magrath and his wife, Susan Thon; Ken Keller and his wife, Bonita Sindelir; Nils Hasselmo and his wife, Ann Die Hasselmo; Mark and Judy Yudof; Bob Bruininks and his wife, Susan Hagstrum; and Eric and I all had dinner at Eastcliff. While neither Susan Thon (who married Peter after his third wife, Deborah Howell, died) nor Ann Die Hasselmo (who married Nils after Pat died) had lived at Eastcliff, Ann summed up my feelings when she said, somewhat in awe, how remarkable it was that we had all lived in the very house where we were having dinner together. That May evening is among my favorite memories of Eastcliff.

THE KITCHEN AND SERVANTS' QUARTERS

Entering the kitchen from the dining room in the original layout of the home, you would first pass through a butler's pantry with a sink and cupboards. The architectural drawing indicates places to store table leaves and trays in this room. Adjacent to the butler's pantry, with access to the kitchen, was a hall pantry. Next to the hall pantry was a hallway running to the left behind the dining room to the side door vestibule, and to the right was a door to a covered porch, which ran back to the servants' entrance. This hallway and porch allowed servants access to the front of the house and the kitchen and back of the house without entering the dining room.

Through doors from either pantry was the large kitchen, including a thirteen-by-sixteen-foot open space with a stove, sink, table, and cupboards, and an additional hallway about fifteen feet long with a refrigerator, counter, and cupboards. The icebox (which was called a refrigerator back then, before the development of electric refrigerators) was about five feet wide, with a cupboard above it. (It must have been counter height.) A note on the plans, indicating an opening over the refrigerator to the covered porch, reads: "Ice door, exact location later." Another

item not included in modern kitchens is an incinerator door, across a small hall-
way from the so-called refrigerator. Incineration was a common method of waste
disposal in the 1920s. The incinerator was a floor below this door in the laundry
room. The floors throughout the kitchen were indicated on the plans as "lino tile."

Next to the hallway part of the kitchen was a maid's sitting room. This room
had a corner fireplace, oak floors, and windows looking out to the terrace. Behind
the kitchen and sitting room were a hallway, a staircase, and a three-bay garage.

When the house was enlarged in 1930, the kitchen remained the same. The
garage was converted into two maids' bedrooms with closets and a sewing room,
and a hallway. An addition of approximately twelve by thirty feet extended to the
south and included a continuation of the hallway, another maid's bedroom and
closet, and a full bath to be shared by the residents of the three rooms. The addition
also had a linen room, which opened to the stair hall. Prior to the remodel, there
were two maids' rooms on the second floor. These rooms were remodeled into guest
rooms in 1930.

The Staff behind the Impeccable Hostess

What was it like growing up with "servants"? I can't imagine but, as Binky Brooks described, whatever your normal is as a child is normal to you. All indications suggest that the Brooks family's maids, cook, and caretaker were valued members of the extended family. Binky told me:

> I was thinking about how we grew up with this huge place, and to main-
> tain it! We had a cook; Mother didn't cook. She wasn't interested and
> she didn't have to, but she knew a lot about food and recipes. There was
> one girl (we called them "The Girls") who was in charge of downstairs
> and one was in charge of the upstairs. And then there was a caretaker
> who lived above the garage. Each of the three women had their own
> room in back, with a common bathroom. There was a sitting room
> with a fireplace where they could entertain their boyfriends (although
> I know only one of them who had a boyfriend). It was a very good life.
> We got to know their families. We would peek at the boyfriend. We
> never felt privileged or that our life was unusual in any way. It was a
> simple life.

Bertha, the cook, stayed with the family for twenty-nine years; the maids, Alvina and Alice, stayed even longer. Alice's brother, Clarence, was hired as caretaker and chauffeur, and he lived with his family in the apartment

over the carriage house. The staff also included a part-time laundress. More women were hired to serve at parties.

When the family bought property at Gull Lake in the early 1930s, the staff (the cook and two maids) would go there with the family during the summer. They wore uniforms, typically yellow and white at Eastcliff, red and white at the lake. Binky recalled seeing them "come through the woods in their red uniforms and white collars and

Brooks family staff, circa 1925. Courtesy of the Brooks family.

cuffs walking toward the house. They had their own cabin, and sometimes, if the weather was very hot, they loved to sit in canvas chairs, which they'd place right in the lake."

Conley described a dinner conversation that speaks to the comfortable relationship between the family and their employees. He described the beginning of his "lifetime involvement" with Marney Brown Brooks: "My mother asked if I was going to be taking any girls to all the parties that were going on during Christmas vacation. I said I didn't know whom to take. Alice Olson, a long-time employee of Mother's and Dad's, said, while passing the beans, 'Why don't you take out that cute Marney Brown? She lives just down the street.' So it began, and I've thanked Alice ever since."[18]

In 1944, the University of Minnesota Press published a book by newspaper columnist Virginia Stafford titled *Food of My Friends*. It was a reminder of life before wartime rationing—the life America was eager to reclaim. Chapters describe the entertaining styles of "sixty-eight of Minnesota's cosmopolitan hosts and hostesses." Familiar names include Mrs. (Senator) Joseph Ball, Mrs. James Ford Bell, Duncan Hines (the man who inspired the brand), Mrs. Stanley E. Hubbard, Doctors Jean and Jeannette Piccard,

Mrs. John S. Pillsbury, Mrs. Harold E. Stassen, Mrs. (Governor) Edward J. Thye, Mrs. Frederick K. Weyerhaeuser, and, of course, Mrs. Edward Brooks. The chapter "Hostess: Mrs. Edward Brooks" begins with a menu, followed by a line of text:

HORS D'OEUVRES

CLEAR TURTLE SOUP

MELBA TOAST—CELERY—HOT ALMONDS

CHICKEN WITH WHITE GRAPES—PUREE OF PEAS AND LIMA BEANS—
TINY POTATOES IN JACKETS

THIN CORN MUFFINS—GREEN SALAD

WHITE BURGUNDY OR RHONE WINE

FROZEN EGGNOG—NUT PUFFS

COFFEE—LIQUEURS

I asked her to plan her loveliest dinner for twelve, knowing that, as in everything she does, Markell Brooks would produce a dinner so exquisite that others would say, "It's too good to be true."

Kitchen staff, circa 1940. Courtesy of University of Minnesota Archives Photograph Collection.

The chapter continues with descriptions of candlelight, centerpieces, and many sets of china. Markell explained some of her dishes belonged to her "'You shouldn't have done it!' collection," her exclamation after opening gifts from her husband. The description of one set of dishes solved a small mystery for me. According to the book, "The dessert will probably have been something chosen to set off the 'Crown Jewels,' the name she has fondly given to a service of Bristol overlay glass, each service comprising a plate and a large compote with glass petals painted in Dresden floral design." Markell's addendum list to her will is stored in a Minnesota Historical Society archive; the list states who was to receive the "Crown Jewels," among other items.

Recipes follow the text, including cheese puffs ("Among her favorites . . . from an old Southern recipe"), pickled shrimps, French dressing (a recipe Markell got "from the chef at the Café de la Paix in Paris"), vegetable soup ("Served when the Brooks are dining *en famille*. It's full of vitamins"), chicken with white grapes, purée of peas and lima beans, frozen eggnog, nut puffs, and thin chocolate cookies.

Markell was known for her entertaining and her recipes, but, as her daughter Binky said, she didn't cook. (I once visited Binky at her home in Pacific Palisades, California, and *she* cooked a marvelous lunch.) Following Markell's lead, I tried asking a caterer to make her chicken with white grapes for a Board of Regents' dinner, and I announced the source of the recipe. The caterer's interpretation was a little bit of curry cream sauce with a roasted chicken breast on top, neither delectable nor true to the recipe. I recently made the recipe at home, and it was delicious, and Markell's nut puffs were my pandemic shutdown comfort food. Favorite recipes from several Eastcliff residents are featured at the end of this book.

The Presidents Move In

When the Wilson family moved into Eastcliff in 1961, a newspaper article[19] remarked on the new refrigerator and two freezers and a "marvel of built-ins in stainless steel and pecan-colored wood," with particular concern about how to "work the new all-electric stove." Another article[20] mentioned that the walls were pale yellow, the appliances were all stainless steel, and the cabinets were honey pecan–stained birch.

A newspaper article from 1963 quoted Marian Wilson as saying, "A week doesn't go by that one or two events aren't planned." The particular events mentioned were a buffet supper for the San Francisco Ballet; a tea for five hundred; dinner for the Board of Regents; and events for students, wives of international students, legislators' wives, and music, art, and theater groups. There were also many non-University events, such as hosting the annual tea for the Women's Association of the Minneapolis Symphony Orchestra (WAMSO) at Eastcliff in September 1962.[21] Later presidents hosted dancers from a Northrop dance performance along with donors—the Wilsons hosted a full eighty-member ballet company on at least two occasions.

A University alumna recalled to me that as a teenager she visited the Wilson girls for sleepover parties. The young girls would tiptoe down the steps to the landing and watch guests arrive for events. I know that the Brooks children spied on guests from this same landing. The Moos children best recall outdoor parties; they could peek out the windows of the upstairs sunroom.

Mae McBroom[22] was the cook for four University presidents, beginning with the Morrills in the Pillsbury mansion. She was with the Wilsons for their six months in the Pillsbury mansion, and she designed the 1960 renovation to the Eastcliff kitchen. Mae moved into Eastcliff with the Wilsons in February 1961 and shared the Eastcliff servants' living quarters with a maid, Joyce Johnson.

A 1963 *St. Paul Pioneer Press* newspaper article, "Mrs. O. Meredith Wilson Loves Her Job as Hostess," said Marian Wilson relied on a yellow legal pad for event planning. "I love to entertain and enjoy planning the menus to suit various groups," she is quoted as saying. "At the beginning of each week I plan menus and recipes with our cook, Miss Mae McBroom, and decide on tables, flower arrangements, and grocery lists."

In January 1960, shortly after O. Meredith Wilson was hired as the University's ninth president, a photographer traveled to the Meredith home in Eugene, Oregon, to take pictures for an article about the family.[23] One of the photographs showed Mrs. Wilson holding a loaf of her homemade bread. Forty years later, she recalled, "I know practically as soon as we got there, we got from three different companies a great big sack of flour as a gift, which was very cute."[24]

Shortly after the Wilsons moved from the Pillsbury mansion into Eastcliff, an article described a walnut table in the dining room that would seat ten.[25] Mrs. Wilson planned to serve large groups with a buffet, with extra seating throughout the first floor and basement. Mae McBroom cooked for the family as well as events, and it was known in the neighborhood that she had warm cookies ready after school. Miss McBroom had Wednesdays and Sundays off; Mrs. Wilson said she loved to cook and planned to prepare the meals on those days. (We know she had plenty of flour.) President Wilson also cooked; he said that he made "pancakes, steak, and very good trifle."

Marian Wilson and Mae McBroom planned on preparing "a mountain of food" for the eighty members of the San Francisco Ballet after their performance. The previous year, they had run out of food when serving the Canadian National Ballet and they didn't want that to happen again. At a dinner honoring a symphony soloist, Chicken Polynesian was served. The chicken was cooked in an orange sweet-and-sour sauce; crushed pineapple, orange and grapefruit slices, and maraschino cherries were added to more sauce at the end of the cooking time, and the dish was garnished with slivered almonds. For a dinner for student government leaders, Italian pot roast was served with homemade rolls.

During the Moos administration, Mae McBroom and a housekeeper named Minnie shared the servants' quarters in Eastcliff. Miss McBroom seemed the dominant personality. Margie Moos (the youngest Moos) recalled her as a loving presence ("God bless Mae McBroom"). Margie seems to have been the favorite; the other Moos children keenly felt Miss McBroom's disapproval. They remember her regularly saying, "When we used to do things nicely, when the Wilsons were here," or "when things were done properly . . ." Even President Moos felt the scorn, secretly calling her "Mae McGloom." The Moos children were not allowed in the kitchen. One Saturday, when Mae was off duty, Kathy Moos put her hot rollers on the stove to boil and left them too long, so the pot boiled dry. The resulting fire left a bit of a mark on the ceiling. Miss McBroom was not pleased.

Elegant events such as teas and buffet dinners continued during the Moos administration, but the couple also added some informal fun. The basement amusement room, paneled in barn wood, occasionally had animal feeding troughs for presenting food. Picnics were held on the lawn. The children remember that there was always some sort of party going on.

In an article about garden parties, Tracy Moos was interviewed as an expert on parties and a frequent garden party giver. She was quoted saying "When you have bad weather, the party generally turns out better. People aren't posing. Something has happened." She described a Mayfest party at Eastcliff for Mortar Board. The Shakespeare theme was enhanced by banners borrowed from the Guthrie Theater. In the middle of the afternoon event, it started raining heavily and everyone ran inside—"But it was a great party." With the smaller dining room of those days, food would be set out buffet style under a tent and then guests would take their plates inside to eat throughout the house, including the basement.

Tracy was quoted further about events of those days: "Nobody likes teas anymore. And they don't serve tea either; it's coffee or cranberry juice." The menus for parties would be planned by Mrs. Moos and Miss McBroom as "they pore over their joint collection of 150 cookbooks, looking for new foods. A popular entrée for parties at the Mooses' is fruited chicken, a dish that is both 'cheap and elegant.' Made with Major Grey's chutney, the chicken is garnished with fruit. The accompaniment is usually rice. An oatmeal cake laden with raisins, nuts, and coconut has been well-liked by guests and is a favorite of Malcolm Moos Jr."[26]

With this documented proof, no one could ever say that Tracy Moos didn't know how to throw a party! Almost precisely fifty years after she entertained an Academy Award-winning actress, Gale Sondergaard, among others, at an elegant event in 1968, she complimented me more than once by saying something like "You really know how to entertain; I had no idea what I was doing!" I would tell her, with true admiration, that I couldn't imagine how anyone could handle this role while raising five young children at the same time. My research proves she excelled at both. From knowing many people in the role of presidential partner at different universities, I would conclude that we all do the best we can, and if anyone makes it looks effortless, it is an illusion.

In May 1980, Eastcliff was featured as the cover story in *Twin Cities* magazine.[27] It was likely Diane Skomars Magrath's knack for promoting the University that gave Eastcliff its most prominent article in a non-University publication. Diane is quoted in the article: "This house was built to be used. It has a very distinct personality. It loves people. It shines when we're entertaining." Diane opened up Eastcliff to others to host events, and she sent a memo to academic departments at the University inviting them to use the president's residence for meetings, retreats, and seminars.

In the late 1970s, Diane and Sheldon Goldstein, director of the University's media resources department, developed the concept of a half-hour, magazine-style television series called *Matrix* to promote the University. Stanley Hubbard, of Hubbard Broadcasting, agreed it was a great idea and gave *Matrix* airtime on KSTP. Actor and University alumnus Peter Graves, best known for the television series *Mission Impossible*, agreed to host the show. *Matrix* ran for six years, with thirteen episodes each year. Each episode featured three stories. In 1982, after the third season's taping, the Magraths hosted a dinner to honor Graves. For the event, Diane and her friend Marilyn Tammen (wife of the dean of agriculture) drove to Dayton's department store. Diane parked illegally outside while Marilyn went in and told someone in the store that the president's wife needed to borrow the store's tall golden Oscar sculpture for a very important event. Two workers carried the statue to Diane's waiting car. Gopher and Major League Baseball star Dave Winfield later hosted *Matrix,* and a reception with about fifty guests was held in his honor, but apparently without any borrowed statues.

By the time of the Magrath administration, Mae McBroom had the four rooms in the servants' quarters to herself, and two sisters who lived elsewhere were hired as cleaners. The Magraths were Mae's fourth University family, and Sandra Magrath wrote about Mae McBroom in a "Notes from Eastcliff" column in *Minnesota Alumni* magazine in September 1976:

> Despite her Scottish name her outlook is more Scandinavian, for she learned at the knee of her Norwegian mother. She is willing to try almost any kind of food and is usually most successful; further, her love of fine tableware is seen in the lavish care she gives to ironing up the table linens and polishing the silver. Her artistic ability is quite evident in the way she arranges both our food on plates and platters and our flowers in vases of various shapes. For the many dinner parties we have, whether it be for sixteen or sixty people, she can call several women in the community, some who have worked with her for years, to help in preparing and serving.

The two cleaners, Evelyn Prest and Thelma Ramberg, were called "the cleaning sisters." Peter Magrath claimed he couldn't tell them apart and called them "Velma and Thelma." A caretaker lived in the carriage house and took care of the grounds. By 1980, Cheryl Anderson had replaced "Velma and Thelma."

After Sandra and Peter Magrath divorced, Mae reportedly enjoyed cooking and caring for the newly single president. In 1976, Peter Magrath was forty-three years old, and Mae was sixty-five, so I like to imagine that she thought of him as the son she never had. And after serving two large families, cooking for just one man would have been a respite.

When Peter met and married Diane Skomars in 1978, Mae McBroom helped plan the wedding and made the wedding cake. After the wedding, Mae retired, and Peter and Diane left on their honeymoon. While they were gone, University personnel hired a new cook and housekeeper. Later, as part of budget cuts, the position was eliminated. University Food Services began preparing food for Eastcliff events on the campus in St. Paul, and the family cooked for themselves.

Diane Skomars Magrath brought bright energy to Eastcliff entertaining. She continued entertaining in the basement "barn room" with themed parties. Diane recalled that when new tablecloths were needed, she bought sheets and her friend Marilyn Tammen sewed them into circles. Dinners began with a social time, including wine, mineral water with lime, and a punch or grog. After about forty minutes, the menu was read, the theme explained, and the guests would proceed to their assigned tables.

In January 1983, Diane was the honorary editor for *Minnesota's Greatest and Best Recipes: A University of Minnesota Cookbook*, a fundraiser for the David Winfield Development Fund for recreational sports at the University. The final chapter of the cookbook is a description of entertaining at Eastcliff and includes eight menus with recipes. Diane wrote that Ruth Wirt, the administrative food operations manager at the University dining center on the St. Paul campus; Robert Ledder, the director of food services; and Marilee Ward, from the president's office, met with her each month to plan the next thirty days of official Eastcliff meals. Ruth adapted and created the recipes, Bob researched beverages, and Marilee kept track of all events and handled invitations. Diane wrote to me recently that Marilee was "absolutely invaluable," and "any success I had can be attributed to the work and dedication of Marilee, Ruth, and Bob."

Over the course of the Keller administration, the dining room, the pantries, the space that had been the outer hall, and the larger part of the kitchen was used to create a larger dining room, with a half bath and coat closet. The space that had been the kitchen hallway and porch was made into a small family kitchen. Two of the maids' bedrooms were converted into a catering kitchen. The former maids' sitting room, now a breakfast room, was not changed except for the flooring, which, along with the flooring in the family kitchen and catering kitchen, is now glazed terracotta tile.

The family kitchen has two kitchen sinks in white countertops over white cabinets with tall white cupboards above. The gas oven and range top are in a peninsula. There is a refrigerator along the partial wall near the dining room and a dishwasher along the opposite partial wall.

Parties for Everyone

Ken Keller and Bonita Sindelir hosted monthly faculty dinners. The first was held in February 1985 while Keller was interim president. The second was on

March 13, 1985, the day that Keller was elected president. There was a break from these dinners while the Eastcliff dining room was under construction. The final one (there were at least seventeen) was on March 8, 1988. Five days later, on March 13, 1988, President Keller resigned, so the dinners spanned his entire presidency. The menus were different for each dinner, as were the speakers and the guests. These dinners were to help faculty from different disciplines get to know one another. President Keller said then, "There are a lot of faculty. Figuring out how to give them a sense of belonging is one of the biggest issues at the University. People are used to the isolation of their departments. Isn't that a shame? Most of us are attracted to the University because all these things are going on. Then we don't take advantage of the diversity."[28] To invite a diverse group, a computer randomly generated sixty-five invitations each month. Of those, around fifty faculty members attended. Keller joked that at that rate he could invite everyone by 2010.

The food at each dinner was appealing, but the real attraction was the presentation one faculty member gave which stimulated conversation of the other faculty members from different disciplines. In my experience, the faculty at the University of Minnesota are excellent, interesting, and generous with their time. As an example, the first of these dinners featured Christopher Sims from the Department of Economics. Twenty-six years later, in 2011, Chris Sims won the Nobel Prize in Economics, along with faculty colleague Thomas Sargent. We hosted a dinner for Tom in February 2013, when he was awarded an honorary doctorate. He is a charming man, very easy to talk to even though he is brilliant. The same can be said of fellow Nobel Laureate in Economics (2000) Daniel McFadden. Dan, who received his BS in physics and PhD in economics at the University, visited Eastcliff with his wife Beverlee, an artist. At another economics dinner, I was awed to be in the presence of four Nobel Laureates from the University, including Lars Peter Hansen (PhD 1978), who received the honor in 2013. I was impressed that the dinner was a real party—friendly, happy people and delightful repartee. I mentioned that I didn't know economists were so much fun, and someone explained that they typically aren't but it's a particular feature of Minnesota's economics department.

The December dinner for Regents was always a special evening. No dinner could top the one Ken and Bonita hosted in 1986. The main course was Greek stew with apricots and prunes. Then there were after-dinner sweets and cheeses in the garden room where guests could view ice skating in the back yard! The invitation stated:

> Bring gay blades, strong ankles, padding, warm clothes, and your sense of fun. Skating will be after dinner, if you want to plan layered or

alternate attire. If you cannot join in the skating, viewing will be good from the sun porch where warm drinks will be served to those who cheer appropriately.

That dinner was on December 11, and the rink was used again on December 30, for skating after the president's staff dinner.

Meals through the 1980s were coordinated by Marilee Ward in the president's office. Bonita met weekly with Ms. Ward and monthly with Bob Ledder, director of University food services. A wonderful chef, Dick Seibert, was hired by food services to cook for events. I asked Bonita about the creative menus (and flaming desserts), and she gave credit to Dick: "He worked with me to plan the menus and was filled with creative ideas. Any flaming desserts were, I am sure, his idea. I had a favorite dessert recipe, Martha Stewart's red currant tart, and Dick brought red currants from his neighbor's yard." University food services provided servers for events and often Bob Ledder came himself.

There are no records of events at Eastcliff from Ken Keller's November 1985 inauguration until a small dinner in April 1986—that invitation was to "Dinner at Eastcliff (such as *they* are)". An invitation a week later stated: "Please come for Chinese take-out in our construction zone at Eastcliff on Sunday, April 13, at 6:00 p.m. followed by the China Ballet at Northrop at 8:00 p.m."

Regular events resumed with four dinner parties between May 24 and 30, 1986. The May 26 pre-opera dinner was interesting to me because of the guest list: Ken and Bonita were joined by Russell and Beth Bennett (Russ was chairing the University's capital campaign), James and Sheba

Ken Keller, Bonita Sindelir, and their son, Jesse, in the living room of the family quarters at Eastcliff, November 1985. Photograph by Bruce Bisping; courtesy of the *Minneapolis Star Tribune*.

Freedman (James was the president of the University of Iowa), and two couples who had previously lived at Eastcliff: Conley and Marney Brooks, and O. Meredith and Marian Wilson. The May 30, 1986, dinner was before the very last performance of the Metropolitan Opera at Northrop. The menu before the performance of *Carmen* included gazpacho salad, paella, and Spanish wine.

Ken Keller and Bonita Sindelir were well traveled, and their menus reflect that. They also appreciated wine; wine (often French) was occasionally suggested on menus by name and vintage. Foods go through popularity phases, but even the oldest menus I found from the 1980s don't sound dated, with a few exceptions. Flaming desserts were often served at elegant dinners; I haven't seen that in a while but would welcome its return.

Richard Sauer was named as interim president after Ken Keller stepped down in March 1988, and he served until Nils Hasselmo was appointed in December. As interim president, he and his wife, Betty, didn't move into Eastcliff. Ken Keller and Bob Bruininks also served as interim presidents before being appointed president; neither lived in Eastcliff while serving as interim. Interim President Sauer resumed events at Eastcliff with a reception for the Brazilian ambassador to the United States in late May. Curiously, while the event request form states "fish or poultry (no red meat)," they served pork. Maybe it really was considered "the other white meat."

Many events were scheduled for Eastcliff in 1989 before Nils Hasselmo took the reins of the presidency. Those event forms included a note advising groups to make alternate arrangements in case Eastcliff was not available after the new residents moved in. Not to worry: January 1989 may have been the busiest January ever for Eastcliff as the schedule included events that had been previously scheduled as well as events added to introduce the new president to the community.

Pat Hasselmo suggested that the twelve Regents be invited to Eastcliff on each of the Thursday nights following committee meetings, before the full board meetings on Friday mornings.[29] Pat said later, "I think it was important for them to see how we entertained, to have a feeling of what we were doing with the president's home in connection with trying to broaden the University community." These dinners now regularly include other guests, such as the Faculty Consultative Committee, University of Minnesota

Foundation (UMF) and UMAA leadership groups, Regents, professors, agricultural leaders, business leaders, healthcare leaders, Minnesota private college presidents, legislative leaders, and so on.

A Regents emeriti dinner was held for the first time in 1987. The Hasselmos hosted a second one on February 21, 1989. It then became a tradition and is now regularly held in June. An attached sticky note on that second dinner event sheet asked to let so-and-so know who was to be seated next to another so-and-so, which I found amusing. While the group is typically collegial, there are some long-standing conflicts, and we arranged the seating to try to assure that everyone had an enjoyable evening. The Regents emeriti dinner is a small thank you to those who served the University so diligently, and they are a wonderful group. Minnesota Supreme Court Justice (and former Viking football "purple people eater" as well as former Regent) Alan Page attended the dinners, and his presence elevates any gathering he attends. I also adored seeing Josie Johnson any time I could. She regularly attended the Regent emeriti dinners starting in 1989. Josie was a civil rights activist, the University's first Black Regent, and too many other firsts to list: she is most definitely a first-class human being.[30] Former governor Wendell Anderson was another former Regent who was interesting to meet. We were thrilled to welcome all former Regents back to Eastcliff, and over time this included those with whom we had previously served. We continued the tradition of seating everyone in a large tent on the Eastcliff lawn, until I became worried that someone might break an ankle on the uneven surface of the lawn. We placed a smaller tent on the terrace so that some guests could sit in the dining room and some on the terrace, with remarks delivered in the doorway. After we moved out in May 2019, the Eastcliff Technical Advisory Committee had the lawn resurfaced so that functions held on the lawn would be safer.

Pat Hasselmo established another tradition, based on her strong affinity for students. She had a master's degree in higher education administration, preparing to be a dean of women before Nils's career changed her path. In 1990, Pat had the bold idea of hosting a commencement open house. Nils remarked later, "I told her the University graduates almost eleven thousand students every year, and she said, 'Let's invite them all.'" The first year there were two events for General College graduates and University College graduates, in the morning and midday prior to commencement ceremonies. The menu consisted of eight hundred assorted tea cookies and punch made from Pat's own recipe. The next year the event was expanded to two dates, inviting all University graduates.

In the early 1970s, Malcolm and Tracy Moos, along with University Relations, invited several hundred people to Legislator–Editor–Broadcaster days. These events included lunch at Eastcliff followed by a Gopher football game.

They had to figure out how to feed a meal to a very large group, which was well beyond the scope of the Eastcliff kitchen. Tracy suggested they buy boxed meals from North Central Airlines, so each guest was treated to a basket lunch, including wine, on the Eastcliff lawn.

Before the first home football game of 1989 (against Nebraska, twenty-two years before they joined the Big Ten), the Hasselmos hosted a lasagna dinner for three alumni couples (including Ted and Ginny Brooks), six faculty members, three legislators, two mayors, three members of the University Foundation, the University of Nebraska president and three Nebraska regents, plus all their spouses. After the meal, buses delivered the guests to the Metrodome. The pre-game meals before every home game that season followed a similar plan, with Regents in regular attendance, the visiting team's president invited, and a mixed group of donors and legislators. Before morning games, Pat's quiche was served. The next year they again hosted meals before every home game, and the following year, and the following year—for nine years.

In addition to the many University events the Hasselmos hosted, the couple also hosted events associated with Scandinavia, and Sweden in particular. This included a dinner for the Swedish Consulate with the Swedish delegation. Other events included receptions for the ambassador of Denmark (Peter Dyvig), the rector of the University of Gothenburg (Jan Ling), the rector of the University of Iceland (Sveinbjörn Björnsson and his wife, Gunlaug Einarsdóttir), the U.S. ambassador to Sweden, and the Finnish ambassador to Sweden. The king and queen of Sweden visited the University, but I don't have any record of them visiting Eastcliff. Nils Hasselmo was the 1991 Swedish American of the Year, as awarded by the Vasa Order of America, and he had received the Royal Order of the North Star from the King of Sweden nearly twenty years earlier.

By 1993, Linda Fox, in consultation with Pat Hasselmo and with assistance from Claudia Wallace-Gardner, was coordinating all the Eastcliff events and hiring the caterers. There were handwritten notes in the event files from the first few months that are still pertinent today: "Program was *way* too long; guests were standing for 45 minutes!" (A common problem for events—academics like to speak in forty-five-minute increments, which is particularly difficult if guests aren't seated.) "Do you know what the Regents are having for lunch?" (We also checked this, so that lunch and dinner weren't similar.) "Bowls of nuts on outside tables not a good idea—squirrels climbed up on the table to eat them and would not be chased away. (Left footprints on tablecloth!)" I love picturing these little footprints, even though we had a similar problem with those squirrels' fat, sassy descendants eating the pumpkins in our fall decorations.

The dinners throughout this era typically had forty to forty-eight guests—one long rectangular table of ten to twelve and four round tables of eight or nine. Some dinners had five rounds. The rectangular table was table 1; President Hasselmo typically sat at table 2, the round nearest the kitchen; and Mrs. Hasselmo typically sat at the round nearest the entrance door, which was table 3, 4, 5, or (rarely) 6.

Poached salmon with cucumber sauce was a favorite during the Hasselmo years, as well as "walleye pike," a Minnesota favorite now called just "walleye" (with a tone of reverence). Desserts were a bit lighter than previously, including simple desserts of ice cream, "light" cheesecake, or "Grandma Leaver's Cranberry Pudding." In Decembers of 1989 and 1991, the Regents were treated to elaborate Swedish Holiday Smorgasbord dinners. Daughter Anna Hasselmo, home from college, was drafted to dress as Saint Lucia.

There were no Eastcliff events at the beginning of the Yudof presidency, as Eastcliff was undergoing renovation. During their first fall in Eastcliff, Mark and Judy Yudof began hosting what became an annual children's Halloween party. Also among the first Yudof events at Eastcliff was a reception for the Berman Family Chair in Jewish Studies, which related to the Yudofs' personal interests. Similar events included luncheons for the United Jewish Fund and Council, Lion of Judah—Ruby Lion, and Israel Bonds. A planned event for the American Israel Public Affairs Committee (AIPAC) was moved elsewhere when President Yudof discovered that guests were expected to contribute to AIPAC in order to attend. As he said, "We never, ever charge anyone admission to Eastcliff."

There are many instances of community leaders being invited to Eastcliff. Mark Yudof's "fireside chats" were specifically for consensus building. An invitation to labor leaders began, "To assist the University of Minnesota in developing a consensus regarding academic priorities that support the state's economic development and facilitate technology transfer from the University to the private sector, you are invited to a fireside chat. Please join some of your business and industry colleagues . . ."

As with the fireside chats, Mark Yudof put his own spin on other gatherings: legislative breakfasts became pancake breakfasts, and donor gatherings became five-course gourmet dinners for intimate groups of four to six.

While the Hasselmos, either due to personal preference, their Swedish heritage, or cost considerations (or perhaps all three) served fish regularly, beef and lamb were frequently on the Yudof menus. Whenever beef was served, there was one meal of fish for Judy. She kept strictly kosher and was, impressively, the first female president of the United Synagogue of Conservative Judaism.

Professor Hy Berman described a dinner when Mark Yudof was president-elect. Mark compared Minnesota to Texas, saying "I'm going to like it here. I mean, this president's house is just five blocks from a kosher butcher shop. In Austin I have to go all the way to Chicago to get kosher food."[31] An early menu during their tenure requests that the salad have "no bacon, please." President Yudof was said to dislike zucchini and that vegetable appeared to be banned from Eastcliff menus. And no matter what dessert was served, President Yudof was given a bowl of berries. One invoice stated: thirty-three beef meals,

Mark and Judy Yudof walk on campus. Courtesy of University of Minnesota Archives Photograph Collection.

one fish, thirty-three crème brulées, one bowl of berries. Why the berries? Whether by his choice, or Judy's choice for him, he was dieting. At a dinner in 2001, President Yudof's remarks (as recorded in the event file) included, "I'm certainly not going to talk long. I don't know about you, but I'm very hungry. It's no wonder, really. I've been on a constant diet for the past two decades. Actually, I've lost a total of 645 pounds. As one wit would have it, I should be hanging from a charm bracelet. Instead, I'm ravenous almost all the time." Mark Yudof, whom I certainly would not consider overweight, was beloved for his charm and sense of humor.

Susan Hagstrum and Bob Bruininks hosted many events of all types. They were also generous in offering Eastcliff for University events, welcoming other University staff members to serve as hosts. Susan told me, "One party we were happy to allow was the annual Student Association event when the students would dress up in cocktail attire and celebrate a year of activity at the U. We would arrive home late from an event on campus and see them very happily celebrating in the living room and garden room. We loved it when students chose to come there."

Susan had a special connection to the neighborhood, and the University, even as a child. Her father had grown up about ten blocks from Eastcliff in Merriam Park. Susan grew up in Mendota Heights, a St. Paul suburb. Her father owned a men's clothing store in St. Paul, so when her mother took her shopping in Minneapolis, they took along a shopping bag from Frank Murphy dress shop in St. Paul to hide the evidence of having crossed the river. (This may sound strange if you aren't a Minnesotan, but if you are from St. Paul, shopping in Minneapolis is the only part of the story that sounds bizarre.) While Susan rode her bicycle past Eastcliff as a young girl, she never imagined that she would one day live in the house herself—she thought a princess lived in Eastcliff.

In 2003, Susan had a stated goal to "highlight the historic value of Eastcliff, its place in University life, and the opportunities for more fulsome and valuable connections to the community," with an aim to "use the house for functions beyond the large public receptions or high-end dinners."

With President Bruininks's wonderful accomplishment of rebuilding a football stadium on campus, it became much easier to host guests at football games. Bob and Susan were able to serve as hosts in the Regents/President Suite at the stadium for the 2009 and 2010 seasons, and we did the same during our eight years. Joan and Gary Gabel now follow that same tradition.

President Bruininks was previously the dean of the College of Education and Human Development. Susan Hagstrum was on nine different boards and committees while living at Eastcliff. One series of events brought their interests together perfectly. Beginning in early 2003, they hosted several conversations, receptions, and meals for the President's Initiative on Children, Youth, and Families, of which Susan was a member of the steering committee. The culminating event was a reception in 2008 to honor the many accomplishments and contributions of the initiative.

In fall of 2011, Eric and I hosted one of our first dinners at Eastcliff for tribal nations leaders. Leaders from twelve Minnesota tribes attended, and I appreciated that some had very long drives from the White Earth Reservation and the Red Lake Band of Chippewa. Chancellors from the other four Minnesota campuses attended as well. The dinner featured walleye and wild rice pilaf made with rice hand-harvested by Ojibwe communities on the White Earth Indian Reservation using traditional methods. I remember most that during our dinner conversation, leaders from the Leech Lake Band of Ojibwe offered to teach me to ice fish using a spear. That never came to pass, but, if either of you is reading this, I'm still available and interested.

When Eric and I were at the University of Delaware, President and Mrs. David (Louise) Roselle hosted a wonderful party several consecutive years in December. It was there that we first met Senator Joe Biden and his wife Jill, Senator William Roth, business and community members, donors, and other faculty members. We found the party to be a wonderful way for people to form deeper connections to a university community, so we created a similar guest list at Minnesota. Eric's chief of staff, Amy Phenix, suggested that December was already too busy for most people, so we held the party in mid-January for four years. We enclosed the terrace with a tent and heated it with portable heaters, and we celebrated winter. The fourth year, we created a warm, wonderful Minnesota cabin: Pam Hudson found a fake stone fireplace online, we moved our own rugs down from upstairs, we installed a photograph of a wolf diorama from the Bell Museum behind a large window frame, and we made other accommodations to bring the North Woods to Eastcliff. Due to the cost of the event, we discontinued the parties after the fourth year, and then held similar (less expensive) outdoor events in the summer for a few years.

The food served reflects the hosts, and therefore the hosts should have final say about the menu. But we had very capable people coordinate events with the caterers, and I was happy for them to do their jobs. Jill Christiansen worked part time organizing Eastcliff events and coordinating my calendar. I believe she was very efficient, in part, due to her other job of raising four children. Jill resigned after two years with us when her children's schedules became more complicated. Patricia Hall joined us at the end of October 2014. She was a former basketball player, so her event sheets referred to the day of an event as "game day." When Patricia moved to a new position, Pam Hudson joined us. Pam had worked in the Board of Regents office for many years, so she brought historical insight to her work with us. When Pam retired in 2017, Bethany Fung took over events from the University of Minnesota Foundation (UMF) office. Bethany is a true event planner, and she works with a wonderful staff at UMF who are willing to help out when extra hands are needed. This approach worked well and has continued into the Gabel presidency.

We used a variety of caterers for several reasons. Some seemed better suited (and had better prices) for certain events—whether their sweet spot was a reception or a large dinner or a smaller meal. We were always budget conscious and had to solve for that challenge. A variety of caterers also gave us more variety in the food served. We self-catered some events, buying food and re-plating (for example, buying breakfast items from the grocery store or take-out lunch from Cafe Latte in St. Paul). Bob Bruininks and Susan Hagstrum regularly used Kafe 421 at Eastcliff. When I first came to know Georgia Sander, the owner of Kafe 421, I asked Nick Bantle, who provided great service as a butler at Eastcliff for many years, if she really was as nice as she seemed. He agreed that she absolutely is; she is good to the people who work with her.[32] She is a Greek mother who makes sure everyone is well fed.

When we visited the University campus in Rochester, Regent Patty Simmons had us over for dinner and used a chef named Justin Schoville. The first dish was an egg custard, baked in the eggshell. Perhaps it was lightly scented and flavored with truffle, or perhaps with bacon. Whatever it was, Eric and I each took one bite and said together, "We need to get him to cook at Eastcliff!" Justin catered many great meals at Eastcliff, but one of his more memorable meals was one that we didn't eat. It was planned for May 2, 2013. That morning we learned that there was a blizzard in Rochester, and all the snowplows had already been put in storage. Justin, to his great dismay, was trapped. Georgia at Kafe 421 graciously served a meal for thirty-six with only a few hours' notice. Justin was able to return the next week for a different event.

We began using University Dining Services a lot more when local celebrity Scott Pampuch became the executive chef. Scott focused on foods from local farms and sourced produce from Cornercopia, a student-driven, organic farm on the St. Paul campus. We loved that while it lasted, which was until Scott moved on to other ventures.

One of the caterers we used had a great reputation and served good food. He was always very warm and friendly to me. For one dinner that he catered, we had three guests who canceled late (flu season), so I mentioned to the servers afterward that they must have eaten well that night. They were typically there from about 4:30 to 9:00 p.m. for a 6:00 to 8:00 event, and would eat leftover appetizers or surplus food between courses. The servers said that they ate nothing; the caterer bagged up all the appetizers *and* the paid-for unserved meals and took everything with him. When pressed, they admitted that he was arrogant and unpleasant to work with. We never hired him again, but we are fortunate that the Twin Cities offer many choices.

We found one great caterer by chance. We were at a dinner at the home of Augsburg University president Paul Pribbenow and his wife, Abigail. The food was all vegetarian (the dinner was in honor of a Hindu Nobel Laureate) and was really good. I asked a server, "Who is the caterer? It's fabulous." They replied, "Yes, it's Fabulous." I said, "Yes, it is, but do you know the name of the caterer?" "It's Fabulous," was again the reply, then "Fabulous Catering." It was a "who's on first" moment. We added Fabulous Catering to our Eastcliff rotation.

I went to many scholarship luncheons at McNamara Alumni Center on campus, and we hosted several such student events at Eastcliff. A fun annual event for us was hosting the Bentson Scholar picnic each Labor Day weekend, filling the Eastcliff lawn with brilliant young people. The Larson Scholars were also fun to host, and for the Shakopee Mdewakanton Sioux Community Scholars, we were able to hire Sean Sherman, the "Sioux Chef," and had an honor drum song ring out through the neighborhood. For the Kaler Scholars, I made lasagna myself. (I also made pecan pie a few times for events, but otherwise I was grateful not to be the chef/caterer.) We became close to Goldy Gopher's support staff and had dinner with them every year. One of our last events at Eastcliff was a reunion for members of this group, shortly after Goldy and I had worked together to write a book, *What Should I Be When I Grow Up? by Goldy Gopher.*[33]

While I will eat almost anything that is served to me, I am pickier about what I cook or serve to others. I don't buy or serve veal. Those little lamb lollipops? I shudder to think of how young that animal was, so they're out. (I joke that I can barely eat baby carrots.) We really like fish; I rarely cooked it myself at Eastcliff as I didn't want the smell of fish to waft down to the next day's guests. During our first year, we hosted a dinner for the Minnesota Business Partnership and offered a choice of steak or halibut; of thirty-three guests, twenty-nine chose fish and only four chose beef, so I felt comfortable serving fish regularly.

I always asked that at least one appetizer be vegetarian and that there be vegetarian options on buffets. We asked guests to let us know of food restrictions (for dinners, we often ordered an extra vegetarian, kosher, gluten-free meal in case someone forgot to reply). Minnesota is an important pork-producing state, but pork is problematic for religious reasons, so we offered pork as one of two entrée choices rather than as the sole entrée. During our tenure, gluten-free was requested more and more, and we were mindful of that on buffets. Eric is sensitive to shellfish, so we understood well to be cautious about it and other common allergens.

Food and menus go through trends. Beets became very popular; I liked red beets and golden beets served together so that we could call them "maroon and gold beets," representing the University's colors. (Our friend Nancy Lindahl taught us to offer maroon or gold wine.) "Airline chicken breast" became a thing—doesn't that sound like overcooked airplane chicken? "Airline style" is a boneless chicken breast with the first wing joint attached (airline = with a wing), which keeps it moister when cooked. It was fascinating to look at all the menus served through the years, and see the trends come and go.

Early in the Gabel administration, entertaining at Eastcliff had undergone three distinct phases. First, the house shut down for electrical repairs in late May of 2019. (We had moved out early, and had one last event, a pool party for the Brooks family, in June with only the pool house open for guests.) The event lawn was also refurbished during this time. There were no events in July or August, which would have been a slow time anyway, but the repairs were extensive enough that no events were held in early September.

A September 20, 2019, inauguration reception began a busy time of Eastcliff events including dinners and receptions, advisory committee socials, a winter open house, and more. The Board of Regents Thursday events were occasionally receptions rather than dinners to accommodate more guests.

This second phase, known as normal life at Eastcliff, was expected to last many years. Then with the unprecedented challenges of the novel coronavirus pandemic, Eastcliff, like the rest of the State of Minnesota, was practicing responsible social distancing. While the University community was hard at work on cures and solutions to help combat Covid-19, Eastcliff returned to its roots as a family home rather than a part-time event center. As things have currently returned to "normal," I think we are all mindful that our new normal is ever evolving.

THE CATERING KITCHEN

When caterers see the catering kitchen for the first time, their eyes light up. It is well situated for a team preparing a meal for forty. (It is decidedly inconvenient for preparing a family meal.) The counters are all stainless steel. There is a large workstation in the center of the room, a separate counter-height table for lining up plates, two large sinks for doing dishes, and a separate handwashing sink. Appliances are all professional/industrial, including a very large gas range with two large ovens, two large refrigerators, two floral refrigerators (floral arrangements are reused for weeks), a small freezer, plate warming drawers, a large icemaker, a garbage disposal, and a dishwasher with multiple insertable racks that cleans and sterilizes in seven minutes. A small room off the kitchen (formerly the maid's sewing room) is now a pantry, holding beverages and serving pieces. A small room in the back contains racks of glassware and a cabinet that holds enough seven-piece place settings of maroon-and-gold-trimmed fine china to serve eighty-four, as well as assorted other dishes.

After Ken Keller was elected president in March 1985, a special issue of *Minnesota Alumni* magazine had an article titled "Not So Private Lives."[34] It began by commenting that Ken, Bonita, and two-year-old Jesse would enjoy the fenced grounds with a swing set, then continues:

> Last fall Sindelir woke up from a nightmare. She had dreamed that they had been invited to stay the night at Eastcliff—the Magraths were still living there. They went upstairs to bed and walked into a cavernous room with missing floorboards. Jesse went running off, and Sindelir chased after him. She had almost caught up to him when he fell through a crack in the floor. She woke up just as Jesse was about to hit a concrete slab in the middle of a grassy area. "You don't need a Freudian analyst to figure out what that one means," she says.

Jesse survived the Eastcliff renovation. The Keller presidency did not.

I have read dozens, maybe hundreds, of contemporaneous articles about the 1980s Eastcliff renovation, many interviews conducted five to ten years later that have the benefit of hindsight, and the minutes of the Board of Regents meetings.[35] There is little disagreement on the facts (except *What did the regents know and when did they know it?*).

At the request of the Regents, President Magrath appointed a committee to recommend renovations to Eastcliff. The Magraths moved out of Eastcliff at the end of November 1984, as he would become the president of the University of Missouri system effective January 1, 1985. Kenneth Keller, vice president for academic affairs, became interim president of the University on November 1, 1984. The Board of Regents passed a resolution that the interim president would not be a candidate for president.

On January 10, 1985, a special meeting of the Board of Regents was held at the request of Governor Rudy Perpich for the purpose of discussing the focus of the University before final budget decisions were made. His staff members stated that "the University cannot be all things to all people; some hard decisions will have to be made" and "resources are essential in order for the University to achieve world-class status," but a "sharp focusing" was necessary. (Ken Keller[36] recalled the governor saying that the University was "running amuck. It makes no decisions. It only grows. It has no control. It has no idea of what it ought to do," and "I think what you ought to do is close a bunch of units," including dentistry. These quotes— not surprisingly—did not make it into the official minutes.) According to the minutes:

> President Keller stated that he would accept the challenge to present ideas to the Regents that draw on the planning process and that leave flexibility for the new president to set directions. He also stated that he would be happy to work with other higher education systems to coordinate the various missions. Governor Perpich stated that the University has to be the flagship educational institution in the state, and indicated his Administration wants to work with the Administration of the University to achieve this goal.

Ken recalled later, "I commented earlier that we'd done seven years of planning even though we didn't have a plan. We did know what all the issues were, and I knew what the issues were. The fact is that there was a need to put it together, but we had done enough of this that, in fact, I could put together a plan in a month." The next month, Ken submitted the plan, *A Commitment to Focus*. I mention the *Focus* plan here because it influenced Ken being the president, and I believe it also influenced Ken *not* being the president. (Both issues are relevant to Eastcliff's history.) On one hand, the newspapers and the public embraced the plan. Regent David Lebedoff, who was chairing the presidential search committee, shared the document with a prospective candidate who suggested he should hire the author of the report. On the other hand, the plan, which called for reducing undergraduate enrollment, was controversial; some Regents and some legislators did not support the plan and did not support President Keller.

On March 13, 1985, Kenneth H. Keller was elected as the twelfth president of the University of Minnesota. His contract stated:

> The President is required to live in Eastcliff as a convenience to the University, and the University will provide maintenance and utilities as well as appropriate staff for the house and grounds.

The Nightmare Renovation and Resignation

Ken Keller and Bonita Sindelir had already been entertaining at Eastcliff during the interim presidency, and plans were under way to renovate

Eastcliff. Ken asked that the planned renovations be completed before he moved in; the estimate was a couple of months. Five months later, the Keller/Sindelirs moved in, and the work had yet to begin.

The Regents toured the house in September for the "Eastcliff deferred maintenance and renovation project," now scheduled to be completed in February 1986. The architectural drawings for the dining room and catering kitchen remodel by Leonard Parker Associates were dated October 15, 1985. The request for bids for construction went out on Halloween—perhaps a foreshadow of the fright to follow. Once the work began, it continued for two and a half years, then was halted before it was fully finished.

According to a long, cheerful, November 9, 1985, newspaper story[37] with photographs, the work—paid for by the University of Minnesota Foundation and University Food Services with no taxpayer dollars—was estimated to cost $463,000 (plus an extra $150,000 mentioned later in the article, for a total of $613,000). The upstairs floor refinishing and the painting upstairs were complete, but the family was washing dishes in a bathtub as the kitchen was under construction. The story mentioned that the Pillsbury mansion had been torn down because the remodeling and repairs were deemed too costly. Architect Leonard Parker stated of East-cliff, "The home is a university treasure and should be treated as such. To replace it would cost at least $1.2 million, and that's forgetting the in-trinsic artistic, aesthetic value of the house." The work to be completed included repairing the wood floor and wood-and-concrete support system at the west end of the house; upgrading the electrical service; expanding the small dining room into the current kitchen area; building a small family kitchen; constructing a larger catering kitchen in the former servants' quarters; energy-saving improvements, such as new windows and doors and glass doors for the eight fireplaces; exterior repair and repainting; and redecoration and maintenance costing an additional $100,000 to $150,000 from the building maintenance budget.[38] All the renovation occurred while the Keller/Sindelir family, including a toddler, lived in the house. Besides regularly doing dishes in the bathtub, a smoke alarm went off once and a plumber reported it was "just some toxic fumes from downstairs." Men in hazmat suits removed asbestos. The scope of the project increased, with cost overruns for unexpected problems.

By 1988, the catering kitchen was built and equipped, at a cost of $187,000. (It has been widely called a $600,000 kitchen.) The dining room was expanded to seat forty-eight rather than twelve. It was extended to the north into the former screened arcade and east into the former kitchen; a large bay window was added with a built-in marble-topped buffet cabinet. A small family kitchen was built, and a patio was replaced and expanded to provide outdoor entertaining space for 150. These projects cost a total of $466,994.

Landscaping work was required to correct drainage problems. The rotting fence was replaced, at a cost of $41,000 (it's a looong fence). The entire house was equipped with central air conditioning, which was first listed in reports as costing $44,900, then $123,000, and finally $191,000. Insulation work was upgraded to include asbestos removal. The exterior was painted at a cost of $250,000. Lead-based paint (ten or eleven coats) was scraped from the house and disposed of as hazardous waste, at a cost of $800 per barrel, adding $110,000 for paint removal. (Yes, $350,000 is indeed a slow, expensive paint job.) The flooring in the living room was repaired, and the flooring in the entry and dining room was replaced. One example of unexpected expenses: under the living room carpet, many of the birch floorboards had become fragile or rotted. Workers were not surprised to find rotten I-beams, but no one anticipated that in 1921 the builders had filled in the interstices with concrete for better support. Workers had to chip out all the concrete before replacing the rotten wood. Usable boards from the dining room were used to repair the living room floor, so the dining room floor had to be fully replaced. Rotted wall studs were replaced. A new ceiling was installed in the living room. The electrical and heating systems were upgraded. The work took more than two years longer than intended, and the ongoing maintenance during those two years was included in the final renovation costs. The work estimated to cost $644,477 totaled $1,266,251 (plus an additional $180,441 for work not included in the estimates). None of the funds came from taxpayer money, or tuition. So where did the extra money come from?

Early in the Keller presidency, the vice president for finance and operations, David Lilly, began consolidating little pockets of money from all around the Twin Cities campus. For example, if funds were set aside for a project, and the project came in under budget, money remained in a reserve fund. That money could be invested. If cash was set aside for a future project, that money could earn interest before it was spent on its intended purpose. These moneys were consolidated into a contingency fund, or central reserves. While the fund seemed surprisingly large at fifty to sixty million dollars, it was a reasonable five to six percent of the annual consolidated budget of the university, which was over one billion dollars. The interest on the central reserves generated three to four million dollars a year, which became discretionary funds to be used for one-time needs. Some use of discretionary funds was approved by the Board of Regents, but there was (and still is) disagreement as to whether the Regents understood at the time what these funds were and where they came from.

I'm explaining the central reserves because it is possible the Regents, and certainly some members of the press, found it confusing. Quoting Ken Keller:

> If you look at the reporting that went on [regarding] the reserves, you can take a set of headlines over a two- or three-week period that have the reserves varying from $60 million to $200 million. The issue there was that reporters didn't understand the difference between encumbered funds and reserves. Encumbered funds are merely funds which we expense at an early stage and then pay out over time but they're not reserves in any sense. They're part of budgeted money that is used over time. I saw headlines that the secret funds are $220 million. As I said, they were in the range of $50 million to $60 million and they were just what I said they were. I think, actually, David, particularly, deserved a lot of credit for understanding the need to bring those kinds of reserves into where everybody could see how they were being used or how the interest on them was being used.[39]

On January 7, 1988, the *Minnesota Daily,* the student-run newspaper, ran a story by Mark Fischenich headlined "President's house gets needed repairs" with the continuation headed "Eastcliff maintenance: price tag attributed to years of neglect." The story included: "Costs rose when workers discovered unexpected problems like rotting wood and ailing pipes." And: "Several University Regents agreed that the renovation project was necessary, and they did not wince at the price tag. 'You don't repair Eastcliff by going over to Knox Lumber and buying a couple of cans of paint,' said Regent Wally Hilke, continuing, 'It's really a consequence of letting the repairs go for too long.'"

Then on February 3, the *St. Paul Pioneer Press Dispatch* ran a story that renovations were double the original $694,000 estimate, and the Regents were not aware of the costs.[40] The next day, the *Minnesota Daily* story,[41] "Eastcliff valued at about half the renovation cost," stated: "The $1.3 million expenditure is also nearly double the 1988 estimated market value, $693,000, according to records from the Ramsey County Assessor's office. The sky-rocketing cost of the project has shocked some University Regents who claim they knew nothing about the extent of the expenditures. State

lawmakers said the disclosure could adversely affect future University funding requests."

Regent David Roe is quoted in the story saying, "This will have a full
hearing. I'm very unhappy." Regarding a 1985 letter with cost estimates of
less than $700,000 from David Lilly: "Nobody remembers the letter David
Lilly sent," Roe is quoted as saying. "Nobody remembers [any discussion
of the project]." (The original estimate of around $600,000 appeared *in
the newspaper* in November 1985, following the Regents' *official tour* of the
proposed work in September.)

The same day as the second *Daily* story, February 4, 1988, the *Star Tribune* weighed in with a story titled "$1.26 million bill for renovation of 'U'
president's house questioned," including, "Regents were not notified of cost
overruns . . ."

Stories began appearing regularly (there were at least thirty stories in
February in the *Star Tribune* alone), including a Sunday, February 7, column
questioning why Eastcliff needed a $650,000 *kitchen.*[42] The headline attacked
on multiple levels: "Ken Keller's kitchen: Focus mainly on status at remodeled Eastcliff." Other articles centered on what was likely President Keller's
overriding concern—that negative press would damage state support for
the University and a Commitment to Focus. A 1989 story in *University of
Minnesota UPDATE* said that in this period "newspapers ran 23 straight days
of front-page bad news about the University, not to mention unflattering
editorials, letters, and poison-pen columns."[43]

Ken Keller marveled, "When we corrected the columnists and said, 'The
kitchen actually cost under $200,000,' they said, 'If you think the number
means anything, you don't understand what the issue is about.'"[44]

On February 29, 1988, Keller gave an interview to the *Star Tribune,* explaining some of the news discrepancies and mentioning the very successful
$325 million capital campaign. To give Minnesota Campaign the credit that
it did not get in that article, in 1987 the University ranked first among public
institutions for private contributions, in the top five for all universities. The
interview was printed above a large photograph of eight students protesting
in front of Eastcliff, with the headline "50 students stage a demonstration
at Eastcliff, call for Keller's ouster."[45]

The Regents authorized an external audit of the renovation on February 12, 1988.[46] After stating it was important to wait for the full audit, they
accepted a partial report at a public meeting on March 4, creating more
headlines. The final report was presented at the March 10 meeting of the Regents' physical planning and operations committee. The report found nothing illegal but stated that University procedures were not followed, and no
one was asking the questions they should have asked. Regents allowed the

Eastcliff renovation to proceed without formal approval. If the approvals had been official, normal University procedures would include monthly progress reports, including problems and cost increases. The president didn't ask questions about costs.

According to the minutes of the Board of Regents committee of the whole (all the Regents) meeting the next day, President Keller "noted that the audits disclosed some management problems within the University, and he accepted responsibility for those problems. Dr. Keller stated that he was not prepared to resign and that he would like to be a part of the successful implementation of Commitment to Focus, and he asked the Regents for their support and help in finishing that agenda. President Keller presented several recommendations to address the issues raised in the audits." The Regents voted on and approved resolutions to "address the issues," including a management study of the University's Physical Plant Operations. Regent Lebedoff then commented on the recent problems and stated that the basic solution was better communication between the administration and the Board of Regents. On behalf of the Board, he extended an apology to the people of the state.[47] The meeting ended without a discussion of the agenda item *Commitment to Focus—Academic Priorities* "due to time constraints."

On Sunday, March 13, 1988, three years to the day after he was elected as President, Kenneth Keller resigned. He said, in part:

> What makes me most unhappy is that this very bad story has completely taken attention away from a very good story: the University's attempt to focus its activities, build its academic strengths, and work cooperatively with the rest of higher education to provide Minnesotans with opportunity, choice, and quality in postsecondary education.
>
> I have said recently that I thought I could learn from the mistakes of Eastcliff, improve the management of the University where it's needed, and get on with the important job of completing Commitment to Focus. I have also said that if I felt my presence would hurt more than help in accomplishing that task I would step aside. As painful as it is for me to say, I now believe that to be the case, and I am informing the Board of Regents this evening that I am prepared to step aside as president as soon as they can arrange for an interim replacement.

The announcement was carried live on the ten o'clock evening newscasts. David Lebedoff, chair of the Board of Regents, responded within minutes: "We're losing a great president, but we must not lose a great program."

He reaffirmed the Regents' support for Commitment to Focus at a Monday morning press conference. Within two hours, Governor Perpich announced he was withdrawing his recommendation to the legislature for twenty-three million dollars in University funding. While he maintained his support for Commitment to Focus, he said funding should come from the University's fifty-eight-million-dollar reserve fund.

The weekend before Ken Keller resigned, a paid advertisement was published in one of the newspapers with several hundred signatures of University faculty, asking him not to resign. He received four hundred to five hundred letters of support following his resignation. He described the advertisement and the letters as very meaningful and helpful.

There are many interviews, conducted as a sort of postmortem, in the University's digital archives that shed light on all that happened, from a broad range of participants who were there and involved. Their statements uniformly support Ken Keller. They describe opposition to Commitment to Focus among some Regents, the legislature, and the public, both due to populism (all Minnesota students should be admitted to the University, even those unlikely to succeed) and miscommunication about what excellence would mean for the institution. (The plan later succeeded, even though its author did not.) There was a circulation competition among the local newspapers, with each paper trying to print the juiciest story, and the city papers jealous of the student *Daily* getting a scoop. When the newspapers began calling the central reserves a "slush fund," some of the Regents disavowed any knowledge of the reserves, even though they had received regular written reports. There were also reports of antisemitism: Ken Keller, who is Jewish and had been on faculty at the University of Minnesota for over twenty years, was regularly called an Easterner or a New Yorker. (President Magrath came from New York, but no one called him a New Yorker. A few months after the resignation, a regent who had opposed Keller was twice accused in the press of making anti-Semitic comments.) The most damning stories were about racism in the University's Physical Plant Operations, and opposition to Keller for promoting two Black men to be head and second in the physical plant. ("[O]ne of the subterranean issues in the ouster of Keller was the deep resentment of the blue-collar trades groups in the Physical Plant who had two black men saying there were going to be major changes in this organization and that was more than that culture could stand."[48]) The workers were said to purposely slow down the work at Eastcliff. (The $350,000 paint job is an example: When Keller expressed concern about the cost of paint removal, a Regent who was a union leader verbally offered to have the union do the work for free, then the University was billed $110,000.[49] The same leader, with another Regent, insisted that the Black supervisor be fired.) It's highly likely the disgruntled workers (and the Regent accused of anti-Semitism) sent the story of cost overruns to the *Daily*, which started the negative news cycle.

The forced resignation was not about a $600,000 kitchen, although people still recall that. As mentioned earlier, Keller told newspaper columnists, "The kitchen actually cost under $200,000," and they responded, "If you think the number means anything, you don't understand what the issue is about."[50] It remains the most infamous chapter in Eastcliff's history.

In 1993, Ken Keller called the events scar tissue rather than festering wounds, and he joked about Clark Kerr's comment when he was dismissed as chancellor at the University of California: "I leave as I came, fired with enthusiasm." In 1997, Keller said, "Things move from passion to remembrance." Ken and Bonita currently divide their time between Bologna, Italy, and the Twin Cities, where he is a distinguished emeritus faculty member in the Department of Chemical Engineering at the University. [51]

After President Keller offered his resignation on Sunday, Richard Sauer was elected interim president the following Wednesday. He held the position through the end of the year. When Nils Hasselmo was elected the thirteenth president of the University of Minnesota, he was asked if he would live in Eastcliff. He responded, "Yes. I understand it's in good shape."[52]

Friends of Eastcliff

What, you may be asking, was done to make sure that this "unfortunate fiasco" would not happen again? ("Unfortunate fiasco" was Pat Hasselmo's apt term for the situation.) The Regents' meeting minutes from 1988 show that the Regents discussed forming a committee in February, then in March they set up a committee to consider setting up a commission. In May, the committee was making initial plans to study the concept, and in June the support services department was researching and evaluating data from other schools. In August, the Regents approved three recommendations: (1) Keep Eastcliff; (2) the office of support services and operations should run it;

(3) an Advisory Committee of volunteers should raise funds to support it. In September, the regents voted to appoint a Regents' Technical Advisory Committee for Eastcliff to advise the volunteer Advisory Committee.

According to the May 1989 Board of Regents'' meeting minutes, the Advisory Committee had been formed in December and had met. The minutes then refer to a Resource Committee as the committee to fulfill the fundraising function (the charge of the Advisory Committee). The September 1989 minutes state that the Regents were considering membership and functions of the Resource Committee. In November 1989, the purpose of the committee was approved, though it's not clear which one. A meeting was reported in May 1990.

Soon, the technical committee became known as the Eastcliff Technical Advisory Committee (ETAC), and the Advisory Committee/Resource Committee became Friends of Eastcliff (committee). Eastcliff donors were also called Friends of Eastcliff. In 2014, the Friends of Eastcliff committee was repositioned as an advisory board and renamed the Eastcliff Advisory Board.

Pat Hasselmo, the presidential partner who was living in Eastcliff when these procedures began, described the process in a 1994 article: "The Board of Regents decided that work on certain aspects of the house should be financed through private fund-raising. Eastcliff should be treated like any other University facility for basic maintenance; the fund-raising is for any of those things that are special and out of the ordinary and have extra cost implications." The article then explained that the regents formed the Friends of Eastcliff committee to explore alternate funding sources, which created the Eastcliff Legacy Fund. The Eastcliff Technical Advisory Committee included volunteer consultants from University departments, including architecture, facilities management, landscape architecture, and interior design, to implement cost-effective house maintenance, repairs, and improvements.[53]

Nils Hasselmo was known to joke that when he was interested in leaving the University, he would just remodel Eastcliff. In an interview in 1998 with Professor Clarke Clifford, after Nils was no longer president, Pat Hasselmo spoke candidly in describing the Friends of Eastcliff fundraising committee:

> It was in place but it hadn't done anything. It was in place because of the unfortunate fiasco surrounding the Kellers' experience with trying to update the house and do absolutely needed improvements. That never should have been turned upon them as a negative. It was one of those situations that, clearly, got out of hand for all of the reasons that I'm sure have been discussed on your tapes.

Professor Clifford replied, "I hate to say it, there are a good number of hours on that subject." Pat Hasselmo continued:

I'm sure there are. Once that whole tragic situation had happened, the Regents had set up two committees to manage the president's home, Eastcliff. One was to make all of the decisions so that, presumably, the president and the president's spouse and family wouldn't have made any of the decisions that could come back to haunt them. That committee was functioning and was making all decisions about what was done at Eastcliff. The other committee had been designated to raise private funds to support what was needed at the house. That committee had been set up and had met a few times but never had gotten off the ground. I finally was so frustrated by that that I said to Barbara Muesing, who was the executive director of the Board of Regents, "Barbara, you have to tell the board to either make a commitment to go ahead and see to it that something happens on this"—it was chaired by a Regent—"do something with it, or else just dissolve it. It's an embarrassment to have community people come and meet three times a year, talk about what is going to be done, and then nothing ever happens." I thought it was an embarrassment. Barbara and I sat down and decided to kind of take things into our own hands. We began a very specific effort to get something started.

Before I read any of this, I had found Pat Hasselmo's old files at Eastcliff and learned that she was the one who really started Friends of Eastcliff. She conferred with her colleagues at other universities regarding fundraising for official residences and did fundraising for the Eastcliff Legacy Fund. The committee began meeting regularly. They ran advertisements in University publications asking people to "Join Friends of Eastcliff—The Eastcliff Legacy Fund is being initiated to ensure that Eastcliff, like all the public places of the University's Twin Cities campus, is preserved for future generations to enjoy." They hosted a reception in October 1993 and celebrated the original donors as charter members of the Eastcliff Legacy Fund. By November 1994, Friends of Eastcliff had raised $100,000 from the Brooks family and $33,000 from 233 new donors. Pat said, "We are especially grateful to the Brooks family for their continuing interest in and involvement with Eastcliff."

One of the strategies for gaining community support was to let people see what the infamous remodeling accomplished. In August 1988, Interim President Richard Sauer had an open house for seventy neighbors. There was precedence, as Diane Magrath had graciously opened Eastcliff to many people, including any group who requested a tour. Early in the Hasselmo administration (April 1989), a "Musical Home Tour" to benefit the University's music performance hall included touring three homes in either Minneapolis (including admired community member and art patron Dolly Fiterman's home) or St. Paul (including Eastcliff), with a musical performance in each home. The Eastcliff tour encompassed all three floors and culminated in a fifteen-minute concert in the living room. Other Eastcliff open houses were held that spring.

A community-wide open house was held that fall and included newspaper reporters. A front-page story headline (albeit below the fold) in the *Star Tribune* read: "Lavish wasn't the word for what the public saw at Eastcliff." A visitor was quoted as saying, "It's a beautiful house and not gaudy. It's obviously not lavish. I've been to King Ludwig's castle in Bavaria and this . . . this would be servants' quarters there." Another guest said, "It's a home that every Minnesotan should be proud of and it's not pretentious." And another said, "I thought it would be more 'Wow!' It's just a lovely old house. Very nice, very appropriate."[54]

Tours continued during the Hasselmo administration, with open houses for the public and special requests accommodated. The public relations helped. Ten years after the ill-fated remodel, a 1997 article about upcoming renovations was titled "Summer brings long overdue overhaul to 'U' mansion." Nils Hasselmo was quoted as saying, "If you have to live in public housing, this is the best" but the paper stated Eastcliff "looked shabby last summer when it was opened for public tours."[55]

In 2001, a Holiday House Tour benefiting Minnehaha Academy included a quick tour of the first floor of Eastcliff. In April 2007, Eastcliff was part of the Minneapolis and St. Paul Home Tour; among the 5,300 visitors who attended the tour, Eastcliff was a top-visited home with 747 visitors.

Beginning in 1995, an annual Friends of Eastcliff Garden Party has celebrated donors who contribute to the care of Eastcliff. The party is held on the terrace and among the gardens.

In 2004, Susan Hagstrum started a book club for Friends of Eastcliff donors (and to encourage others to become donors). The first book featured was *Saul and Patsy* by award-winning author Professor Charles Baxter. Each meeting featured an author with a connection to the University, and every author attended the meeting that featured his or her book. Susan continued the club throughout their tenure and said, "I'm the host, but Bob always attends as well, so it's an opportunity to have a conversation in the president's living room with the president present."

Eastcliff has remained in the news. Over the years, each remodeling project is reported in the newspaper, and mention is often made of the problematic Keller remodeling. A 1992 newspaper article reported, "Now a committee of officials and citizens keeps tabs on every penny spent at Eastcliff."[56] A 1996 article stated that Eastcliff was undergoing $200,000 worth of repairs and enhancements. The article continues, "But don't worry . . . It has been approved. The largest home improvement project since 1988 . . ." [57]

Nearly fifteen years after the Keller era renovations, the *Minnesota Daily* was still making mention of breaking the story. A 2002 article reported the 1980s expenses "according to an exclusive *Minnesota Daily* report on Feb. 11, 1988." Renovations during the Hasselmo administration were listed as totaling nearly $200,000, and during the Yudof administration, from 1997 until 2000, the remodeling cost approximately $1.35 million.[58] A 2006 article reported, "They're spiffing up Eastcliff: Unlike 1988, this detail work on the U president's house won't bring any surprises."[59]

In 2019, more than thirty years after the electrical improvements were discontinued during the catering kitchen addition, we moved out early and Joan Gabel moved in late to allow electricians to replace more of the 1920s wiring that was still in the house, as well as replace the sixty-year-old boilers. When the plans were announced in 2018, a newspaper reported:

> Mike Berthelsen, vice president of university services, told the Board of Regents on Thursday that Eastcliff needs new heating infrastructure and electrical wiring, which could cost as much as $970,000 . . . Regents urged Berthelsen to consider additional upgrades that the mansion may need but might become politically untenable once a new president is living there.
>
> In 1988, Kenneth Keller resigned after spending $1.5 million renovating Eastcliff and another $200,000 on his campus office.[60]

Shortly before the work began in 2019, another newspaper reported:

> Eastcliff has also been a source of controversy. A scandal involving $1.5 million renovations to the residence forced President Kenneth Keller to resign in 1988.
>
> After the scandal, the University took renovation decisions out of the hands of presidents. Instead, the Eastcliff Technical Advisory Committee—a group of faculty, administrators, and University members— recommends improvements to the property.
>
> Renovating Eastcliff during presidential transitions can help public perception, a concern raised by several Regents at a meeting last semester. "Where the public seems to attach a concern is when there's

a resident in the building," Regent Darrin Rosha said at the meeting. "This is really the time [for renovations]."[61]

Hmmm, good idea. Let's give Ken Keller the last word on this: "I want it to be clear that in the contractual agreement that I reached with them [the Regents], in the contract, it says, 'These repairs will be done to Eastcliff before the new president moves in.' It just didn't get done."[62]

THE OFFICE

The Eastcliff office has changed little since the room was built in 1930. Originally part of the maids' quarters, it has a full bathroom with bathtub—a feature not found in many offices. There was live-in staff at Eastcliff until 1978, so the room remained part of the staff living area. After that, it became an office, in succession, for Linda Fox, Dana Zniewski, Jill Christenson, Patricia Hall, Jim Bossert, Pam Hudson, and Kristia Davern. Kristia remodeled the office in 2017, with previously owned built-in furniture, so that it would function more effectively as an office for one full-time staff person and shared space for the multiple workers who came to Eastcliff for events.

This office has never been used as an office by the University president's partner. However, in writing about the unusual situation of having a paid employee working in an office in someone else's home, this seems an apt place to discuss the role of the presidential partner and the history of official residences for university presidents.

After leaving Minnesota for the University of Missouri, Diane and Peter Magrath gave a presentation and wrote an article, formatted as letters to each other, for the Association of Governing Boards. When beginning again in Missouri, Diane set out a new "motto" of goals for herself that may have been tongue in cheek but reveals good insight into her life as the president's partner:

Number 1: Do not be sick; it does not pay. I was ill two times in six years and missed two events. The first time I was ill, the rumor was that I was pregnant, and it took months to disprove it. The second time I had the flu so badly I could not stand up, and I was going to miss the opera and a dinner. You suggested that I sit during the receiving line.

Number 2: Do not be tired; fatigue is not tolerated.

Number 3: Do not be afraid; it does not help. Remember that time Mo and I drove up to the garage in the dark and the police person was waiting in an unmarked car? "May I help you?" I asked.

"A disgruntled employee has threatened to shoot the president and reportedly followed him home."

"Where is the president?"

"Out jogging."

And number 4: After an encounter with new folks, let's not ask each other anymore "Do you think they know who we are?" Because who we are is an ordinary family in an extraordinary job, and that's my mission—to keep us ordinary and the keep the job extraordinary.[63]

The University of Minnesota is a member of both the Association of American Universities (AAU), which includes the sixty-two leading research universities in North America, and the Association of Public and Land-grant Universities (APLU), which is an organization of 238 public research universities, land-grant institutions, state university systems, and higher education organizations. The National Association of State Universities and Land-Grant Colleges (NASULGC) was a precursor to APLU, which began in 2009. Both the AAU and APLU have meetings for member presidents/chancellors and have been having meetings for spouses/partners of those leaders since the 1970s. The spouse/partner groups offer friendship, support, and professional development for those of us in the role.

Diane Skomars Magrath was at some of those first meetings of partner groups. Bonita Sindelir provided an article for the first NASULGC partners' manual. Pat Hasselmo was chair of the NASULGC Partners' Council. Susan Hagstrum was chair of the APLU Presidents' and Chancellors' Spouses/Partners Council and was active in AAU. Susan gave me the excellent advice to become involved in the groups. I also became chair of the APLU group—for multiple terms, for complicated reasons—and then chair of the AAU group.

Diane Magrath and Joan E. Clodius, whose husband was the NASULGC president, recognized that it would be helpful for partners to know more about the experiences of others in the role. In the early 1980s, Diane teamed with University of Minnesota researcher Dr. Roger Harrold and Marilee Ward from the president's office to survey 104 spouses of presidents of public institutions. That research led to a book that Diane and Joan coedited.

The President's Spouse: Volunteer or Volunteered shared the research findings and a collection of essays from those in the role. With Diane's permission and the assistance of Laura Voisinet, a partner at Georgia State, a free pdf download of the book is on the presidential partners' page of the APLU website.

My involvement in the APLU and AAU partners' groups led me to want to redo the survey Diane had conducted, with an expanded emphasis on official residences. Two particular conversations sparked my interest in learning more about the residences:

1. In 1977 I had attended an honors students' reception at the residence of the University of Tennessee chancellor. I remember vividly that there was an ironing board set up in the kitchen—which made me understand that I was actually in Mrs. Reese's *home*. In 2011, when I met the UT chancellor's wife, Ilene Cheek, at an APLU meeting, I shared that I had been in her home thirty-four years earlier. Ilene told me that the residence had been deemed too expensive to keep, was left sitting empty, had fallen into disrepair, and therefore UT hadn't been able to sell it. I shuddered to think something like that could ever happen to our beloved Eastcliff.

2. At another meeting, a spouse of a president proudly shared that she told their university that she didn't want to live in the official residence and they should sell it. Then she said, "You're welcome!" as if we all welcomed getting rid of an official residence.[64] (Sadly, the house has since been razed.) I love Eastcliff—but I wondered if others felt differently about their official residences.

Presidential Partners

While I wanted to update the presidential partners survey, the project seemed more than I could do alone, particularly since I also wanted to write a book about the history of Eastcliff. I wondered if I could interest a graduate student in the topic. I serendipitously mentioned the idea to Gwendolyn Freed while we were chatting at an event. Gwen, besides being a lovely person and a friend, is the director of development at the Humphrey School of Public Affairs at the University and has a PhD in educational policy and administration. She thought the role of presidential partner was under-researched in higher education, and she was interested in working with me. Gwen suggested seeking advice from her thesis advisor, Professor Darwin Hendel; I was honored when Darwin said he would like to join us on the project.

In 2016, Gwen, Darwin, and I completed the largest survey to date of presidential partners, with 461 respondents in both public and private institutions. Our study was also the first to include responses from a substantial number of males (seventy-seven) in the partner role. The percentage of female presidents is higher than the percentage of male partners: the American Council on Education (ACE) survey of college and university presidents from 2011 reported that seventy-two percent of female presidents are currently married, compared to ninety percent of male presidents. In our study, twelve partners (nine females and three males) reported that the president's gender was the same as their own. Our 141-page report, *The Lives of Presidential Partners in Higher Education Institutions,* is available online through the University of Minnesota Digital Conservancy.

Love, Marriage, Baby Carriage: The First Three Families

Marian Wilson, Tracy Moos, and Diane Skomars Magrath lived at Eastcliff during the full era of second wave feminism and demonstrate the changes that occurred during those two decades. Marian Wilson (whose maiden and married names were both Wilson) was a twenty-year-old student at Brigham Young University when she met her future husband, a history professor and the college debate coach. Tracy Gager, a student at Goucher College, was on a blind double-date in 1945 when she met her future husband, a young professor at Johns Hopkins University. (Mac was not Tracy's date, but they connected. He did not date students, but since she went to a different university, he made an exception.) He proposed a week after they met. Diane Skomars was a divorced mother in her mid-thirties and director of the University student activities center when she met her future husband, the University president. All three women married their husbands within a year of meeting them. All three were seven or more years younger than their husbands. Marian and Met Wilson married in 1938; Diane and Peter Magrath married in 1978: two administrations apart, but forty years apart in marital expectations.

When Met Wilson became president of the University of Minnesota, his wife was described in the *Minnesota Daily* as "an attractive brunette whose smile is surely one of her husband's chief assets"—yes, even the student newspaper wrote of women in that way in 1960.[65] Tracy Moos was portrayed by the press, in my opinion, as a lovely, quiet, and behind-the-scenes mother and hostess. Tracy had a dynamic personality but played the white-gloved role expected at the time. Diane Skomars, the second wife of Peter Magrath, was described in the newspapers as the modern woman she was.

Marian and Met Wilson had six children, with four at home and two in college when they moved into Eastcliff. Tracy and Malcolm Moos had five children, ages seven to fifteen, when they moved into Eastcliff. Both families had multiple children in the house throughout their years at Eastcliff. Diane Skomars Magrath had a three-year-old daughter when she married Peter and moved into Eastcliff. Peter and his first wife, Sandra, had a daughter in college; they had been married twenty-two years when they divorced in 1977.

The Next Six Families

Bonita Sindelir and Ken Keller moved into Eastcliff with their two-year-old son, Jesse. (Ken's two older sons were away at college.) Patricia and Nils Hasselmo's two sons were working adults when Nils was elected president. Pat stayed in Arizona for six months while their youngest child, Anna, finished high school; Anna was a rising college student when she and Pat arrived at Eastcliff. Judy and Mark Yudof's children were out of the house when Mark began his term; their son was a working adult and their daughter was in college. Susan Hagstrum and Bob Bruininks's three sons were all adults when Bob became president. Our younger son was beginning his last semester in college when we arrived at Eastcliff, and shortly thereafter both sons were working adults. Gary Gabel stayed in South Carolina at the beginning of Joan's presidency so that the youngest of their three children could finish high school there. Their oldest child, and only daughter, was a working adult, and the middle child was starting his last year of college. During the March 2020 stay-at-home period of the coronavirus pandemic, Gary and their two sons moved to Minnesota.

Every president and partner who lived at Eastcliff had children, but in recent administrations they have been adult children. Since 1988, no young children have lived at Eastcliff, although Hasselmo, Bruininks, and Kaler grandchildren have visited.

These changes in number of children reflect demographic trend of smaller families over the time period. Since the discontinuation of a mandatory retirement age, presidents and partners have gotten older on average, and therefore they are more likely to have older children. (In Diane's 1984 study, 15 percent of partners were over age sixty, compared to 51 percent in my 2016 research.)

Working—at Home and Beyond

Marian Wilson, with six children, and Tracy Moos, with five children, were (more than) busy full time at home prior to their arrivals at Eastcliff. Diane Skomars Magrath worked full time at the University but quit when she and Peter married to serve full time in the role of presidential partner. Bonita

Sindelir was a lawyer working full time in the office of general counsel at the University; she reduced her paid employment to half time and also used vacation days to accommodate the demands of the partner role.[66] Pat Hasselmo had already given up paid employment before Nils became president; she had been associate dean of students for women at Gustavus Adolphus College and was director of alumni relations at Augustana College when she met Nils. She served on the Golden Valley School Board and Metropolitan Council when Nils was on faculty at the University. Judy Yudof had also given up paid employment during Mark's career moves. While living at Eastcliff, she remained involved in her volunteer roles, many established prior to moving to Minnesota, most notably with the United Synagogue of Conservative Judaism. She became the first female international president of that New York–based group in 2002.

Susan Hagstrum was working on her PhD in educational policy and administration, with a focus on language acquisition, when she met and married Professor Robert Bruininks. She worked in administrative positions in Minnesota schools, including as assistant superintendent. She recalled being so busy while Bob was interim president that after rushing from work to an event at Eastcliff, she greeted guests and introduced herself as the "interim wife of the president." While she continued working for a while after Bob was elected president, she cheerfully and tactfully said she recognized she was "missing all the fun" and quit paid employment.

I enjoyed a long career as a graphic designer, and I kept one large project (Kids Count in Delaware Fact Book) that I worked on remotely when we moved for Eric's position as provost, and again when we moved for the presidency. After burning the candle at both ends for a few years, I contracted shingles as a sign from my body that the demands at the University were too much for me to continue paid employment. Then I started writing, with no deadlines.

Gary Gabel began his working life as a graphic designer, then received his EdD (a connection with Susan Hagstrum) and has been working in education for more than twenty years. He is currently a K–12 administrator.

In 2016, fifty-three percent of female partners reported that their employment had changed as a result of their spouse/partner becoming president. Gary Gabel is like the majority of male partners (sixty-six percent) who did *not* change employment status, but like most "trailing spouses" in a move, he may pay a career price for moving. Gary, as a partner working full-time, also follows the gender divide on working partners: Whereas sixty-one percent of females were not employed outside the role, only twenty-two percent of males were not employed outside the role.[67]

A Full-Time Volunteer

The University of Minnesota has been fortunate to have had many presidential partners who volunteered long hours for the University. I am fortunate to know all the partners who lived at Eastcliff except Marian Wilson and Patricia Hasselmo. Unfortunately, I have only been able to talk with a few people who knew Marian Wilson, but I feel that I know Pat Hasselmo quite well from talking with others who knew her, reading about her, and reading notes in old files about her work. I know her to be a gracious, hardworking person who was modest about taking credit. While I couldn't interview Pat, she was interviewed in 1998. Excerpts from that interview will give you a snapshot of what the partner role is like. Pat said:

> I have said sometimes in speeches that growing up as a minister's kid in a big church was really pretty good preparation for ending up as a president's wife at a university.

Pat complimented the work of Diane Skomars Magrath, saying it gave her a picture of what the role was like:

> I watched her doing it her way and got a sense of what her concept of it was, how she and Peter had worked out their plan as a partnership and how they executed it to a large degree because we were involved so much . . . I think that was very helpful to me. After my position as director of alumni relations and the jobs I had held while Nils was in graduate school at Harvard, I really from that point on had done largely volunteer things, like being on the school board and the Metropolitan Council. I was prepared coming back to Minnesota, then, to focus my energies and interests on the university and made that commitment. I wasn't interested in trying to pursue my own professional interests at that point. I spent a lot of time on university matters.

Pat reflected on the event procedures:

> I think there's quite a varying degree to which presidential spouses turn that over to someone who is employed to do the mechanics of it and set it up. We had a house manager who was in charge of events, sending out all of the invitations, and getting responses, and so on; but, I felt that I wanted to have a very key role in that; so, I didn't just turn it over to her. I was very involved in the issue of who was invited and being sure that we had the right combinations and didn't miss people who were important. . . .
>
> The development people for the respective colleges would often come and request that we hold an event. In those cases, they were the

ones who put together the list of people that they wanted to include. There were times when it was somewhat out of my hands; although, I always tried to look at that, too, to see that it was going to be put together in a way that seemed to me to be the most optimal way of functioning. A lot of what we did was cultivating people with the hope that they were going to be financially supportive of the University.

There was very close communication [with the Minnesota Foundation] . . . When we went out on behalf of the University for President's Club events, for example, all over the country, then, there were people who would fill us in about whom we were going to see and what their background was, what their interests were.

I agree wholeheartedly with Pat's description of fundraising:

Fund raising and hoping for support from these people is . . . one of the really satisfying things about being in a presidential role. You meet so many wonderful people who are *so* committed to education, education at all levels but certainly, in this case, to higher education and who are so interested in giving back to the community of higher education according to their means and how well they have done. They, by and large, are just wonderful people. It's just a privilege to have gotten to know them, whether they do anything. It's really special to have met them and have a chance to thank them and encourage them to keep on doing more of the same, hopefully.

Pat described the schedule as the hardest part of the role. I felt the same way. At my last AAU meeting, I said that my least favorite thing was that we were so busy (and tired) that I occasionally felt like I "had" to go somewhere as I was getting ready to go. Once I was there, I recognized I was fortunate to "get" to be there. I'm sorry that we were so busy that I couldn't relish every moment. The events at Eastcliff were never a problem; it was just that there was so much to do in addition to them. Pat described the schedule concerns:

Sometimes . . . he was so exhausted, he didn't want to talk about anything. It is stressful. That's the hardest thing about that role. The interesting thing to me was that I kept saying to Nils in the beginning, "We have to get a handle on this schedule for our own sake." He kept saying to me, "It's going to get better. It's going to better." Every year, it was more out of hand.

People asked me if I ever got to see Eric; I would reply, "I probably see him more than I ever have, but he is across a crowded room or sitting at another table at dinner." Pat described this as well:

We were together a lot in public situations. We were not together privately very much. I have often said that I would have hated being in
that role if our children had been young or even still at home. I think I
would have found that very stressful because of the lack of time on his
part, more than anything. He just wouldn't have had time . . .

Pat spoke about her work as chair of NASULGC, and how she tried to improve the role for others:

I decided a couple of years before Nils stepped down from the presidency that I would at least try, within the University of Minnesota,
to establish the idea that there was a title, which gave the role some
status, and to see to it that there were certain defined things that the
Regents would expect to give . . . for example, something as simple
as a library card, a parking permit so that I could go to these events
and park anywhere on the campus, coverage for insurance for liability,
some of which can be very important. All of these things were spelled
out, at one point.

I benefited from, and was grateful for, Pat's efforts. After Board of Regents
chair Linda Cohen noticed that I was a very active volunteer for the University in the partner role, she offered me the title of "University Associate."

At the conclusion of the interview, Pat was asked if she wanted to add
anything. She answered as I would have, if I were as articulate as she:

From time to time, I'm asked to speak to one group or another and I
have always tried to say in absolute, genuine sincerity that the opportunity for Nils and me to serve as the presidential couple at the University
of Minnesota was one that neither of us would trade for anything in the
world. It was exhausting. It took a toll on our personal lives in the sense
of time together—but, it was so interesting and so exciting. We met
absolutely wonderful people, endless numbers of people, who are so
committed to the University in so many ways—I'm talking within the
institution and also from without in the community. It was a pleasure
to have the opportunity of meeting them and getting to know them
better and to have the feeling that we were a part of the opportunity
of leading the University, and trying to do the best that we could in
that role was an incredibly wonderful opportunity for us. We are very
grateful for that and always will be.

In the 2016 research, eighty-four percent of presidential partner respondents reported being satisfied in the role.[68]

The Tradition of the University President's House

The U.S. tradition of a college president's house goes back to the country's first degree-granting institution. When Harvard College was founded in 1636, it followed the English collegiate tradition of students eating, sleeping, and studying together, with faculty living in residences alongside their students. Since headmasters were allowed to marry, schools provided houses that would accommodate their families. The president's house was one of only four buildings at Harvard in 1655.[69]

Other colleges in colonial America also followed the English system and provided houses for their heads—and continued to provide houses for presidents even after other faculty were allowed to marry and live off campus. The College of William and Mary, the second oldest college in the United States (chartered in 1693), claims the oldest president's house still in use, built in 1732. Eleven U.S. presidents, from George Washington to Dwight Eisenhower, have been guests in the home.

I visited the official residence on the University of Missouri campus in Columbia while on a visit with the APLU partners' council. It's a beautiful home right in the middle of campus; the doors are locked so that lost students don't inadvertently wander in. I learned from presidential partner Ann Deaton that when the university was founded as the first state university west of the Mississippi River, the state provided its first appropriation of $10,000 (in 1867) in part to build a home on campus for the president. Housing the president was so important that it was the first thing they did.

At the University of Minnesota, when the first presidential couple arrived, the wing of Old Main that was offered to them as a home was already inhabited by wild turkeys. They respected the squatters' rights of the turkeys and moved elsewhere. (Are the turkeys I regularly see on campus, crossing the road in front of Pioneer Hall, descendants of those birds? We can imagine so.)

Minnesota's second president bought a home near the first president, and the third presidential couple was given a residence at the Pillsbury mansion, which housed seven presidential couples (including the Wilsons, who lived there eight months before moving into Eastcliff). Eastcliff is currently home to her ninth presidential family.

The amusement room in the basement. Photograph by Patrick O'Leary. Courtesy of University Photographer records, University of Minnesota Archives.

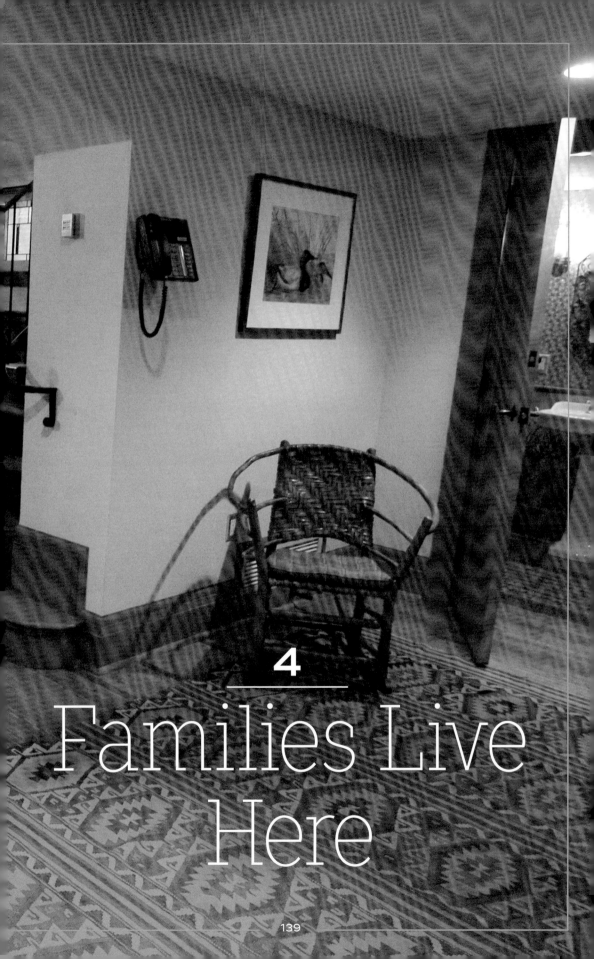

4
Families Live Here

In the 1921 and 1930 floor plans, *the back stairs and the entire back of the house were for the staff. On the second floor, there was a door between the family bedrooms and the servants' hall and stairs. The back stairs connected the servants' hall on the second floor to a short hall on the first floor behind the maids' sitting room. Below those stairs is another set of stairs that lead to the basement and laundry room. There is still a sign at the back entrance of the house indicating that it is the service entrance. We used that entrance and the back stairs almost exclusively, and appropriately so, as we felt that our role in the house was to be of service to the University.*

A few feet inside the service entrance door is the door to the basement. At the bottom of the basement stairs, past an open area containing racks of glassware, are two doors and a long hallway. At the far right is a door opening to small half bath with storage closets; another door from the half bath opens into the laundry room. The center door opens to a storage room listed on the 1921 plan as a "fruit room." At the left is a corridor more than fifty feet long. In the 1920s, one door opened off this long hall to the north into the laundry room. Over time, a door was added into what was originally a coal room, then a sauna, and is now used for storage. Continuing to the west end of the long hall is a door into the "amusement room."

Basement floor plan, 2020.

THE BACK STAIRS AND LOWER LEVEL

Heading up the back stairs from the first floor to the second, there is a large landing to the right near the top, then the stairs continue up to the left. That landing wasn't there in the 1921 floor plan—instead, there was a closet off the upstairs maids' hall with drawers and shelves. This was likely a large linen closet; when the maids' bedrooms were relocated downstairs in the 1930 addition, a linen closet was added downstairs. Before we arrived, Bob Bruininks and Susan Hagstrum had coat racks on the stairs landing. We thought that was an excellent place for coats and installed metal clothing bars for that purpose.

The landing near the top of the back stairs on the second floor had its best use when Monette Magrath used it as a puppet stage and invited guests to sit on the stairs to watch the performances. The audiences included University Regents and others who had been invited to dinner. When Monette was quite young, the puppets would, at times, face her rather than her audience.

Monette's grandmother claimed that Monette said, at age three, that she wanted to be an actress. Monette doesn't recall that early ambition, but at age four she would perform as the dying swan from *Swan Lake* in the Eastcliff living room. Diane recalls her being very serious about the scene, holding her composure and her audience. Monette is now a film, television, and theater actress. She is most known for her performance as Lady Bird Johnson in *All the Way* on Broadway, opposite Bryan Cranston; *All the Way* won a 2014 Tony Award for best play.[1] In 2019–20, Monette was standby for Mary-Louise Parker in *The Sound Inside* on Broadway. When Monette was a child and saw people on tours at Eastcliff gazing into her room, the little girl would ask, "Why are all these people coming to see *me*?" And now, just as Monette foretold as a child, people do go to see *her*.

The large laundry room in the basement currently contains two sets of washers and dryers and a large metal-topped table that was in the house during the Brooks days. In the front corner of the room is what looks like a large metal cupboard about eight feet tall, five feet wide, and eight feet deep. Instead of doors, it appears to have very tall, narrow vertical drawers. I saw similar contraptions when I toured two famous Minnesota mansions,

Glensheen in Duluth and the James J. Hill house in St. Paul: it is a Chicago-Francis dryer for drying clothes. Each of the vertical drawers pull out and contain long metal rods inside, perpendicular to the drawer face. Clothes, sheets, or tablecloths were hung over the rods, then pushed back into the drying chamber, which was heated. This dryer is no longer functional, but it is not worth removing. Eastcliff also had an outdoor clothesline area, which in 1960 was a paved pad near the back service entrance.

The next doorway along the long corridor opens to the elevator/storage room. In the 1921 floor plan, this room was the fuel room with two coal chutes to outside, and it opened only to the boiler room.

President O. Meredith Wilson visited a sauna at the University's Grand Rapids experiment station early in his presidency and was inspired to ask that a sauna be installed at Eastcliff. The sauna was added to the former fuel room (the boiler room has remained where it always was). The sauna continued to be in use during the Moos administration as both sons, Malcolm Jr. and Grant, were on the University High School wrestling team. Their good friends and neighbors, the three Lillehei brothers, were also on the team (the team of twelve wrestlers included three or four sets of brothers). The entire team would come to Eastcliff to use the sauna, hoping to sweat off extra weight before matches. A docent handbook for Eastcliff tours states that Diane Skomars Magrath said that she was "accused of marrying Peter for the sauna because she is a Finn, and she says it is true." Diane also commented that the room "may be in use; if door is closed, call and ask," so clearly saunas were enjoyed regularly during the Magrath years (and possibly during tours). I don't know if the sauna fell into disrepair during the intervening twenty years, but in 2001, when the elevator was installed, the sauna was removed. The room is now used for storage.

Before walking through the back door of the amusement room, take a look behind you down the long corridor. Grant Moos described the appeal of the hallway when he was eleven years old: "There couldn't have been a longer hallway in the world." Grant described his family to me as "the *Beverly Hillbillies* with books." In a 1988 article he said, "We were a bad-dog version of the Clampett family, except we came from swarthy New York City to the stoic Midwest. My dad was no Jed, but you could make a good case that the rest of us were a lot like Granny, Jethro, and Elly May."[2]

The Moos family had moved from New York, but they already had a strong affinity for Minnesota. Malcolm Moos was born in St. Paul and grew up by Como Lake. In 1959, while he was serving in the Eisenhower administration, Malcolm and Tracy bought land at Ten Mile Lake in Hackensack, Minnesota. The family began spending summer vacations at the family cabin there prior to moving to Minnesota. Malcolm, reportedly, once shot a rabid raccoon near the lake cabin.

The family had a .22-caliber varmint rifle, and Grant believed that he needed to learn how to shoot it. He recalls his younger self thinking that learning to shoot the gun was the responsible thing to do in case *he* encountered a rabid raccoon, and he considered himself safety oriented. He piled firewood at the end of the long hall in Eastcliff to protect the back wall. Elder brother Malcolm was likely involved, although Grant refused to incriminate him in the story. After rifle practice at the shooting range had ended, and the firewood was removed, the boys discovered that firewood does not offer adequate protection against rifle fire. Fortunately, only the wall was damaged.

THE AMUSEMENT ROOM

The Brooks family and their guests would use stairs next to the front door to go down to the amusement room; the staff would go down the back stairs by the kitchen and walk down the long corridor past the laundry room. In the 1920s, at the bottom of the front stairs to the left was a wall with a door. Behind the door was a storage room, and then the hallway. In the 1930s, the storage room was converted to a bar. To the right of the stairs was, and is, a room nearly thirty feet long and nineteen feet wide. At the far end of the room is a fireplace. To the right of the fireplace is an arched door to a small closet where the dumbwaiter used to be. Beginning in the late 1960s, the room was known as Helen's Pig Barn and later as the Barn Room. The room was rumored to be paneled with used wood from a pig barn.

"Edward was a jovial host holding court in 'the Bar,'" Marney Brooks wrote of the room next to the amusement room. "This haven was his bailiwick, a comfortable room on the lower level, with silver-leafed walls, painted with colorful tropical birds, which eventually ended up at Longshadows, the house Markell built at Long Lake in 1960. The bar itself was adorned with all sorts of humorous trappings, including a large picture of a Gibson Girl whose eyes moved almost imperceptibly from left to right and back, causing bewilderment for some who might have had one too many."[3]

Edward called his Gibson girl *Mona Lisa*. I have seen a photograph of

Amusement room, circa 1925. *Left:* Edward in the amusement room bar. Courtesy of the Brooks family.

her, and I would describe her as a bit horrid, reflecting Edward's sense of humor. Photographs of the bar show elegant paintings of diving birds, on silver leaf, but *Mona Lisa* was also there. Edward's account ledger notes expenses for making over the bar and putting in a new sitting room in October 1936.[4]

The Brooks children later recalled their favorite amusement room memories as parties where around fifty boys and girls came dressed in costume. "Several times during the middle and late 1930s, the Brookses were hosts to children's masquerade parties. These were held in the basement known as the 'amusement room.' At the masquerades, everyone came in costumes."[5] The Brooks children had a wide variety of costumes to choose from, as their parents had travelled widely, and Markell brought costumes home from around the world.[6]

The amusement room was likely used less after the Brooks children grew up, and it was not mentioned as being renovated during the 1960 makeover of the home. The house upkeep was modest following the Wilson remodel. One woman I met, who had been a student during the Moos administration, told me that she remembered Mrs. Moos showing her a hole in the floor that was covered by a rug.

During the 1960s, students protested the Vietnam War outside Eastcliff and the SDS threatened the president. Malcolm and Tracy Moos decided that the amusement room, without windows, would be a safe place for meetings with faculty during protests (and it was a much larger room than the dining room). But the room needed to be updated. Tracy told me she sourced new barn wood and used it to panel the room. The fireplace was

Left to right: Ted, Binky, Conley, and Dwight Brooks, dressed for a masquerade party. Courtesy of the Brooks family.

faced with Minnesota field stone and granite. She added a pig weathervane and named the room Helen's Pig Barn in honor of Helen Grant—who was *not* a pig farmer but rather a cousin of Malcolm Moos and beloved by the family.[7] The room was a comfortable space for events, and the Moos children still recall it as "a really cool room."

A newspaper columnist at a small-town Minnesota weekly wrote that "the house could not be considered a showpiece" and "it's casual and lived in." She goes on to say:

> We toured the Moos home on Editors' Day last year, but we missed the basement recreation room which is called "The Pig Barn," and it is most interesting. Its walls are paneled with gray barn-siding from the Pig Barn at the Faribault, Minn. farm of Mrs. Moos' cousin, Helen Grant. The weathervane from the same Pig Barn has a prominent place as the visitor approaches the recreation room. A Buffalo Robe on the floor was rescued from the same Pig Barn. A graceful bouquet of wheat, a gift from famed scientist Norman Borlaug, fit beautifully into the decor. Dr. Borlaug won the Pulitzer prize in agriculture for producing the staff of life strain of wheat which helped the entire world. [8]

This story seemed to stick. Even though Nobel Laureate Norman Borlaug is incorrectly said here to have won a Pulitzer Prize, the idea of an actual pig barn installed at Eastcliff was another story for which exaggeration was more eagerly accepted than the truth. Tracy had both a great intellect and a wicked sense of humor, and she found it all quite funny. I admired her for being truer to who she was than caring about what other people thought, and I suspected she got a kick out of people underestimating her. Later I came across an Eastcliff brochure, which Tracy likely wrote, that described the basement paneling as "fumigated barn wood." Tracy admitted to me that reusing barn wood proved that the family was frugal, so it seems that she had both the first and last laughs over the barn wood.[9]

In May 1972, amid protests against the Vietnam War, President Moos met in the Eastcliff basement with Governor Wendell Anderson, Minneapolis Mayor Charlie Stenvig, members of the Minnesota National Guard, and University Regents regarding demonstrations on campus. This was likely the important meeting that occurred after the governor arranged to send the National Guard to campus, as described by former governor and then chair of the Board of Regents Elmer L. Andersen, who was present at the meeting. President Moos was concerned about student safety and insisted that the National Guard could not come to campus armed. The head of the guard insisted that they never went unarmed. In a heated exchange, Moos prevailed. This was *before* the tragedy at Kent State.[10]

Peter Magrath also conducted meetings in the basement, but not for security reasons. He had been hospitalized with Guillain-Barré syndrome and was bedridden at Eastcliff for a few months. He continued to conduct University business, albeit while horizontal, and held meetings from a bed in the amusement room.

At Ken Keller and Bonita Sindelir's faculty dinners, the professor's talk was in the amusement room. They also used the room for a Regents Professors' dinner in 1988 that sounded particularly delightful. The University's college bowl team won the national championship in 1987.[11] The members of that team joined the Regents Professors for dinner at Eastcliff the following February. After dinner, everyone went to the basement for an unannounced college-bowl type game, with teams of students and professors competing. The group returned upstairs for dessert.

In a second phase of the Yudof renovation in 1998, the amusement room was renovated with new mission-style millwork, bookcases, and banquettes of quarter-sawn oak. When the barn wood was removed, it was obvious why it had been added, as the stucco was in disrepair. Barn wood had covered the windows; now they are framed in wood and covered with period-style stained glass (for below-grade windows, the stained glass is a practical, as well as elegant, solution). The stone around the fireplace was removed and the fireplace was returned to its original design. A powder room was added where the bar had been, and air conditioning was another welcome upgrade. A 1920s pool table with open leather pockets was purchased from an auction house in New Orleans and outfitted with new slate and new felt. Mark Yudof played pool with students during Eastcliff student events.

The Brooks family had their family Christmas tree in the amusement room, and it should come as no surprise that Eastcliff was decorated tastefully and lavishly during the Brooks days. Family remembrances include the scent of evergreen from pine boughs throughout the house. A small photo album (given to me by Conley Brooks Jr. and left in the walnut den) bears witness to these memories. Christmas Eve activities included the entire family piling into the car for a drive along Summit Avenue to admire the Christmas lights. The two older boys, Conley and Ted, distinctly remembered their grandfather, Dr. Dwight Brooks, coming for breakfast on Christmas morning and eating very, very slowly—or so it seemed to the boys. They thought he did so intentionally, as they could think of nothing except getting downstairs to the amusement room and unwrapping the presents under the tree.

A newspaper columnist described holiday decorations at Eastcliff during the Moos administration as "early American style with garlands of greens on the banister to the second floor, and three trees trimmed with popcorn necklaces, strings of cranberries and gingerbread boys and girls baked by Moos Housekeeper, Mae McBroom. Mrs. Moos gave instructions on the decorating before leaving on a trip to California with her husband."[12] An annual December event at Eastcliff, going back to at least the Moos and likely the Wilson administration, has been the University of Minnesota Women's Club (UMWC) holiday tea. (The tea was a favorite event for both me and the Eastcliff staff during our tenure.[13]) In December 1969, the tea was previewed in a Minneapolis newspaper: "Mrs. Malcolm Moos and the governing board of the University of Minnesota Faculty Women's Club are giving a Christmas tea for the members at 1:30 p.m. Thursday at Eastcliff, the university president's home. There will be no program, but everyone has been asked to bring a gift for a child at University Hospitals."[14]

In 1972, the same columnist described a more inclusive event: "University Hospital Volunteer Association will stress both Christian and non-Christian holiday traditions at its membership tea." The article goes on to describe the cookies made by housekeeper Mae McBroom: "She found an old family recipe for a sugar cookie that is decorated with three raisins to indicate the Trinity, and also a recipe for what she called a Hebrew biscuit, brushed with honey and sesame." Quilts were used in decorating, including one as a tablecloth on the dining table; an old pickle crock was used for the spiced cider; and a blue enamel pot held coffee. The "house was fragrant with spice and pine . . . Mrs. Louis Wannamaker was reminded of a 'country church fair where everything is so interesting.'"[15] Tracy bought the quilts from the Salvation Army store. In recent years, the event changed to ask for gifts for a hospital patient, not just children. The only year the event was not held at Eastcliff appears to be 1985, when Eastcliff was under renovation.

During the Hasselmo years, the holiday tea desserts included dozens of Swedish cookies (krumkake, finska pinnar, syltkakor, sandbakkels, mazariners) and a French bûche de Noël. Recipes were available for the cookies. During the Yudof years, there were several types of tortes. During the Kaler years, I augmented the desserts with my own homemade fudge.

The Kellers had a Christmas tree in the walnut den. The Hasselmos decorated heavily for Christmas each year, with a tree in the garden room and another upstairs in the family living room. Bob Bruininks and Susan Hagstrum moved into Eastcliff in December 2002, just in time to decorate. Two young girls, Abby and Ellie, from their Minnetonka neighborhood, had helped them decorate their tree in the past. The girls were invited to help

Robert Bruininks and Susan Hagstrum. Courtesy of University Photographer records, University of Minnesota Archives.

at Eastcliff. Susan wrote to me: "As they arrived to help that wintry day, their parents reported that the younger girl said, 'I guess Bob really is the President because he now lives in the White House.' This is a favorite memory of ours."

The Bruininks/Hagstrums got their Christmas trees from the University's forestry club, and we did as well. They displayed the tree in the corner of the living room, and we did too, for our first seven years. When Bob and Susan moved out, they donated beautiful pine garlands they had used in their Minnetonka home prior to living at Eastcliff. They hang so beautifully around the entrances to the dining room and living room that they seem custom made for Eastcliff.

During our second December at Eastcliff, I thought that in place of the budgeted live garland in the porte cochère, we could buy yards of artificial garland from Bachman's nursery and decorate the entire fence, the porte cochère, and the stair rail. I enjoyed the decorating, even though I recall the many hours required to tie dozens and dozens of large bows. I wanted one for each fence post, to accompany the garland. We festooned the stair rail with garland and placed a poinsettia (a gorgeous "tapestry" variety of poinsettia with variegated sage and ivory leaves) purchased from Bachman's on each step next to the wall. It was truly beautiful—until irregular watering took its toll. After a few years we bought "forever" poinsettias. The poinsettias inspired us to get mini-poinsettias for the dollhouse stairs, which led to our getting mini-pumpkins for the dollhouse, which were then followed with regular-sized pumpkins for the regular-sized stairs in October. Art imitates life, then life imitates art.

One year we were on a development trip to China, and I was gone for the early decorating. Pam Hudson, in her first year as my scheduler and the Eastcliff events coordinator, recruited her sister to help with the decorating. I returned to see the most magnificent garlands all along the stairs and over the mantel, gleaming with countless maroon and gold ornaments. "What ornaments," Pam asked, "do you have to put on the tree?" Of course, these were to have been the ornaments now on the garlands. That year I decided we'd use my personal ornaments, although many were handmade and others were truly Christmas themed rather than just University colors.

Our last year at Eastcliff, we were traveling (again) with our good friend Bob Burgett (again) in China, this time over Thanksgiving and into December.[16] On Thanksgiving Day, we joined a large group of Chinese alumni from U.S. schools, including three full tables from the University of Minnesota, for dinner in a hotel ballroom in Shenzhen. The buffet included turkey along with various Chinese dishes. All the Eastcliff decorating was left in the very capable hands of house manager Kristia Davern, part-time housekeeper Hannah Barrows, and Foundation events planner Bethany Fung. Rather than place the tree in the corner of the living room, we decided to leave the corner door available for crowd flow during the always-popular faculty/staff winter open house. So instead, that year there was a twelve-foot tree displayed in the two-story bay window over the stairs.[17]

You may wonder why we would have a "Christmas" tree, as Minnesota is a public institution. It is true that the president's office faced criticism one year when someone placed a red candle next to a green candle on a table in December: red and green were deemed religious. We didn't use the H-word (holiday) for gatherings between Thanksgiving and New Year's

The Kalers, December 25, 2018. Courtesy of the Kaler family.

Day; we had "winter celebrations." When guests visited us at Eastcliff they were welcomed by beautiful winter decorations that included a Christmas tree with secular, ecumenical, and interfaith decorations; a menorah; stained glass featuring the word "shalom"; and a Santa figure with a little girl's wish list that said, "Beat Wisconsin" (given to us by our friends John and Nancy Lindahl). When it comes to celebrations and religious observance, I prefer celebrating everything to celebrating nothing. As Eastcliff is a home, the displays can reflect the preferences of the residents. Ken Keller is Jewish; his and Bonita's decorations included a Christmas tree in the walnut den. Mark and Judy Yudof are also Jewish; they displayed menorahs and chose not to have a tree.

Eastcliff is such a beautiful home, and it is almost fairy-tale beautiful when decorated for winter celebrations. It was a real joy to welcome guests into the house in December.

THE STAIRCASE

Leaving the amusement room, we walk up the stairs and arrive on the first floor into the entry space right by the front door, directly under the grand curved staircase landing. The grand Georgian staircase is the visual centerpiece of the house. The skill of architect C. H. Johnston Jr. is on full display in the elegance and graceful proportions. The steps open wide at the bottom, then narrow as they follow the curved wall up to a landing over the front door, then curve up again to the open second floor. The curves remind me of a nautilus shell. The railing is made of wrought iron and is sturdy but includes a delicate pattern evoking vines. The balustrade is made of curved wood. The craftsmanship is remarkable.

Above the landing, high over the front door, is a two-story bay window. The bay windowsill is about three feet deep and eight feet wide (too high and deep for a window seat, although my granddaughter and I climbed up to watch the snow on a few occasions). Custom-made planter boxes to fit the seat were in the attic, although we preferred not to block the light and didn't use them.

For nearly forty years, when Eastcliff was a private home, Markell Brooks walked down these steps each morning for breakfast. Did she take their beauty for granted, or did she continue to appreciate their elegance? I think the latter, as she shared that elegance with her granddaughters. Marlow

The main staircase in the entry. Photograph by Patrick O'Leary. Courtesy of University Photographer records, University of Minnesota Archives.

Top of the main staircase. Courtesy of the Brooks family.

Brooks recalls that she and her sister Sky, Markell's first two granddaughters, were treated to an imaginary trip on the ocean liner *Queen Elizabeth*, complete with dancing at a ball as guests of Empress Eugenie. The young girls had their choice of their grandmother's gowns to wear for the occasion. They ate dinner at a table set with fine china on the staircase landing, pretending they were on the drawbridge of the grand ship, looking out over the water.[18] For the less imaginative, looking from the stairway down into the actual surroundings of the home is quite elegant enough.

Guests to the home gravitate to the staircase for photographs. It's a beautiful backdrop. Fortunately, most do not feel a gravitational pull *up* the stairs. They would soon encounter a velvet rope attached to a stanchion post with a single word: PRIVATE.

Imagine seven lovely young women wearing long, sapphire-blue velvet gowns descending the Eastcliff grand staircase. Each carries a bouquet of pink and red camellias. They are followed by a proud father and a glowing bride wearing a gown of silk and Bruges lace, with a short train. She is wearing a veil and, because it is 1965 (December 27, to be exact), the veil is attached to a pillbox hat.

The bride was Constance "Connie" Wilson, second child of President and Mrs. O. Meredith Wilson. Her attendants included her older brother's wife and her two younger sisters, Mary Ann and Margaret. These sisters had giggled with their girlfriends on the landing of these stairs as they peeked at their parents' guests arriving for fancy parties. The Brooks children, twenty years earlier, had done the same thing.

Connie Wilson and David Bennion were married in front of the garlanded fireplace at Eastcliff. The bride's grandfather (Marian Wilson's father), a judge from New York, performed the ceremony. Most of the furniture was removed from the living room to accommodate seventy guests. The groom and his brother entered the living room from the sunroom/garden room.[19] A dinner at the Campus Club, on the fourth floor of Coffman Union, followed the ceremony. The rehearsal dinner the night before had been held at Eastcliff.

A year and a half later, second daughter Mary Ann Wilson and John Hansen had their wedding reception at Eastcliff. They were married on June 24, 1967, at Nokomis Heights Lutheran Church, with John's father, Reverend Alfred Hansen, a former pastor of the church, officiating. Mary Ann wore the same dress her sister had worn. In contrast to the deep blue gowns worn by the bridesmaids in her sister's winter wedding, Mary Ann's four bridesmaids in the summer wedding wore long, pale pink dresses with empire waists, and "pearl-trimmed hats designed by milliner Roberta Myers, wife of artist Malcolm Myers of the university studio art department."[20] A *Winona Daily* newspaper article described a busy penultimate week for President Wilson, followed by his daughter's wedding. His last day in office was six days after the wedding, so the wedding reception was most likely the last event the Wilsons held at Eastcliff.[21]

The next University family at Eastcliff was the Moos family with five children, ages seven to fifteen. When they arrived in Minnesota, the children were photographed for *The Minnesotan* (later *Minnesota Alumni*) magazine posed along the staircase. The photograph seems meant to evoke the von Trapp family from *The Sound of Music*, yet Grant Moos wrote that "having us storm in after President O. Meredith Wilson and his family was like having Marie Osmond as the warm-up act to Twisted Sister."

As we ascend the stairs, you will see a wrought-iron gate at the top on the landing. This gate serves as a reminder to guests that upstairs is private space, and a reminder to pets to stay upstairs. I regularly said a silent thank you to Diane and Peter Magrath for this gate, as they had it installed. Peter told Diane that you can ask for housing adjustments only when you move in or when you move out, so the Magraths paid for the gate themselves.

During the Magrath years, tours were allowed upstairs. The bedrooms were described in a 1980 *Twin Cities* magazine article as "comfortable and homey." The article ends with a description of "the one additional feature that may best sum up the agreeable marriage of Eastcliff's public and private functions. You will find it at the top of the circular stairway in the front of the house. It is, improbably enough, a black wrought-iron gate . . . fitted with a heavy, key-operated lock . . . the gate ostensibly divides the official and unofficial sections of the home. . . ." The final sentence of the article: "The gate is almost always open."[22]

Land of 10,000 Coats

I first visited Minnesota in October 1979. Eric and I had met, and fallen in love, that summer in Tennessee. I visited because I missed him and because long-distance phone calls were expensive—and, frankly, if our relationship wasn't real, I was going to cut my losses. I was wearing a thin leather coat, and it was already very cold (to me, at least). We married in late December then drove to Minnesota, arriving on January 2, 1980.

Minnesotans say that there is no bad weather, just inappropriate clothing. I was inappropriately clad. During my first years in Minnesota, I had a cloth coat. I had a knee-length sweater. I wore them both together. I had neither the money nor the knowledge to do better. We didn't have a garage, and I was often very cold while digging out our Volkswagen Beetle and then driving with the windows down because the defroster was not designed to deal with Minnesota winters. Yet that Volkswagen was apparently better in the snow than my KSTP coworkers' cars, as I was one of the few who made it to work after an overnight blizzard. I still remember that as a source of pride for a Southern driver.

When I returned to Minnesota three decades later, people kindly explained to me that during a Minnesota winter you dress for warmth, not fashion. A big puffy down coat that makes you look like the Michelin Man is socially acceptable. Even fur is acceptable in Minnesota.

Winter events at Eastcliff are complicated by the necessities of de-icing sidewalks and finding places for coats. Years ago, I recall hosts asked women to put their coats on the beds in one bedroom, and men would put their coats in another bedroom. Was this to avoid the impropriety of men and women together in a bedroom? I never knew.

There is now an open coat closet in the dining room at Eastcliff. During large winter events, we would also put a coat rack in the elevator and keep the elevator doors locked open to recreate the coat room that had been there before the elevator. For very large winter events, we added coat racks in the walnut den.[23]

Prior to the 1980s dining room remodel, there wasn't a coat closet on the first floor. Tracy Moos told me that during their tenure in the 1960s and 1970s, guests went to the top of the stairs, turned right, and placed their coats on the bed in the master bedroom. I was grateful that hundreds of strangers didn't visit my bedroom, but during the Moos years there was once a more unusual complication. Kathy Moos used the bedroom on the left at the top of the stairs. That room adjoined her sisters' room next door through the bathroom. Another door connected that bedroom to the next bedroom, which was Grant's room. Grant was just a year younger than Kathy, and the two regularly played pranks on one another—that they could access each other's bedroom without going into the hall may have made certain pranks almost irresistible. They vividly remember one that backfired.

Tracy, Kathy, and Grant recalled to me that Mrs. Brinkerhoff, the wife of a university vice president, arrived late for an event at Eastcliff, as she had just come from the beauty parlor after having her hair done. Tracy instructed her to leave her coat in the bedroom at the top of the stairs. At the beginning of the event, many guests were going upstairs at the same time and following each other to the bedroom on the right. Mrs. Brinkerhoff, not having others to follow, understandably thought the designated bedroom was the closest one, the door to the left—Kathy's bedroom—although the door was closed. She opened the door—and was immediately doused by a bucketful of water that Grant had propped over the door in wait for Kathy. Kathy was in the hall, about to fall victim herself, when she saw what had happened to Mrs. Brinkerhoff. "The poor dear" (as Kathy described her) was now both late and with her perfectly coiffed hair dripping wet.[24]

Master bedroom, circa 1940. Courtesy of the Brooks family.

5
The Private
Life Upstairs

Standing on the large landing at the top of the stairs, there is a west–east corridor straight ahead and a door to the right into the master suite. The corridor has an arched ceiling and plaster walls, and there are three bay windows with window seats along the south wall. Doors in the north wall opened to four bedrooms and three closets. In the original floor plan, a door toward the end of the corridor separated the back staircase and two maids' bedrooms from the family bedrooms. After the 1930 renovation, this door was removed, the maids' bedrooms were expanded to the south to create two larger bedrooms for guests, and a sunroom/sleeping porch was added. The current corridor continues past a door on the left that opens out to the back stairs, next to another door that opens inward to reveal the stairs to the attic. A door to the sunroom is on the opposite side of the hall. At the end of the hall, two steps descend to a short hall leading to the two guest bedrooms.

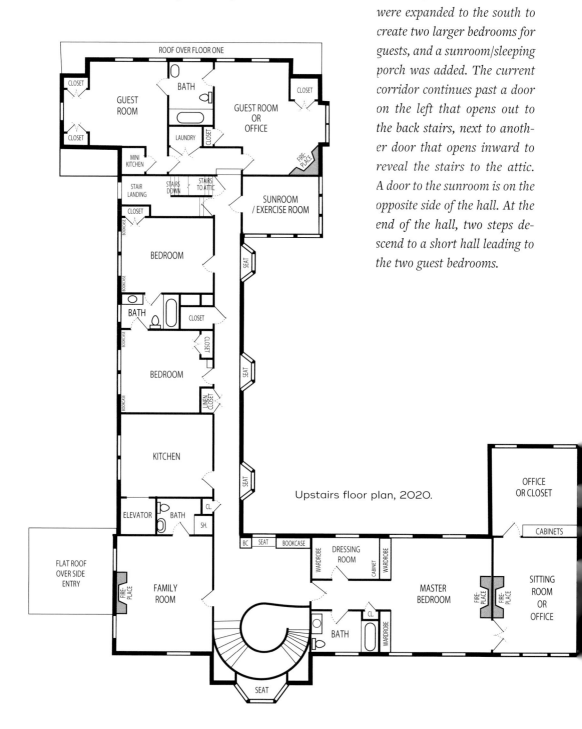

Upstairs floor plan, 2020.

THE MASTER BEDROOM SUITE

Entering the master suite, you walk through a very short hallway with a door to a closet/dressing room on the left and a door to the master bathroom on the right; a second door on the right conceals a small closet. Straight ahead at the back of the room is a fireplace faced with gray marble and a painted (white) mantel. Behind you as you look at the fireplace are built-in wardrobe closets. We know what the master bedroom looked like in the 1940s both thanks to a few photos, and because members of the Brooks family worked with Barbara Bentson to recreate the room in the Eastcliff dollhouse. And we know what the bedroom looks like today. This room has neither received, nor needed, much renovation.

The master bedroom was described in detail in a November 1931 issue of *The Amateur Golfer and Sportsman* magazine, when Eastcliff was featured as "The Home of the Month." The article described the entry and living room, but curiously (at least to me) the master bedroom received the most detailed description. Perhaps that was because Edward and Markell Brooks entertained regularly, so the first floor and lawn were well-known, but no one else had access to the bedroom. About six months after we moved into Eastcliff, University Relations was getting requests for access to the house. It was decided that we should have one interview, with WCCO's Amelia Santaniello and Frank Vascellaro.[1] During the interview, knowing that another news outlet was asking for access to the upper level, I said, "People do say 'I've never been upstairs.' And I'm thinking, I don't know, do you invite people up to your bedroom? It just seems sort of awkward, and it just doesn't seem like your home if people think they can go in your bedroom."[2]

Imagine the room in 1931: "Mrs. Brooks' boudoir is delightfully done in French period style and is a perfect symphony of softly blended, French grey woodwork, ashes of roses[3] walls, and dainty embroidered French blue satin draperies," gushed the magazine article. It continues: "The twin beds with their low, rounded headboards are in antique French grey with dainty floral motifs, and a single canopy of embroidered French blue satin hangs from a metal swan's head fixture, draping the two beds as one. Bedside tables of decorated antique French grey to match the beds are used at the outer side of each bed." The Eastcliff dollhouse reproduces this crown-like fixture over the beds. The bedspreads, as shown in Brooks family photographs and described in the article, are "dainty cream-colored embroidered lace over

Dollhouse master bedroom. Courtesy of Eastcliff records, University of Minnesota Archives.

ashes of roses silk, and the gauze glass curtains at the windows are in ashes of roses shade with plain rosy moiré side draperies and lambrequin of the same richly embroidered blue satin as the bed canopy." The original of the dusty rose carpet in the dollhouse is described in the magazine as "a delicate violet shade."

The Eastcliff dollhouse has five miniature fans decorating the wall in the master bedroom which were created to match fans that Ginny Brooks inherited, and an additional miniature fan on the dresser that was created in 1940 by Elsa Mannheimer. Barbara Bentson told me that Markell Brooks collected fans and owned a fan that had belonged to Eleanor Roosevelt. I found a photograph of the Roosevelt fan, made of apricot feathers, in a catalog for a 1974 Minnesota Museum of Art exhibition, *Lace, Fans, and Photographs.*[4]

The Wilsons' bedroom, described when they moved in after the 1960–61 updates, was rosy-beige and white. I have no further bedroom descriptions, and rightly so.

While Diane Skomars Magrath lived in the house, she wrote that there was a secret hiding place used to hide valuables in the master bedroom (which she used as a living room). It was a hidden compartment in the far corner closet behind her piano. Diane gave a televised tour of the house and showed the hiding place—then she had to move her jewelry, as the place was no longer a secret. (I myself was never able to find the hidden compartment.)[5]

The walls of the house are thick, so this room is quiet. Nonetheless, shortly after we moved in, I was awakened early one Sunday morning to screaming, then quiet, then screaming, and so on—but these were hap-py-sounding screams. I guessed what was happening before I looked out the window. The course of the Twin Cities Marathon, as well as several other races, passes right in front of Eastcliff, and we regularly heard the cheers. Spectators gather in front of the Eastcliff fence.[6]

In 1998, while living in Eastcliff, Judy Yudof interviewed members of the Brooks family. During the interview, Binky recited part of a sonnet:

> This is the house where gentleness abides;
> Builded upon the mutual love of years.
> It stands serenely firm against the tides
> Of shifting fates—impregnable to fears.

Then Binky said, "I've always felt that poem goes with the house, so whoever lives here is *protected* by that. So, it can change, and still everybody can be himself, but the house will be flexible enough to adapt to different ways of perceiving it."

Judy said that people asked her if she was frightened in Eastcliff. "The first few nights I was alone in the house," she said, "I admit to an overactive imagination, and then I didn't give in to that anymore. I honestly feel very serene here, and I don't understand why, because it's an awfully big place. There's something about it that I feel okay."

Binky replied, "It's that foundation of love, it grows." One of her broth-ers said that the sonnet, titled "Eastcliff," was framed and hung in Markell's bedroom. The full poem, written about the house by family friend Barbara Austin Foote, is reprinted at the end of this book.

THE SUNROOM

The sunroom off the master bedroom, at the south end of the house, was designed as a screened porch. With screens on three sides, it would have been more comfortable to sleep here on hot summer nights than in the bedroom. Within five years the room was turned into an enclosed sunroom.

Markell Brooks used the sunroom as an office, and some presidential partners have done the same. In 1931, the room included an antique inlaid desk made from an old German organ (Mr. Brooks bought it in New Orleans), as well as an oversized chaise that Mrs. Brooks used for twenty-minute power naps, before they were known as a thing.

The 1931 article described the room: "Across the front of this sunroom is a row of casement windows leaded in green, and at one end of the room is a small tan marble fireplace with green mantel and hearth. The carpeting of the room is green, and all of the woodwork. In one corner is a chaise so enormous and comfortable looking as to be more properly classed as a large lounge. It is upholstered in a very delicate salmon-colored figured chintz as that used on several of the small lounge chairs."[7]

The room now has wood floors, built-in bookshelves, and the same lovely fireplace.

THE SITTING ROOM

When the south porch on the first floor (now the garden room) was expanded in 1926, the fourteen-by-fourteen-and-a-half-foot space above the addition was built as a screened porch (this is also when the larger upstairs screened sleeping porch was enclosed as a sunroom). In 1935, the room was remodeled into what Edward described as a bed/sitting room. Walls, windows, and heating vents were added. This room apparently had a sink at that time, as there were expenses for plumbing and a marble bowl. The cypress wood paneling was added later, as the 1935 expenses include painting but no paneling. The paneling has a medium reddish stain. (Being from Tennessee, I thought the cypress looked like cedar, but without the characteristic scent.) Bookshelves were added in 1997.

Mr. Brooks slept in this room, and it was here, on December 8, 1954, that he had a heart attack and died. He was sixty-five years old. Markell became a widow at fifty-five. It is difficult to summarize a life well lived in a few paragraphs, but obituaries attempt to do just that:

> Edward Brooks, 65, president of Brooks-Scanlon, Inc., pioneer lumber firm, died Wednesday.
>
> He had been president of the company 15 years. He also was a director of the Northern Pacific railroad and senior director of Powell River Co., Vancouver, Canada, largest newsprint mill in the World.
>
> Born in St. Paul, he was an army captain in the engineers corps during World War I and served in France 18 months. He lived at 176 N. River boulevard, St. Paul.

Survivors are his wife, Markell, three sons, Conley, vice president of Brooks-Scanlon, Wayzata; Edward, Jr., master of Grosse Point school, Detroit, Mich.; Dwight, 2nd, in the air force at Great Falls, Mont., and a daughter, Mrs. John D. Krafchuk, San Francisco, Calif.

Arrangements for memorial services are not complete, but a service is planned for Saturday at Unity church, St. Paul.

After the memorial service on December 11, 1954, Conley and Ted scattered Edward's ashes over Gull Lake.

President Wilson was the first of several presidents to use Edward's room as a home office. The room was described as quiet, with a new teakwood desk and swivel chair. The 1960 floor plans list only this room as being air conditioned.[8]

O. Meredith Wilson, as the new president with a vivacious wife, was a cause for excitement in the Twin Cities media. His hiring was front page news in January 1960, followed by more articles when he took office July 1. After six months described as spent "living out of suitcases," the family moved into Eastcliff in February 1961; that created another flurry of articles. As the Magraths would later joke, "They love you when you come; they love you when you go."

Barbara Flanagan, women's editor of the *Minneapolis Tribune*, wrote an article titled "'U' Head's Family Is Settled" on February 14, 1961, and a follow-up article in mid-March. The *St. Paul Pioneer Press* ran a large article with color photographs on February 19, 1961. President Wilson's mother was the feature of a *Minneapolis Star* article on February 24.

University historian Ann Pflaum, who knew the Wilsons, still describes two sentences from that Flanagan article in March as being the epitome of the home life of a university president with a large family. Wilson, in his new office, was frequently interrupted by a ringing phone. He didn't yet know how the intercom worked, so he couldn't ask someone else to pick up the phone. "When the phone rang—more than once—it was the president of the University of Minnesota who answered. It was never for him."[9]

Peter Magrath also used this room as a study, as he found it to be quiet and peaceful. But phone calls continued at all hours. Diane wrote:

I have been known to take the phone off the hook when my "coping batteries" are running low. Peter insists on being open about our phone number and its listing. Lucky for me most people don't know how to spell our last name or whether we live in St. Paul or Minneapolis. However, when a major issue arises, the phone starts ringing with vigor. Our family tries to be patient about the phone but we will only talk to people who identify themselves. That generally cuts the calls in half.[10]

Diane recalled that during the search for a football coach, the calls didn't stop until midnight and began again at 5 a.m. When Peter proclaimed that he would quit if Lou Holtz said no, ten-year-old Monette cried to Diane:

"Where will we live?" she asked. "I'll have no friends."

"Are you worried that your friends like you for the house and the pool and because your daddy is the president?"

"Yup!"

"But Mo," I said, "that's not true. Besides, you'd have the opportunity to find out who your real friends are."

"I don't want to take the risk," she said.[11]

Even during the Hasselmo administration, using a home landline was common and home phone numbers were typically available to the public. Anna Hasselmo told me that she got a kick out of answering the phone whenever she was home from college, and her parents were happy to have her do so. The most frequent calls she answered were students calling throughout snowy nights to ask if classes were going to be canceled. They were not. Another memorable call was from a woman complaining that she had taken her child to the dental school for care and had received separate bills for the child's top and bottom teeth.

Sometimes a call is better than a visit. Some of the 1980s cost overruns during the Keller remodel were due to lead paint removal. Ten years later, in August 1997, when a painting subcontractor had hired nonunion painters to work at Eastcliff, Local Union No. 61 announced a picket of Eastcliff to protest the University's use of "non-licensed people for the lead-paint project." The University responded that there was no longer lead-based paint at Eastcliff.

The University police monitored the situation and declared it a non-event. Eastcliff was unoccupied, as the Yudofs had not yet moved in.[12]

The Yudofs were home for the next (actual) protest in January 2002. American Indian activists erected a tepee on the front lawn of Eastcliff (outside the fence) to protest the University's plan to purchase five-percent viewing rights to the University of Arizona's large binocular telescope. The telescope is on Mount Graham, which members of the Apache tribe consider sacred. Jim Anderson, a spokesman for the American Indian Movement, was quoted as saying, "He'll see this tepee when he wakes up in the morning, like the people of Mount Graham see the telescope when they wake up to pray."[13] After the protest, Judy noticed burn marks on the grass from a fire in the tepee.

Protests against the telescope were mentioned in an October 4, 2002, article in *The Native American Press,* which also mentioned a banner hung on the KSTP television tower on September 25. The article referred to protests at Eastcliff and at KSTP. It doesn't specify if the Eastcliff protest was the one in January or if there was a later protest in September. In September, Bob Bruininks was interim president, and no one was living at Eastcliff.[14]

Bob Bruininks used the cypress-paneled sitting room as an office, and Susan Hagstrum used the adjoining sunroom as her office. They used cell phones, rather than answering a home phone, and the frequency of telephone calls had been reduced by email.

When we first moved in and I was unpacking, I had an uncomfortable feeling that I was being watched. I saw a car parked in front of the house and told Eric. He explained that we were, in fact, being watched—by campus police. A disgruntled employee had displayed some bullets in a meeting and named one of them for President Bruininks. The police watched Eastcliff until June 30 (Bob's last day, a day on which he very unfortunately broke his femur while on vacation). After that day, it was deemed that the house no longer needed protection.

I used Edward's room as an office for a few years; Eric had his office at the opposite end of the second floor. As a thoughtful gift for my birthday one year, our son Sam converted Edward's sitting room into a clothes closet and I moved my office into an empty bedroom (bedroom three).

While we used cell phones rather than a landline, the doorbell worked through the landline telephone: pushing the doorbell rang the phone, then the sound of the visitor came through the phone. One night we were awakened around 3 a.m. by a man screaming into the intercom.[15] By itself not particularly alarming, except I had experienced an incident one morning a few weeks earlier when I was walking the dogs. As I headed up Dayton Avenue, a man up the hill was walking down. As I crossed the street to the opposite sidewalk (our dogs required the full path), the man began screaming that I should be afraid because he was going to harm me severely (my delicate interpretation of his expletive-laced rant). I turned and walked away on Otis Avenue (toward Marshall, so he wouldn't know where I lived), and dialed 9-1-1 on my cell phone. When I explained that a man was threatening my life at the corner of Otis and Dayton, the dispatcher responded that my cell phone had incorrectly routed the call to Minneapolis police. Hold—and hold—and hold for St. Paul.

To paraphrase what my friend Tracy Moos said regarding the SDS bomb threats they experienced, he said he was going to kill me, but he didn't. I, like Tracy, took it in stride. But when I heard the man screaming at our door, I asked campus police if I could see the videotape. (Indeed, the Eastcliff security system has a videotape, so don't be ringing the bell late at night.) My would-be attacker on the street was skinny and bedraggled; the intercom screamer looked younger and more robust. Both threats seemed random, not personal. We were very fortunate in this, and in many ways, during our eight years at Eastcliff.

A brief shout-out here to the University of Minnesota campus police department. We had several unfortunate incidents when someone in the family set off the alarm (not to be naming names, but Sam Kaler) and the police officers who responded were always helpful and unfailingly polite. Once or twice a year, Eric would go on a ride-along with the campus police. He learned that a lot of students make poor decisions after 2 a.m. The ride-alongs reinforced what he already knew: the University has an outstanding police department. They *serve* and *protect* students.[16]

My immediate reaction after the tragic murder of George Floyd was that if not for concerns about coronavirus vulnerability at our ages, Eric and I would join the protest rallies. We regularly make contributions to organizations that seek justice and support underserved communities.[17]

I recall my shock and dismay when I first glimpsed racism in Minnesota in the early 1980s. Returning to Minnesota in 2011, I recall an early visit to the north side in Minneapolis, when an elderly Black woman warned me that my husband was talking about the achievement gap (which is better described as the *opportunity* gap) between white students and students of color in Minnesota, and I better be prepared, because no one who talked about that ever survived in the Twin Cities. Eric did focus attention on the problem, and helped make progress, but it is a complex, long-standing problem that needs all of us to work together. During the 2020 protests, windows on our Minneapolis condominium building were covered in plywood, and within a few days, murals were created honoring George Floyd and Black Lives Matter. One read "It's not just the police." I agree; it's on all of us.

While Eric was president, I remember him lying awake at night during a rash of thefts, worrying about student safety. Although the thefts were in Minneapolis rather than on campus, the campus police solved the crime ring to protect students.[18] A campus policeman stopped a serial rapist when the Minneapolis police were part of the problem. Minneapolis police and the police union, as a whole, had long been known to be a problem, particularly regarding people of color or sexual assault victims. The campus police had a different goal—protecting students, *all* students.

When I read that during a protest on campus on June 7, 2020, a student organizer said, "If MPD is guilty, UMPD is guilty," I wanted to reply, "No they are not. Life is not that simple." The article concluded: "SDS ended the gathering with a call for a week of action, encouraging people to decorate Joan Gabel's mansion with signs, banners and sidewalk chalk urging her to remove cops from campus."[19] The new SDS had already "visited" Eastcliff before this call for action, and did so again after. On June 1, after a week of widespread daily protests following Floyd's murder, the SDS protested at Eastcliff.[20] President Gabel met with the protesters in front of the house. A protester stated: "Joan, I have a question. Are you open to limiting the amount of money you give to police and redistributing that money to student organizations like MSA, BSU, and multicultural organizations on campus as well as mental health resources? Is that something you're open to?"

President Gabel replied, "What I'm open to is getting the resources to the organizations that you describe while also investing in your safety . . . where we disagree is that you see it as an either–or, and I see it as a yes–and. And I think it's okay that we disagree. I want to try to find a compromise within that space. I don't want to change your mind, that's not why I'm here, but I do want to find common ground with you."

Protesters are heard chanting, "Whose mansion? Our mansion. Whose f—ing mansion? Our f—ing mansion." Another protester asked that campus police be defunded and "What we really need is more mental health services that help create a safe space for us." Yet while the University has prioritized funding for mental health services for students, the chant of

"Our f—ing mansion" was clearly intended to make a family feel unsafe in their home.[21] President Gabel is an ally on the side of justice and equality. I see it as self-aggrandizing when protestors make demands and attack proponents, rather than working for positive change. Fortunately, the majority of University students are actively working for justice. For example, many students volunteer by mentoring and tutoring young students in under-resourced communities, which in turn may increase diversity on campus.

When a call went out for volunteers from the University's law school to help defend the 2020 protesters, more than a hundred law school students signed up in four hours. These students, and so many more, reinforce my often-stated opinion that University of Minnesota students give me hope for the future.[22]

Upstairs floor plan, 1921.
Drawn by the author from
C. H. Johnston Jr.'s plans.

THE BEDROOMS

The four bedrooms, labeled on the 1921 architectural drawings as bedrooms one, two, three, and four, were the Brooks children's bedrooms. When the young family moved in, Conley was a baby and Markell was pregnant with Ted. After Binky was born, but before Dwight, Binky was in bedroom one, Conley and Ted were in bedrooms two and three, and bedroom four was the guest room. Dwight was born in 1929, and bedroom two became his room. Conley and Ted moved to bedrooms three and four.

The first two bedrooms shared a bathroom between them with doors entering from each room, as did (and still do) the last two bedrooms. The first bedroom (Binky's) is the largest and has a fireplace, and the other three are similar in size.[23] It is my conjecture that the largest bedroom, closest to the master, was used as a nursery for Conley and Ted, and the boys moved to other bedrooms as they became older. At some point, a door was added to connect bedrooms two and three. (Perhaps so that Dwight, when he was older, could share a bathroom with his brothers rather than his sister.) In 1935, paneling and bookshelves were added to bedrooms three and four. In 1937, bookshelves were added to bedrooms one and two, and paneling was added to bedroom two. The walls of bedroom one (Binky's bedroom) were painted with tree branches and chickadees.

When O. Meredith Wilson became president, Meredith "Met" Jr. was twenty-one and a junior at Harvard, Connie was eighteen and a freshman at the University of Oregon (so home only on school breaks), Mary Ann was sixteen, John was fifteen, David was ten, and Margaret was eight. Met didn't need a regular bedroom at Eastcliff but likely used a guest room on occasion.

Connie and Mary Ann shared bedroom one, which was painted gray. Margaret was in bedroom two, which was paneled in bleached oak, and shared the bathroom that was between her room and her sisters' room. All the Wilson women shared a professional hairdryer in that bathroom. John was in bedroom three, which was paneled in knotty pine with a light finish. David was in bedroom four, paneled in cypress wood (at some point the paneling was painted white).

The four younger Wilson children all went to University High School, and some went on to the University of Minnesota. Mary Ann was a student in one of the first classes taught by a young professor named Nils Hasselmo. At the end of President Wilson's tenure, the youngest two children were seventeen and fifteen, so there had been teenagers in the house all seven years of the Wilson presidency.

The Moos family moved into Eastcliff in 1967. Malcolm Jr. was fourteen, Kathryn "Kathy" was thirteen, Grant was twelve, Ann "Simmy" was nine, and Margaret "Margie" was seven. The three older children attended University High School, and the younger two were at Visitation Convent School. Like the Brookses and Wilsons, the girls used bedrooms one and two. Kathy had the first bedroom, and her little sisters shared the second bedroom. Simmy later wanted her own room and moved down the hall into the sunroom. Grant was in bedroom three and Malcolm Jr. was in bedroom four.

The Moos children all attended the University of Minnesota. The eldest, Malcolm, received his undergraduate degree from Stanford University and his medical degree from Minnesota. Kathy started at Macalester College, then transferred to the University. Grant started and finished at the University. Simmy and Margie moved with the family to Santa Barbara, California, at the end of Malcolm's presidency. The family later returned to Minnesota and the girls eventually attended the University.

Two presidents used what the Brooks family considered the master bedroom as a family living room and used bedroom one as the master, the Magraths being the first. Sandra Magrath referred to the long corridor as "Motel Alley" because there were so many bedrooms for guests—of course, they were the first Eastcliff family to have only one, rather than four, five, or six children, so previously the rooms were full of family. Sandra and Peter's daughter, Valerie, was away at college and didn't live at Eastcliff.

Two years after Peter and Sandra divorced, Peter married Diane Skomars. Diane's daughter, Monette, whom Peter adopted, was three and a half years old when she moved into bedroom two; she was ten when the family moved to Missouri.

The Keller/Sindelirs didn't move into Eastcliff while Ken Keller was interim president, and they waited a few months (for the promised finish of the remodeling) after he was elected president to move in. They used the master as their bedroom, and their son, Jesse, used bedroom three. That bedroom was halfway down the hall from the master suite, but Jesse used that to his benefit by navigating the long wooden hallway on his rubber-wheeled fire truck. Ken Keller's two older sons were away at college when he became president, Drew in graduate school at Princeton University and Paul finishing a chemical engineering degree at Johns Hopkins University.[24] Jesse was two when he moved into Eastcliff and five when the family moved out. Ken and Bonita's daughter, Alexandra Amelie, was born after their years at Eastcliff.

Upstairs hallway, circa 1925. Courtesy of the Brooks family.

The Hasselmos, like the Magraths, used what had been the master bedroom as a family living room and used bedroom one as their master bedroom. Anna Hasselmo, like Monette Magrath, used bedroom two. While a student at Gustavus Adolphus College, she lived at Eastcliff during breaks, then lived at Eastcliff full time for three years after college. The Hasselmo sons, Peter and Michael, were adults with homes of their own (in Philadelphia and Boston), but they visited regularly for summer vacations and holidays.

When Mark Yudof assumed the presidency, he and Judy lived in an apartment near St. Anthony Falls for three months while Eastcliff was being redecorated. Their children, Seth and Samara, were adults, so they did not move with them. Samara had just finished her freshman year at Southern Methodist University in Texas. She stayed at Eastcliff the summer after her sophomore year. Seth, exactly six years older than Samara, graduated from the University of Pennsylvania in engineering and was working as an illusionist while the Yudofs lived at Eastcliff.

While Bob Bruininks served as interim president, Bob and Susan commuted to events from their Minnetonka home, staying overnight (in the room labeled guest room one) when the schedule was hectic. Bob was elected president in early November 2002, and they moved into Eastcliff in December. Their three sons were adults. Robert Todd was living in San Francisco, Brian was in Seattle, and Brett was in graduate school at the University, so none of them lived at Eastcliff, but they visited regularly, as did the next generation of Bruininks boys. Bob and Susan's oldest grandson, Henry, was born two months before Bob's inauguration, so he stayed at Eastcliff when he was just eight weeks old. Two years later, baby brother Wilson joined Henry in Seattle, and four years after that came littlest brother Ike. For Bob and Susan's retirement celebration, three sons and three grandsons were at Eastcliff. A fourth grandson, Zane, joined the San Francisco Bruininks after Bob and Susan left Eastcliff.

When Eric and I arrived at Eastcliff, our older son, Charlie, had just graduated from law school at George Washington University; our younger son, Sam, was about to begin his final semester at Auburn University. Charlie visited (in bedroom four) during his four years living in Santa Barbara. He and his wife, Lisa, stayed with us briefly before moving into their house in St. Paul. Sam visited (in bedroom three), while working in Utah and South Dakota, then moved into Eastcliff (in guest room one) for a couple of years before buying a house in Minneapolis. He has since moved to San Francisco. Our toddler granddaughter, Ophelia (Charlie and Lisa's daughter), used that guest room as a nap room when she stayed with me after Sam moved out.

When Joan Gabel became president, Eastcliff was undergoing extensive electrical repairs. She moved into Eastcliff in November. Joan and Gary's

Joan and Gary Gabel. Photograph by Erin Benner.

daughter, Grace, had graduated from the University of Missouri (where Joan had been a dean) and was living and working in Seattle. Son Jack was a rising senior at the University of South Carolina (where Joan had been provost). Younger son Luke was a rising senior in high school. Like Pat Hasselmo before him, Gary Gabel planned to delay moving until their youngest child could finish high school. However, the coronavirus pandemic changed everything. With students throughout the United States studying at home, Gary, Jack, and Luke all moved to Minnesota in March 2020. Jack and Luke each finished their senior years at Eastcliff, living in the two guest rooms.

Walking into bedroom one, there is a fireplace straight ahead, with a column of shelves on either side of the fireplace. The mantel and the shelves are painted white. There is a window on the west wall, and windows on either side of the fireplace. Out of the right window is a flat roof over the porte cochère. This was Binky's room, and she told me that a neighborhood boy would sometimes climb up to the roof to visit her.

From the 1920s through 1970, there were two doors on the east wall, the first opening to a closet and the second opening to a bathroom with another door into the next bedroom. In 1970, the closet was removed and the space used for a bathroom, so that bedrooms one and two each had a bathroom. In 2001, to make room for an elevator, the bathroom opening into bedroom two was removed and the bathroom opening into bedroom one was remodeled with a shower rather than a tub.

As described earlier, the Brooks, Wilson, and Moos families, with multiple children living at home, used bedroom one for children. The Magrath and Hasselmo families used the room as a master bedroom and used the master as a family living room. The four other presidential families have used this room as a family room.

Bedroom two was converted to a family kitchen at the end of the Bruininks/Hagstrum tenure. Eric and I were forever grateful to have a private place to cook and eat meals. When we gave Joan Gabel her first tour of Eastcliff, her face lit up when she saw that there was a private upstairs kitchen.

Eastcliff's Children

Anna Markell Brooks is a remarkable woman. The third of Edward and Markell's children, she was born in 1926. Now in her nineties, she told me that she was called "Binky" as a child and expected to use her real name as she got older, but she remains Binky. She is petite and absolutely beautiful. I asked her if she thought she looks so young because she is such a spiritual person. She said no, it was because of the alignment of the stars when she was born.

Binky remembers a lovely childhood. She says the Brooks children didn't realize they were privileged; they had a simple, happy life. As Binky got older, her father explained that money was a responsibility and taught her to keep track of all her expenditures. They discussed her expenses and bank balance on a monthly basis.

There was one great sadness of her early years. In 1942, at age sixteen, she met a young air force officer. I would say they fell in love at first sight. Binky, being more poetic, described it this way: "I felt suddenly catapulted into a vortex of feelings. The magnetic pull was overwhelming . . ."[25] He wrote to her father regarding a date with her after the war. The officer was killed in action. That loss remained with Binky. In 2015, when telling me about her wedding reception at Eastcliff, she said that her husband was a good friend, but she knew that she would never truly love anyone again after she lost her first love, although they were together in person only one time. (Her marriage ended in an amicable divorce.)

In the summer of 1945, Binky was studying music and piano performance with Egon Petri (a famous German/Dutch pianist) at Mills College in California. She lived at La Maison Française in Berkeley, along with members of the Budapest String Quartet and their wives. Several years later, the Quartet was playing in the Twin Cities, so Edward and Markell invited them to Eastcliff.[26] The afternoon was informal, and cellist Mischa Schneider and his wife arrived carrying their child in a laundry basket. Binky recalled to me with amusement that her father asked her to go up in the attic to see if they still had an old Stradivarius up there. He asked the violinist, "It wouldn't bother you if some of the strings were broken, would it? I know it has been lying around there for a while, and it probably isn't in good condition—but that wouldn't faze you, would it?"

After college, in 1949, Binky traveled with friends in Italy. Although traveling in post–World War II Europe was complicated, she made her way to Austria for the Salzburg Music Festival. When the festival ended, she was determined to stay in Austria and began studying music at the Salzburg Mozarteum. After studying there for two years and depending on her parents for support, she wanted to become more self-reliant and support herself. After a brief job in Paris, she returned to the United States. On the way home, she set up an interview in Washington, D.C., for a government job that would let her return to Vienna as a reports officer at the Austrian desk. She was interviewed by six men, one after the other. And that is how Binky got a job working for the Central Intelligence Agency—yes, the CIA.

She was to tell anyone who asked that she worked in a civilian section of the army. Her two older brothers had served in World War II and her younger brother had just transferred from the marines into the air force. Her father, who served in World War I, was extremely proud that his daughter was to be in the military as well. Although she was not able to tell him who she was really working for, or what she was doing, she discovered that he had bragged to friends that his daughter was "in the army doing some hush-hush work." (Did he guess at the truth, or did he inadvertently stumble upon it through a joke? We'll never know.)

She worked for the CIA for about two years. Binky recalled to me that she met and spent an afternoon with the daughter of a world leader. When her bosses asked her to further develop the friendship to extract information, she was unwilling to spy on a friend, so she never made the arrangements.

A few years after the CIA experience, Binky went on the first of many pilgrimages to India to visit the ashram of Bengali Saint Anandamayi Ma. These spiritual journeys continued for many years. Binky visited her in India twenty-four times and received specific spiritual advice until Anandamayi's death in 1982. Binky was visiting Anandamayi in India when she had the opportunity to travel with a friend to meet the Dalai Lama at his home in Dharamsala. She said, "He has such a sense of humor—tremendous humor. When you look at his face, his quiet face, there is a faint hint of a smile always there. How can he stand what has happened to Tibet? How can he stand it? I guess he just has a historic point of view. There is a peace about him; part of him is just untouchable."

Binky became a very accomplished ceramicist. She told me that in the late 1950s she went to see a man who was supposed to be a psychic seer in the San Fernando Valley. He closed his eyes and then said, 'Well, it's very clear. For the last three incarnations you have been bossed by a father or a husband or some male figure totally. Now, if you don't do something to establish your own identity, then you're just kind of finished as a person. You have to do something, it doesn't matter what, if you can sign your name to it.' On the way home, I stopped by a college and signed up for pottery lessons. Working with clay became my life for thirty years, all because he said I had to sign something. Then I got fascinated. I realized clay does not lie. It is a portrait of who you are right then. You can't keep yourself out of it."

Binky's oldest brother, Conley, described her perfectly in *Turning the Leaves*:

> She has been an angel with extended arms, a caretaker to many people. She also has a mystical side to her and she has an attraction to some of the religious teachers and teachings of India. Through this

interest Bink has developed insights that most of the rest of us do not really know about or even understand. Judging by her physical appearance, her state of mind is in tune with this world.

Bink has a very practical and down-to-earth side, which comes directly from her father, and her artistic and spiritual side comes from her mother.[27]

Binky wrote of her parents' influence in *Turning the Leaves*:

Sometimes, like gifts, traits appear, which unfold and come to flower in a lifetime. More often, tendencies are seen flowing through generations, from potential to manifestation as they are woven into habits, family traditions, and finally human history. Our parents were beings who adhered to the principles of truthfulness and integrity, creating a strong foundation for the lives of all of us.[28]

Turning the Leaves describes the end of Markell Conley Brook's life: "Her heart gave out and she died peacefully in 1971 with Binky at her side. They had just spent a fascinating evening listening to a tape of Joseph Campbell comparing the Hindu concept of the four stages of life with that of Dante's *Divine Comedy*. During her lifetime she had aspired to be a 'great lady.' She was one."[29]

Binky wrote a letter to her family that provides a contrast of her life in an ashram in India to her life at Eastcliff:

Our beds are narrow tables with sleeping bags on top and mosquito netting overhead. We eat (on a stone floor in the dining hall where Maharshi ate with the Brahmins on one side and non-Brahmins on the other) off a plate made of leaves and with fingers of the right hand. We bathe in the heat of the day from a bucket of cold water. We sleep from 9 to 4 under the starriest sky on earth and wake up feeling like children.[30]

Conley and Ted Brooks used bedrooms three and four. The Wilson family also used these rooms for their two younger sons. Then the two Moos boys used these rooms. It's little wonder that when the connecting bathroom was refurbished in 1983, it was referred to as the "boys' bathroom."

Conley and Ted were less than fourteen months apart in age, lived in adjoining rooms, and are together in most Eastcliff stories. As adults, their wives, Marney and Ginny, were great friends, and were the lead authors of *Turning the Leaves,* the history of the Brooks family.

After Eastcliff, Conley Brooks (1921–2013) attended Yale University, leaving just short of graduation in 1942 to join the Army Air Force.[31] During World War II, Conley was a flight instructor in C47 and B25 airplanes, and married Marney Brown. When the war ended, they moved to the Eastcliff carriage house and were living there when the first of their five children was born. In 1946, Conley joined the family business, Brooks–Scanlon, Inc., which at the time was primarily a lumber manufacturing company. Conley had many roles at Brooks–Scanlon, including director, CEO, and long-time chairman, until its sale in 1980. He was then involved in successive Brooks family enterprises including Brooks Resources Corporation (a real estate developer in Bend, Oregon) and Sawmill Private Management, Inc. (a multifamily office in Minneapolis). Conley and Marney's first child, Conley Jr., followed his father in the family business. Daughters Marlow and Sky were born while Conley and Marney were living in Florida. Son Stephen was born after they returned to Minnesota. Daughter Markell was born ten years later.[32]

Conley and Marney had been married nearly sixty-eight years when she died in 2012. When he died the following year, at age ninety-two, his obituary stated, "He was devoted to Marney, and also took great delight in spending time with his two brothers Edward (Ted) and Dwight, both of whom predeceased him, and his sister Markell (Binky)."

Ted Brooks (1922–2004) wrote of his own birth:

> It was in 1922 that Mother not only began to move into the new house, but also began producing me. Apparently, I spent nearly all of my very early life sleeping; "Is it any wonder," my mother was often heard to say, "that Ted was born tired? I haven't had a chance to rest myself since the moving began!"[33]

Ted majored in music at Harvard University, where he was placekicker on the football team. During World War II, he joined the marines and served in Guadalcanal, then Japan and Guam. He was a platoon leader on Okinawa and received a Purple Heart.

Like his brother, Ted joined Brooks–Scanlon when he returned from the war. When Ted told his father that he didn't want to remain with the family business, his father expected him to become a doctor. Returning to school as a pre-med major didn't suit Ted. He went to the St. Paul Academy (SPA) headmaster for advice and was offered a job teaching Latin at SPA. That suited him well. He taught at SPA for ten years and began graduate work at the University of Minnesota. He earned his PhD in classics in 1960. Ted then taught Greek, Latin, and classical history at Macalester College for twenty-five years, and he taught annual courses at the University of Minnesota's Elder Learning Institute after he retired from Macalester. Ted and his wife, Virginia "Ginny" Dahleen Brooks, had two daughters, Katherine Sophie Brooks and Julie Markell Brooks.

When Ted died in 2004, even his death indicated a life well lived. He suffered a heart attack at an evening dinner party, after a full day that included an eleven-mile bike ride. His obituary stated, "He will be remembered as a deeply cultured man whose generosity and sense of humor endeared him to all." His wife, Ginny, died in 2014.

The youngest Brooks child, Dwight, was born in 1929. Conley and Ted were born in 1921 and 1922, so they had several years of Eastcliff memories before Dwight was on the scene.

The two "boy's bedrooms" became the rooms of John and David Wilson, then when the Moos family moved into Eastcliff, bedroom three became Grant's room. This room was the location of a significant event in the lives of the Moos family dogs.

President Moos had always loved dogs. When he first became president of the University, he mentioned in an interview that he knew five previous University presidents. He had gotten to know President Coffman at local dog shows, as Moos had raised Scottish terriers while a student at University High School. The Moos family arrived at Eastcliff with two golden retrievers, Topaz and Lord Boswell. Tracy said they named the male Boswell "because, like the writer, he's a thorough reprobate."[34] While the Moos dogs were beloved pets, accustomed to living with the family, life at Eastcliff brought changes. The dogs needed to spend more time outdoors, out of the way of events. They had doghouses in the yard on the north side of the house. Tracy Moos described them as normal-sized dogs, with normal-sized houses. She recalled the dogs' enjoyment in sitting on top of their houses, like Snoopy. Please picture them high above ground, gazing over the fence and observing the neighborhood. According to Tracy, passersby along Dayton Avenue thought they were some strange breed of giraffe dog.

The dogs did spend some time inside. One day, Grant was in his bedroom

Lord Boswell *(left)* and Topaz hear the Canine College commencement
address, with Kathy and Grant Moos, 1968. Photograph by Powell Krueger;
courtesy of *Minneapolis Star Tribune*.

wrestling with the male dog. The dog performed admirably, but Grant needed to go the hospital for an injury to his forehead. It turned out to be quite a
few stitches, requiring sedation. Grant awoke back in his Eastcliff bedroom.
He was aroused to consciousness by the sounds of seagulls, or so he thought.

As he awoke, he discovered that the sound was . . . puppies! Topaz was
delivering puppies at the foot of Grant's bed. The entire Moos family, and
the Michaels girls from down the street, were in the room watching the
miracle of birth. Topaz delivered eight puppies.[35] While the Brooks family
loved dogs and had two or three at a time over nearly forty years at Eastcliff,
I don't know of another time when ten dogs were living in the house.

During graduation season of 1968, Lord Boswell and Topaz, along with Kathy, Grant, and President Moos, were featured in a front-page newspaper photograph wearing graduation attire. (To be clear, only Boswell and Topaz were wearing mortarboards, not the humans.) The dogs had just graduated from Canine College. The writer, clearly enjoying himself, wrote, "Topaz salivated gleefully at the prospect of continued education. Boswell yawned." President Moos was quoted as saying, "We knew it would be a photo-finish, and as I understand it, they came through without flying colors." Kathy and Grant trained the dogs. The story described the concern with the retrievers passing the class:

> Moos said he first became worried about Boswell when he took him for a walk along the Mississippi River after the dog's second lesson.
> "The dog is supposed to stop when you say 'halt,'" Moos continued, "but Boswell saw a squirrel and almost pulled me over the riverbank."
> At an estimated 80 pounds, Boswell weighs close to two-thirds what the thin university president does. [36]

Even after completing their educations, the dogs would occasionally escape the confines of Eastcliff's fenced yard and run down to the river. Sadly, Lord Boswell disappeared and, despite intense searching, could never be found.

After the tragic loss of Lord Boswell, Topaz gained a new partner in Sandy. Anyone who has raised a retriever knows they can be a handful for a few years. Sandy was a rascal. Perhaps the dogs were allowed in the house more often after Lord Boswell's disappearance, and Tracy also said the neighbors complained about the dogs barking. Whatever the reason, Sandy was in the house while cook Mae McBroom was preparing for an event. There were dozens of rolls in industrial pans cooling on the counter in the kitchen, and Mae was taking a break. Kathy, who considered Sandy as her dog, entered the dark kitchen and flipped on the light. There was Sandy, standing on the high metal counter. Kathy couldn't imagine how he could climb that high, but there he was, finishing off the last of the rolls.

The next litter of Eastcliff puppies (yes, there was another litter—as stated, Sandy was a rascal) numbered five puppies, all of whom, as with the first litter, went on to other good homes.

The Magraths' three pets seemed small in number in comparison to the Moos dogs. Sandra Magrath wrote, "Our 'family' is completed by Teddy, our West Highland white terrier (who barks only at strangers—the mailman and the milkman—but never at University of Minnesota workmen), and Franny and Snowy, a gray tabby cat and an odd-eyed white Angora cat."[37] Later, another dog named Max joined the Magrath family, and Monette Magrath had a tri-colored cat named Mitzi who was strictly a house cat and lived upstairs. The Hasselmos had a cat, Stefan. The Bruininks/Hagstrums had three dogs, in succession. We had two dogs.

By 2021, two more dogs were part of the tradition of family pets at Eastcliff. The Gabel family moved in with little Annie, a toy poodle, who was about ten years old. As occurred in many families who began working from home during the lockdowns, a new puppy joined the family. Ruby, another toy poodle, arrived in September 2020. Both poodles have holiday birthdays: Annie was born on Valentine's Day and Ruby was born on the Fourth of July.

The youngest president's child to live in Eastcliff was Jesse Keller. Ken Keller had become interim president in 1984 and was named president in March 1985. Beginning when he was interim, Ken and Bonita would commute from their house in St. Anthony Park to Eastcliff and elsewhere for events. Jesse was regularly left at home with a babysitter. When they moved into Eastcliff in August, Jesse could at least be with a babysitter in the same building as his parents during Eastcliff events. The house was partially dismantled for the planned renovation, but construction didn't begin until December, and the family was without a kitchen until May. A stove and refrigerator were added to bedroom four, but not a kitchen sink. Dishes were washed in the bathtub for months.

Jesse's bedroom had the benefit of proximity to the sunroom, which he used as a playroom. His room had a trundle bed, and he filled the window seat with stuffed animals. He turned the distance from his parents' bedroom into a fun activity by traveling the hall on his ride-on fire truck.

During those years, the large crystal chandelier hung in the center of the grand staircase. When I told Ken Keller that it had become brittle and had to be removed, he said an earlier removal could have saved him a lot of money. He had paid for repairs due to the almost inevitable damage produced by mixing such a chandelier with a small boy and a ball.

Ken recalls that, when he picked up Jesse from daycare, Jesse would often inquire if it was a "nametag night," meaning the house would be full of guests. He did occasionally attend the events. Bonita shared, "He greeted Judy Dayton at one summer gathering and asked her if she'd like a tour of the gardens. They went off hand in hand."

A year or two after moving out of Eastcliff (recall he was only five when they moved out, so he was reminiscing at the age of six or seven), Jesse was asked what he missed about living at Eastcliff. Bonita said, "He gave it a bit of serious thought and said, 'The service.' Jesse and I would have breakfast together in the little family dining room on the mornings when Ken had the vice presidents over for breakfast meetings. Bob Ledder usually came to serve at those breakfasts, and he'd serve us as well on his way to and fro. I think it was the pancake syrup in the silver pitcher on a tray that impressed Jesse as the kind of thing he didn't see away from Eastcliff."

During their years at Eastcliff, Bonita wrote, "When our four year old in his bedraggled school clothes greeted a visiting chancellor at the door, he shook the chancellor's hand and said, 'This is my house.' Then he added, 'And I'm glad you're here.' That, more than anything, tells me that the University house and family house can work together."[38]

Contributions to the Secret Compartment

During the 1930 remodel, plans were included to add wood paneling to Ted's bedroom (cypress) and Conley's bedroom (knotty white pine). Conley was then ten years old, and Ted was nine; Binky was four and a half, and Dwight was only a year old. The older two boys were offered the option of secret compartments in their rooms. The blueprints include the label "secret door, shelf inside." The bedroom paneling was completed in the fall of 1935, with woodwork from longtime Minneapolis company Lake Street Sash and Door on Hiawatha Avenue. (Binky's and Dwight's rooms were remodeled in 1937.)

During the Magrath administration, Conley Brooks Sr. was at Eastcliff and asked Peter Magrath if he knew about the secret compartments. He showed Peter a dresser drawer compartment with a little bottle that had contained ocean water, long since evaporated.

The hidden compartment in bedroom three is in the top left corner of the wall above the built-in bookcase. Ted had had his appendix removed, and the doctors gave it to him in a bottle. He stored it in the secret compartment so that he could bring it out and impress his friends. That compartment above the bookshelf, behind a small door that blends in with the paneling, inspired an Eastcliff tradition. Diane Skomars Magrath decided that each Eastcliff family should leave a memento in the secret compartment. Although I knew of the tradition, I waited until we were moving out to climb up and discover the mementos others had left.

Diane left the floral wreath that she wore on her head for their 1978 wedding. It was well preserved when I saw it: pink rosebuds and baby's breath flowers, augmented by fabric leaves. Attached to the headdress is a note on University of Minnesota memo paper. A notation at the top reads: "If you find me, please leave for the Magraths to rediscover . . ."

> *date*: November 27, 1982
>
> *to*: (Drawing of a smile)
>
> *from*: Diane Faye Skomars Magrath
>
> This is my wedding wreath from March 25, 1978, Eastcliff.
>
> This is my last night at Eastcliff after living here 6½ years. The house is a good one with no ghosts, no darkness—only a house filled with light & memories of the mere mortals who called it home.
>
> I came with apprehension—one does not move from a five room townhouse to 20 rooms without apprehension—and I leave no regrets. I, like the President, gave it my "all." A Minnesota daughter loved serving her University, her state.
>
> God bless all who follow. . . Our lives are richer because of Eastcliff!

The only University president (to date) to marry while in office was Peter Magrath. After his divorce, Magrath began dating the young, vivacious director of the University Student Activities Center, Diane Skomars. Peter wrote to Diane later (in a 1985 article for the Association of Governing Boards formatted as letters):

> You could be the only woman in America who was given a copy of Betty Corbally's book [*The Partners: Sharing the Life of a College President*] as a gift to read while being courted. That book—and the one that you and Joan Clodius edited for the National Association of State Universities and Land-Grant Colleges [*The President's Spouse: Volunteer or Volunteered?*]—have helped promote understanding of the role, dilemmas, and choices (or lack of them) that face presidents and their spouses and families.

Diane wrote in the same article:

> I should have realized that this was going to be no ordinary marriage when you mailed out 12 notices of our engagement to the Minnesota Regents one hour after you proposed and I said yes. Indeed, when more members of the press than family attended our wedding reception, I should have figured that my life had changed dramatically. But the real shock came with the move to "Eastcliff," the university president's residence.[39]

Peter and Diane were married at Eastcliff after a seven-month courtship.

They walked together down the Eastcliff staircase, accompanied by harp music. They were married in front of the living room fireplace, in a ceremony performed by Reverend Warren Jorenby of the University Lutheran Church. Attendants for the small wedding ceremony were Peter's twenty-two-year-old daughter, Valerie, and Diane's three-and-a-half-year-old daughter, Monette. Valerie and Monette wore matching dresses. The prayer table used in the ceremony had been given to Peter's parents on the occasion of their wedding in Mogadiscio, Somalia,[40] fifty-four years prior. Both Peter's and Diane's parents attended the ceremony. A column in the *Minneapolis Star* prior to the wedding described how the couple were writing their own vows and would not reveal them to each other until the ceremony, and stated that the theme of the wedding would be "A New Day Has Come."[41] Newspaper coverage of the wedding included a large photograph in one paper of Diane throwing her bouquet,[42] and in another newspaper Peter was shown holding Monette while Diane offered her a bite of wedding cake.[43]

After the wedding, Peter and Diane went on a honeymoon to Trinidad and Tobago.[44] Then they immediately became heavily involved in University life and entertaining for six and a half years.

Thirty-five years after the wedding, Diane wrote daily letters to Monette, which were compiled for a book titled *Have I Taught You Everything I Know?* Diane wrote of the wedding:

> You were just four years old and, of course, stole the show. Your favorite teddy bear had lost an eye and so we put a sprig of baby's breath in the socket until we could bring it to the "hospital." You were darling about it.
>
> Before the wedding, there were sirens and I told you, "Someone's got troubles." As the fire truck stopped outside our new home, "Eastcliff," you turned to me and said, "We've got troubles." A fire in the furnace room was quickly extinguished and the wedding went on without a hitch, so to speak.[45]

The smoke was from smoldering coals from the living room fireplace that had been put in a bucket.

In a request for her memories to include in this book, Monette wrote:

> One of my very earliest memories of childhood was during my mother's wedding to then President Peter Magrath. I was 3½ and had run upstairs to my new room in tears for some reason that I don't recall; it may have had to do with a teddy bear losing his eye during the festivities? I think it was my mother who put a sprig of baby's breath where the eye had been, and Peter came up and carried me down the stairs

as I dearly clutched the repaired bear. That sweeping staircase winding around the stunning crystal chandelier will never leave my mind.
I remember being fascinated when it had to be cleaned!

Monette did not leave that teddy bear in the secret compartment. Instead,
she left a pull-toy dog. By the time I moved in, she had returned to retrieve
it. As she described, "When we moved away, I hid a wooden dog toy in a
secret cabinet in that room. I've only been back to the house once, when
I was in college, and we retrieved the dog, but he was hidden for quite a
while. Children always do find the nooks and crannies of a place." Monette
and her darling daughter, Finley, visited Eastcliff again over Thanksgiving
weekend 2018. Unfortunately, we were on a University trip and couldn't
host them in person.

Monette recalled her bedroom:

> It was large for a child. My mother had let me get bunkbeds, but they
> were not ordinary! Each one was a tube, covered in a yellow leath-
> er-like material. Very mod, actually. On the side of each tube was an
> oval opening through which you got into bed. On the end of the bed
> were circular steps to get up to top tube. I always slept on the bottom,
> and friends who would sleep over got the top. Peter read to me most
> nights, and I specifically remember him reading *The Diary of Anne Frank*
> in its entirety, one chapter a night. Besides books, my other form of
> entertainment in that room was a small record player. It may have ac-
> tually been a Mickey Mouse record player now that I'm thinking of it,
> with the needle extending down from his plastic, white-gloved hand.
> I remember listening to the cast album of the musical *Annie* on that
> record player.

Valerie Magrath was a college student when her father became president
and an adult when Peter and Diane married. After a house full of children
with the first three families, Monette Magrath was the first singular child
to live in Eastcliff. That didn't mean that the house wasn't full of children.
Diane wrote:

> I can still hear Monette's Girl Scout troop whooping through the house
> playing hide and go seek. I remember her school class coming to East-
> cliff for a tour, a history lesson, and a dance around the May pole in the
> back yard. At every formal dinner, Monette came down clad in pajamas
> to get goodnight kisses and hugs.

Diane was one of the leaders of Monette's Girl Scout troop, and they had
sleepovers at Eastcliff. My son's Minneapolis next-door neighbor, learning

where I lived at the time, shared what fond memories she had of visiting Eastcliff as a Girl Scout.

Children of faculty families were also visitors. Anna Hasselmo's father was a long-time faculty member who had become vice president for administration and planning. Anna recalled wonderful times with Monette at Eastcliff and how heartbroken she was when her family moved to Tucson in 1983 when her father became senior vice president for academic affairs and provost at the University of Arizona. There was a going-away party for them at Eastcliff. Anna was twelve or thirteen years old, in the middle of seventh grade, certainly a difficult time to move.

When Nils Hasselmo was chosen as the thirteenth president of the University in November 1988, the *University of Minnesota UPDATE* reported, "People are going crazy here. There hasn't been this kind of euphoria in Minneapolis since the Twins won the World Series. Professors are giving each other bear hugs, columns of balloons and a welcoming banner decorate the room, and the marching band is stirring things up by playing the 'Minnesota Rouser.'"[46] Perhaps happiest of all was Anna Hasselmo, as she loved Minnesota, and Eastcliff, and was eager to be reunited with both. She was in the middle of her senior year of high school, so when Nils moved in December 1988, Pat and Anna remained in Arizona until the end of the school year.

After graduating, Anna moved into the same Eastcliff bedroom where she had happy memories of times with Monette. Upstairs, the house looked just as she remembered. The family went to the St. Paul Humane Society and adopted a cat. That cat, Stefan, enjoyed living at Eastcliff and, unlike the human residents, regularly enjoyed staying out "partying" all night. In the hidden cupboard, there is a small, worn, royal blue pet collar with a heart-shaped tag. The tag reads STEFAN—646-7816, ST. PAUL. A story about Stefan, written by Nils, is featured at the end of this book.

With Anna ready for college, Nils and Pat felt that, with an unusual name like Hasselmo, Anna would be better off not attending the school where her father was president. She went to Gustavus

Anna Hasselmo's bouquet, photographed by the author.

Adolphus College in St. Peter, Minnesota, and returned home for summer breaks and holidays. Anna played Goldy Gopher at commencement receptions and Santa Lucia for December dinners. After graduating from college in 1993, she lived at Eastcliff full time until April 1996.

Anna's brothers, Michael and Peter, are eight and ten years older than she is, respectively, and were adults with their own homes when Nils became president. Each summer, the sons, their wives, and children would spend a weeklong vacation at Eastcliff. Peter's daughters, Karen and Christina (Chrissy), loved swimming in the pool. Michael's daughter, Simone, was a baby at the end of the presidency, and son Nicholas was not yet born, so they missed the swimming. The tennis court was also heavily used during those weeks. Peter's and Michael's families also visited Eastcliff together for either Thanksgiving or Christmas each year.

Two other items hidden away in the secret compartment are a dried bouquet of red roses and baby's breath and what appears to be a dried corsage. Attached to the bouquet is a note in red ink, with a heart drawn after the text: "These belong to Anna Hasselmo—I'll be back to find them again someday." I assumed the bouquet was from Anna's wedding, but its history is actually more romantic than that.

The Hasselmos had lived in Golden Valley, a suburb of Minneapolis, prior to moving to Arizona. When Anna returned to Minnesota, she worked summers at Golden Valley Park and Recreation, where she met Jim Williams, who asked her out for a date. Jim was in the role of supervisor, and he therefore seemed more mature than the other summer staff.

Jim arrived with a bouquet for Anna on their first date. As he talked to Anna's parents, Nils asked him about himself and about teaching. Anna said, "Everyone was doing the math in their heads thinking hmmmm . . ." Jim was seven years older than college-girl Anna. "I actually went in Dad's office the next day and said, 'He's old!'" Anna recalled. Nils replied, "Who cares?" While Anna refused to claim that it was "love at first sight," or to say whether she knew he was "the one," she *did* save that bouquet.

The corsage seems to be Pat Hasselmo's, from her daughter's wedding to Jim Williams in 1996. The wedding ceremony was at Calvary Lutheran Church in Golden Valley, but the reception, for 250 people, was at Eastcliff. Talking with Anna about the reception twenty years later, it seemed that Anna worried little about the weather, but Pat was understandably concerned about an outdoor event with dinner and dancing on April 20 in Minnesota. Heaters were in the tents that were set up on the terrace and on the lawn. (Both of our sons were married outdoors, and I believe I was the person most concerned about the weather.)

"Our daughter loved the Eastcliff environment and reveled in Eastcliff," Nils said later. "We were very pleased that she got married at a time when we could have the wedding at Eastcliff. It turned out to be just a splendid event where we had tents in the backyard and had all of their friends and relatives there for the occasion."[47]

Another item in the cupboard is a poem titled "How to Repair President Keller's House" by Leavitt Anderson. It must have been left by Bonita. There are twenty four-line stanzas. The fourth and fifth stanzas give a representation of the whole:

> No space for pots and pans was there,
> The kitchen was so wee.
> Three thousand guests were mortified,
> Because there was no tea.
>
> The Regents all decided they
> Should save the house from shame,
> But failed to vote the needed funds,
> Nor thought of it again.

The final items I discovered in the cupboard were two dog collars. One is brown with a Pacific Northwest pattern; the other is red with a tag saying FOSTER with phone numbers. The brown collar belonged to Bob and Susan's vizsla, Dunbar. He was an old dog when he moved into Eastcliff. After he died, Foster, a flat-coated retriever, moved in. Foster was six years old when he joined the Bruininks/Hagstrum family, and he lived to age eleven, when his collar joined Dunbar's in the cupboard. Jack, another flat-coated retriever, then joined the family. He was still a young dog when the family moved out. Bob and Susan also had two American saddlebred horses, Arthur and Bentley, but they did not live at Eastcliff.

What did I leave in the cupboard? A copy of my first book about Eastcliff, *Rusty Goes Swimming*; a sprig of eucalyptus; a small jar of honey (from my bees, who undoubtedly visit Eastcliff but live several blocks away); and half a University of Minnesota dog leash (chewed through by our dog Lida while being worn by our dog Mo).

THE GUEST ROOMS AND SUNROOM

During the 1930 renovations, the south wall over the former garage was bumped out about twelve feet. This enlargement allowed the modification of this end of the hall from two maids' bedrooms to two larger guest rooms, with a bigger bathroom and an additional half bath, and the addition of a screened porch/sunroom.

During the 1930s, the second-floor sunroom was a porch with screened walls. "[We] had four beds out there," Binky said, "sort of crashed together in a row. When the weather got warm we slept out there." After the miniature of Eastcliff was finished in the 1940s, it was placed in this sunroom.

At some point the screens were replaced by windows, but the 1960 floor plan indicates the room was still unheated when the University took possession of the house. When we lived at Eastcliff, the room was heated with baseboard heaters. There is a thermostat in the room, but it doesn't control the heaters.

The Moos children used the sunroom to watch events taking place on the lawn or terrace. Monette Magrath filled it with pillows, calling it the pillow room, and considered it her special retreat. Jesse Keller used it as a playroom. During the Hasselmo years, Nils and Pat's granddaughters, Chrissy and Karen, would sleep in the sunroom when they came for summer vacations.

Bob Bruininks and Susan Hagstrum had exercise equipment in the sunroom. Eric and I also had exercise equipment there. Susan had called it "the room of good intentions," and we quoted her, also calling it that. Joan and Gary Gabel frequently used the exercise equipment they had in the sunroom, particularly during the coronavirus pandemic days when gyms were closed.

Famous Guests in the Guest Room—Maybe

The south guest room was expanded in 1930, and a fireplace was added in the corner. It's a beautiful fireplace with a surround of handsome marble and a honey-colored wood mantel. The chimney is no longer functional, so the fireplace can't be used. The extension includes a window framed with shelves under a gable ceiling. This gable ceiling reminds me of rumors that

Clark Gable spent the night in this room. While Binky recalled Helen Keller's and Katharine Hepburn's visits in detail, she didn't remember Clark Gable at all.[48] The family story was that Clark Gable had worked for the Brooks family business, Brooks–Scanlon in Bend, Oregon, then later visited the Brookses at Eastcliff.

I searched for corroboration and found that, in 1922, Gable was in his early days of acting and traveled with a road show that went broke in Montana. He made his way to Bend, Oregon, and worked for a while in a sawmill. A 1932 article quoted him as saying that in Bend, "the moon was a beacon light of welcome to a lonely wanderer." He got a job making three dollars a day carrying lumber. "That three dollars didn't mean anything; it wouldn't have meant anything if it had been twenty. It merely kept me from starving. The job wasn't what I wanted to do, so the pay was unimportant."[49]

In 1922, there were only two sawmills in Bend: Brooks–Scanlon and Shevlin–Hixon, and they were two of the largest pine sawmills in the world. Even without the family story that Clark Gable worked for Brooks–Scanlon, there was a fifty/fifty chance that he had. In 1950, Brooks–Scanlon bought Shevlin–Hixon,[50] so at the very least he worked for a company that the family later owned. Not long after working in the sawmill, Clark Gable had roles in silent films. He had his first leading role, opposite Joan Crawford, in 1931.

It is more likely that Edward and Markell met Gable as an actor rather than as a worker in their sawmill. Ted Brooks mentioned actors Katharine Hepburn, Clark Gable, Chester Morris, and playwright Noel Coward as

South guest room. Photograph by Patrick O'Leary. Courtesy of University Photographer records, University of Minnesota Archives.

visiting Eastcliff. These guests would have come to parties that the children wouldn't have attended, being that they were children.

How did they meet all these people? They were probably friends of friends. As described earlier, Edward had a friend from the Mayo Clinic who told him when Helen Keller was visiting. (The HIPPA privacy rules were established in 1996, about sixty years after her visit.) Edward and Markell had many friends in the Twin Cities as well.

Markell had a dear friend with connections from her schoolgirl days at Chicago Latin School. Frannie Coonley (later Underwood) and Markell were in each other's weddings. Frannie, in fact, fainted during Edward and Markell's wedding, so Edward always claimed he didn't know if they were married or not because he kept looking to see if Frannie was going to fall down. The colonial-style house in New York that Edward and Markell admired and used as a model for Eastcliff belonged to Frannie's parents.

Frannie visited Eastcliff regularly and the two women considered each other as best friends throughout their lives. Frannie told Marney Brooks that Edward and Markell always had interesting guests, saying, "Helen Keller and Polly Thompson came, Annie Sullivan and people from the Mayo Clinic and doctors and a big group from St. Paul, and the tennis club."[51]

Marney replied, "I think a lot of them were connections, for instance, Katharine Hepburn came to visit you" [meaning Frannie]. Frannie agreed and added there were also "Cornelia Skinner and John Bowles, who was a beau of mine at one point."

There were connections among these connections. For example, actress Cornelia Otis Skinner was nearly cast for the role of Scarlett O'Hara's mother in *Gone with the Wind*. Katharine Hepburn auditioned to play Scarlett. Clark Gable played Rhett Butler.

Although I am disappointed to not have a firsthand story of Clark Gable's visit to Eastcliff, it seems likely that he visited but unlikely that he spent the night in the guest room. A different (and differently spelled) Gabel did, however: the two guest rooms have been used by President Joan Gabel's sons, Jack and Luke.

If not Clark Gable, then who did stay in the guest rooms (or who else did) during the Brooks years? Markell Brooks's parents visited from Chicago. In addition to Tom and Frannie Underwood, friends Edwin and Marion Austin and their daughter Barbara were regular houseguests at Eastcliff. Markell's cousin Quail Hawkins visited regularly at Gull Lake and likely also at Eastcliff.

In searching for answers, I had read *Turning the Leaves,* transcribed interviews with Barbara Foote and Frannie Underwood, Marney's many writings, newspaper articles, the Brooks family file contents at the Minnesota Historical Society, and a 1972 letter Ted wrote to the University detailing his memories of growing up in Eastcliff. This research was all several years before I heard Judy Yudof's 1998 interview with Conley and Marney, Ted and Ginny, Binky, and Conley Jr. I knew Conley and Marney, albeit only for a short amount of time, and I had talked extensively with Binky and with Conley Brooks Jr. I never met Ted or Ginny in person, so it was particularly wonderful to hear them on the tapes. Although I had already heard most of the stories from Binky, Ted answered two of my unasked questions when Judy asked him about houseguests.

First, did Clark Gable spend the night at Eastcliff? Ted's 1972 letter mentioned Clark Gable having been a guest, but not that he had spent the night. (I had also heard that Katharine Hepburn spent the night; she was at Eastcliff at least twice, but not overnight.) When asked about overnight guests, Ted did not mention Clark Gable.

My second question, how did Edward and Markell travel so extensively while they had young children at home? Markell had brought the children clothing from Austria, Egypt, Greece, Holland, Italy, Japan, and Madeira. International travel was more complicated and time consuming in those days. While the Brooks family had live-in servants, they would have been busy full-time caring for the house rather than for the children for weeks at a time.

As a quick indication of their travel, while it is unlikely that many of their trips would be mentioned in newspapers, at least three were. An article titled "Minneapolis Society Returns North After Winter Travels" on March 28, 1925, shared that

> With the coming of spring and its attendant sunshine, Minneapolis folks who have been away during the cold months are returning daily from trips abroad and from southern resorts of the United States.
>
> Mr. and Mrs. Edward S. Brooks (Markell Conley) of Mississippi River boulevard, who have been making a cruise of the Mediterranean on the Mauretania will land in New York next Friday and will come to Minneapolis a week from tomorrow. They went abroad in early February.[52]

A later column in April mentioned that Edward and Markell were on the *Mauretania* with Mr. and Mrs. Edward Gale, John Woodbridge Avery, and Mr. and Mrs. Russell M. Bennett. In 1925, when Edward and Markell were gone for about two months, Conley was four years old; Ted was three.

In April 1933, it was reported they were preparing to leave for Vancouver, Washington, for two weeks.[53] In 1933, they were on a cruise and in Italy (this trip was not reported in the newspaper). In March 1934, it was reported that Mr. and Mrs. Brooks had just returned from a six-week trip to Europe.[54] The four Brooks children were then ages twelve, eleven, seven, and four. Who took care of the children while Edward and Markell were gone on frequent long trips? Ted explained in the 1998 interview:

> In the early years of this house, Mother and Dad used to travel quite a bit, abroad and in this country. It was their regular practice, when they were off to King George V's coronation, for example, in 1935 [actually, King George VI's in 1936], while they were away there was a woman who stayed in the house to be in charge. Her name was Anna Bell Thomas, and she was a distant relative of my father. She was also the assistant principal of Central High School of Minneapolis, and a member of the math faculty at Central High School.[55] She would come over here when Mother and Dad were away and occupy what we called the south guest room. And that would be her habitat for the three weeks or four weeks, or whatever it was Mother and Dad were away.

> I know, Con and I, anyway, while we would miss our parents while they were away, we didn't shed any tears for one reason mainly. Mind you, this was the very early and mid-thirties when we were in school and beginning to study algebra. We used to hope Mother and Dad would take another trip, especially as exam time came in school, because Miss Bell, as we called her, although she was reluctant to give us any help—we really pressed her so hard that sometimes, just to get rid of us—she would solve the problem or help us. "X-squared plus y-squared equals *WHAT?*" she'd say. "What was that?"

> She was really not a nanny, and not a guest, more a first sergeant or the CEO of the premises while the parents were away. She was a wonderful soul. I think Con and I are, I am, still grateful to her for the help she gave us in algebra.

During the Magrath administration, the south bedroom was named the Waller room for Luckie and Dora Waller. Luckie, a 1926 graduate of the University, was the son of the founders of Luck Land Company. He and Dora lived on a citrus ranch in San Diego. After he died in 1976 and she died in 1982, they left the University three properties worth seven million dollars (as well as bedroom furniture, crystal and silver serving ware, and a clock, all for use at Eastcliff). The properties were sold to provide scholarship support for high-achieving students.

Diane and Peter had a special blue rug from Morocco in the room. While they were visiting Morocco regarding the University's Institute of Agriculture activities, Peter was invited to the king's birthday party, but no women were allowed to attend. Diane went shopping and bought the rug, attributing the purchase to the king of Morocco. Diane used the adjoining, smaller guest room as her office.

Eric used the Waller room as his office while we lived at Eastcliff, keeping work as far from the bedroom as possible. We had houseguests use the adjoining (north) bedroom.

THE ATTIC

In between the door to the back stairs and the short hallway to the guest bedrooms, there is a door to the attic. Open that door, and we climb up steep stairs. At the top of the stairs to the right are various lamps and other leftovers. In the 1940s, there were stacks and stacks of National Geographic *magazines here. Even the well-traveled, urbane Brooks family was not immune to thinking these magazines, containing such spectacular photography, were never to be discarded.*

This space to the right is small, as the attic does not extend over the catering kitchen. To the left, the long, narrow space extends over the family kitchen and dining rooms to the front of the house. The attic then turns to the left, in the L-shape of the house. Continuing along, above the entry and living room, there is currently stored furniture, more boxes, and at the end, over the garden room, the very large crystal chandelier from the Pillsbury mansion hanging from the rafters and covered in cloth.

The Brooks family stored a more interesting item at this end of the attic.

An Attic Filled with Airplanes

During the Brooks days, the long stretch of attic above the kitchen and dining room was filled with Dwight's model airplanes. Imagine the air full of planes, with the low light giving them an illusion of flight. Dwight built his first model plane at age five; he professed this was the beginning of a lifelong love affair with airplanes.

Conley Jr. said, "As a grandchild, one of my favorite places was the attic because—there were lots of things up there—but among the things that were really intriguing were these model airplanes. I used to go up there as a kid and play with those, or look with wonder at them. And he [Dwight] went on and did that the rest of his life." Dwight wasn't just interested in the models: he wanted to fly. "I have a photograph of him when he was in kindergarten in St. Paul," Binky said, "and he's inside an airplane he had made out of orange crates. He's sitting in the pilot seat. It's the cutest thing."

Dwight was too young to serve in the military during World War II as his brothers did. He traveled with his parents during those years. They would regularly get calls complaining they were breaking blackout rules; Dwight would push the curtains aside to look out the window at the airplanes.

At age fifteen, Dwight got a job washing airplanes at Holman Field in St. Paul. His parents bought him flying lessons, which he took with special permission due to his young age. He flew his first solo flight at sixteen. In 1948, when his father told him that no Brooks man had ever been drafted and it was time to enlist, he joined the marines. He served in the U.S. Marines for three years, then transferred to the U.S. Air Force.

Dwight flew thirty-three combat missions in the Korean conflict. He later flew for the strategic air command. Binky recounted to me that one of his training missions in the United States was highly significant: he flew next to a UFO and took photographs. The government told him not to tell anyone and classified the film. Dwight later told Binky. She told me.[56]

After four years in the Air Force, Dwight worked in the family business in Powell River, then in land development in California. He had two children, Dwight Frederick Brooks III and Jennifer Conley Brooks Sykes. His love of airplanes, and of making things, continued as his passion throughout his life. He restored both airplanes and automobiles. He restored and drove what he called the "Quack," a 1942 amphibious jeep. He rebuilt a 1937 SS-100 Jaguar, which he sold in 1974; with those proceeds he bought a 1944 V-77 Gullwing, which he restored and flew in airshows, winning thirty-seven awards. After the success of the Gullwing, Dwight took on what he came to consider his peak achievement: he restored a World War II–era British Lysander airplane. After Dwight's death, his siblings spoke proudly of this achievement.

"He was very creative—making things; he restored old aircraft," Binky said. "At one point he restored a British Lysander, which was at that time the only one flying in the world. So, he was invited by these former pilots to come to a place just outside of London and give a talk about the restoration, and I went with him. He had that audience just riveted. These were all pilots, and he was describing how this thing works."

"He had two wrecks of this plane. Half of them were made in Canada and half in England," Conley added. "He bought two wrecks. One of them

Dwight with one of his model planes. Courtesy of the Brooks family.

was a chicken coop in some field in Canada when he found it. Then he took them to Van Nuys, California, and made one flyable plane. And he flew it."

Ted chimed in, "It was a very specialized plane, the Lysander. It was used for night reconnaissance. At the time of the Blitz, it would fly over the English Channel very low, just off the water, and would land in northern France to drop off agents or to pick up underground [agents]. It could land on a dime and turn around and get back out again."

Dwight donated the Lysander to the Smithsonian National Air and Space Museum. It is on display in Chantilly, Virginia, at the Air and Space Museum's companion facility to the museum on the National Mall.

Dwight continued his model making as an adult—in a big way. He built airplane, ship, and powerboat models that were three to twelve feet long, spending 1,200 to 1,500 hours on each. The boats were all seaworthy; he tested them in his California swimming pool, then in Gull Lake in Minnesota. They ran with gas or electric engines and were operated by remote control.

He built a tugboat, a Norwegian Trawler, a sailboat named *Atlantic*, and a German submarine. When he built the German submarine, he called the German embassy and tracked down a former U-boat captain to help with the interior. This complemented his work on the Lysander, as his brother Ted said: "It was kind of ironic that Dwight, one way or another, worked with a former U-boat captain and with RAF British people. He was universal that way."

Dwight became well-known for his models and was featured several times in *Scale Ship Modeler* magazine. Many of the model boats and planes were sold to collectors during Dwight's lifetime. When Dwight died, according to Conley, "there were forty-one aircraft models and a whole bunch of ship models. His workmanship was the kind you would find in a model in the lobby of General Motors in New York. It was just impeccable—beautifully done and accurate."

The models he made as an adult were not the small size that were in the Eastcliff attic. Some were twelve feet long. As Conley said, "We had a problem. What are we going to do with these models? He'd given one to each of us, 'Take your choice.' But to take one, first of all, you had to get it to wherever you were, and how were you going to keep it? You almost had to set aside a room or something. So we decided we would try to keep the whole collection together and give it to somebody. We finally ended up—after a lot of traveling around—we gave it [the collection of thirty-two ship and boat models] to the Santa Barbara Maritime Museum."

Halloween Parties

"Airplane alley" continued as storage space when we lived at Eastcliff. Along with miscellaneous boxes and furnace filters, there were holiday decorations: Eastcliff's, ours, and others. I found the decorations used for the Yudofs' Halloween parties, including a box of skeletons, which foreshadow the end of this story.

Imagine you are walking through the Eastcliff basement as a young child in costume. The invitation your family received stated that children, up to age six, were invited to "Come tour Eastcliff's spooky basement!" The next year the invitation began, "It has been rumored that Eastcliff, the president's residence, is haunted . . ." Your parents leave you with other small children at the top of the stairs by the service entrance. You walk down the stairs: clop, clop, clop, lots of giggles.

The giggles quickly subside as you hear eerie music and see that the walls are very dark and covered in spiderwebs (black plastic sheeting streaked with white paint). Along the long hall, a mummy hangs in an archway. In the rooms to the right are skeletons and mannequins. Then what had appeared to be a mannequin comes to life. There is a vampire in the laundry room. In the elevator room, severed heads are surrounded by smoke (fake, of course, on dry ice, but still). You try to appear invisible, and indeed the creatures are sensitive; they do not attempt to frighten you *too* much, unless you seem to relish that.

At the end of the hall, there is a door. Perhaps this is the spot where it will be the most frightening of all. There is no turning back.

Through that door, slowly, *slowly*, and there are your parents waiting for you in the brightly lit amusement room.

The Yudofs' next two Halloween parties, in 1998 and 1999, were on Fridays (instead of on Halloween) and included entertainment by the "Teddy Bear Band," cupcakes, cookies, caramel corn, and gallons of hot chocolate and cold apple cider. The third event welcomed children up to age ten. The 2000 and 2001 parties were again on the thirty-first of October and included a face painter along with the band.

I didn't know about the haunted house when we planned a Halloween party our first year at Eastcliff, but I was inspired by knowing that the Yudofs had hosted such parties for families of faculty and staff. Our parties were not scary, and the weather cooperated so that we were able to have them all in the backyard. We self-catered, buying cookies, pretzels, popcorn, and gallons of apple cider. Jill Christenson planned a scavenger hunt the first two years. Then Patricia Hall, also a young mother, added coloring sheets and crafts. By the time Pam Hudson joined as my assistant, the event was so popular that we invited guests to arrive in three different time slots.

The University of Minnesota is well-known for its apple breeding program, most famously for the Honeycrisp apple. Pam and Eastcliff facility supervisor Jim Bossert contacted the Arboretum to see if apples could be donated to the party. Renowned apple breeders David Bedford and Professor James Luby came to slice apples and offer them to the families for a taste test. Dave and Jim are exceedingly gracious and modest: I overheard people telling the apple cutters about the apple breeding program, and they never confessed that they were quite familiar with it. My favorite apple is SweeTango®, but hundreds of Eastcliff Halloween party guests were among the first to test several new introductions, including Minn 55. Minn 55 rivals my beloved SweeTango and has since been introduced as First Kiss® if grown in Minnesota (it's an early apple) and Rave® if grown elsewhere.

Eric and I needed costumes for the parties, of course. Jill told us that the Yudofs rented from the Guthrie Costume Shop, which is available to the public. The first year, Eric, as the sixteenth president of the University, decided to be Abraham Lincoln. As Mary Todd Lincoln, I wore a dress with a hoop skirt.

In 2012, Eastcliff was scaffolded in the fall as the roof was replaced. We were happy to restart the parties in 2013, when Eric dressed as a Gopher football player and I was a superhero: a Gopher women's hockey player, as the team was in the midst of an unprecedented sixty-two-game winning streak. In 2014, I was a honeybee and Eric was a beekeeper. We are big fans of the world-renowned bee research at the University. In 2015, Eric had been joking about getting some "Gopher-alls" (the striped maroon and gold overalls that many students wear to football games), so we dressed as *Gopher Gothic* in homage to the painting *American Gothic*. Our 2016 costumes were my favorite: we were Goldy's parents, and Goldy came dressed as a child.

Each year, we offered photographs with Goldy to families at the party. Goldy was such a draw that people would immediately get in line for photographs. The line got very long. In 2017, Bethany Fung, an event planner from the University of Minnesota Foundation (UMF), joined the planning, along with UMF's Hannah Skog. They cleared the bottleneck with a layout change that sent guests through the

Halloween, 2011. Photograph by Patrick O'Leary. Courtesy of University Photographer records, University of Minnesota Archives.

house, onto the terrace for refreshments, along the sidewalk past College of Design students carving pumpkins, through apple tasting, and then to photographs with Goldy at a beautiful backdrop arranged by University Landcare. Guests could then proceed to the oval garden to join a sack race, draw with chalk on the sidewalk, or play lawn games before being given an apple and prizes and exiting through the front yard. This plan required more volunteer workers than those we regularly had from the president's office,[57] and the UMF staff and interns cheerfully joined in.

With the increase in staffing, Eric and I had the opportunity to expand from a couple's costume to a group costume. In 2017, we all dressed as University of Minnesota apples. None of us was an actual apple; rather, we dressed as the names: Beacon, Fireside, Frostbite™, Honeycrisp, Honeygold, Prairie Spy, Red Baron, Regent, SnowSweet, State Fair, SweeTango®, and Sweet Sixteen.

In 2018, our last fall at Eastcliff, we had to fly to San Francisco for a development trip on the Sunday before Halloween. Word came from the president's office that we would need to cancel the party. I typically do as I'm told, but this time I found a later flight and worked with the events team to plan an earlier party. We came up with a theme of University inventions. As Eric and I needed to leave immediately for the airport, we needed quick-change costumes, so we wore signboards over our clothing. I was the Minnesota Multiphasic Personality Inventory (MMPI). I made Eric's signboard, and on Saturday he attached pages from the local newspapers. It was his last year as president and his favorite costume; he dressed as "yesterday's news."

I never felt that the attic was spooky. Binky said to me in 2015 that "there are psychic footprints all over the place and you are probably tuned to it, sensitive to it." I replied that there were no ghosts at Eastcliff. She agreed there was nothing dark. I would, however, try to avoid going up in the attic if I was home alone. I was worried I might fall and not be found. Besides the narrow entry stairs, it is necessary to step up and over heating ducts, about a foot and a half tall and three feet wide, every several steps. If I carried several boxes and moved quickly, I could get a mini workout. Tyler Larson, who cleaned at Eastcliff (a hard worker and a self-starter), must have found the attic a bit creepier than I did. When a window at the end of the hall kept opening on its own, Tyler was convinced we had a ghost. I went up and discovered that the window wasn't securely locked; locking it banished the ghost. Neighborhood children in the 1930s could easily be forgiven for believing there was a *real* ghost in the Eastcliff attic.

During the Brookses' time at Eastcliff, the Brooks children would take parades of friends up the steep stairs into the attic, down the east-to-west length of the house, then down the north-to-south length. There was a cedar closet along the way. At the end, hanging from a rafter, was a human skeleton.

If one of the braver children, no doubt a Brooks as they were most familiar, touched the skeleton gently, it would slowly rotate so that its one glass eye would shimmer and shine through the dark.

Binky told me the story of the skeleton. She said her grandfather, Dr. Dwight Brooks, was always very serious; she never saw a photograph of him without a hat. He had need of a skeleton for his work. Or, at the least, he had a patient who believed that he had need of *her* skeleton. This patient knew she was dying, and she said, "After I'm gone, if you wait seven years, you can have my skeleton for research."

Apparently, he took her up on the offer.

Binky told me this story a second time when the two of us were with Barbara Bentson. At this point in the story, Barbara asked, "Why seven years?"

I wish you could hear Binky's reply, because it was so Binky: "Don't ask me." Her response indicated that it wasn't her business to know, she just knew what she knew. She did offer a conjecture: "There must have been something about the body deteriorating enough in seven years, and you had time to get adjusted somewhere else."

Binky explained that her father had a close friend named Harry Simmons, who was an official with the St. Paul police department. Mr. Brooks asked "Uncle Harry"[58] to help him disinter the bones after the seven years had passed.

The bones were wired together into a skeleton.

I will henceforth refer to the skeleton as "Bridget," as that is what the Brooks children called her. I have no idea or opinion as to whether that name had any connection to the body that the skeleton had previously inhabited—as Binky might say, "Don't ask me."

Harry Simmons put Bridget in the passenger seat of his police car and drove her to Eastcliff.

When Bridget arrived, Mr. Brooks and his two older sons, Conley and Ted, were expecting her; Mrs. Brooks was not. They had arranged the arrival for a time when Mrs. Brooks wasn't home, and hung Bridget in the closet in the second floor sitting room that held wood. They waited patiently.

According to Binky, "That evening we said, 'Oh, we really should have a fire. It's too cold. Mother, let's have it in your sitting room.' They [the boys] purposely put very little wood to make the fire, so it was almost nothing. Then they said, 'We should get more wood on there. It's your turn, Mother, to get the wood.'"

Her reaction was indescribable.

So, what became of Bridget? The family once loaned the skeleton to Blake School for a class, propping her up in the front seat, once again, for another drive across town; she returned to Eastcliff after the class. In 1954, not long before Edward Brooks died, Conley and Marney Brooks, along with their four young children, moved to Long Lake, Minnesota. (Their daughter, to be named Markell, would be born nine years later.) In 1958, as Mrs. Brooks was making plans to move to Long Lake, Bridget moved to Conley and Marney's barn.

6

Go Outside to Play— and Party

FROM 1922 UNTIL 1930, *the main house included a three-stall garage. In 1930, Clarence Johnston Jr. designed a carriage house for Eastcliff with a five-stall garage on the first floor, an apartment on the second floor, and a full basement for storage. The building is designed in the colonial revival style of the main house, with wide clapboard siding and five dark green garage doors crowned with an*

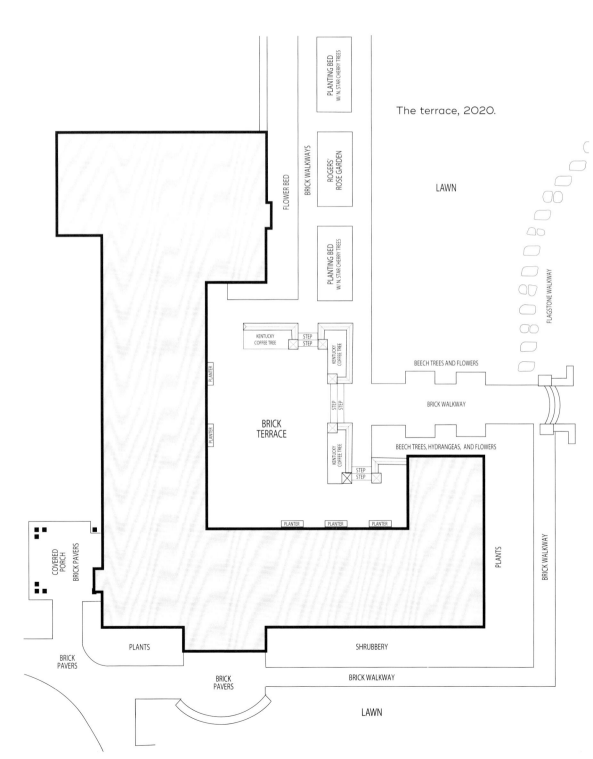

The terrace, 2020.

entablature and dentils. A second-floor dormer window is centered over each ga-rage door. It is, and has always been, referred to as the carriage house—it is too pretty to be called a garage. An entry door on the northwest corner allows access to the apartment upstairs without entering the garage. The apartment is gener-ously sized at 1,320 square feet. In the 1930 architectural drawings for the carriage house, I was amused to see one room labeled "man's room" (I thought man caves and man rooms were recent terminology). I would have been much less amused if the kitchen had been labeled "woman's room," but perhaps all the rooms not labeled for a man were regarded as belonging to a woman.

The carriage house was built in 1931.

THE CARRIAGE HOUSE

Living above the Garage

Why would anyone in Minnesota give up an attached garage for a detached garage? I expect that question didn't bother Edward and Markell Brooks. Their family had expanded to fill all their bedrooms, and they enjoyed having guests. Their live-in help included three "girls," as they always called them: Bertha cooked, Alice and Alvina cleaned (one upstairs and one downstairs) and served meals. They needed the extra space taken by the original garage. I don't know when they hired Clarence, Alice's brother, as chauffeur, but eventually Clarence was both caretaker and chauffeur. He, his wife Mona, and their children occupied the apartment above the garage.

Another reason not to cherish an attached garage: the Brooks chauffeur could pull up to the covered porte cochère door and the family could enter and exit the car there. Arriving back home, Clarence could then quickly enter his home from the warmth of the garage—and the garage was likely warm. The heating oil costs for the carriage house (again, from Mr. Brook's careful ledgers) weren't a lot less than for the house. The garage is still kept above freezing in the winter to protect the pipes and the items in storage.

The application for Eastcliff's inclusion in the National Register for His-toric Places suggests another reason for the carriage house and its place-ment: "By the time the garage was built in 1930, the neighborhood to the east had become more fully developed. Gone was the heavily wooded area that had attracted the Brooks family to the site. The new garage was intended to buffer the estate from the encroaching neighborhood to the east."

The Brookses wrote of those days in *Turning the Leaves*: "Everyday life at Eastcliff for the most part was orderly and pleasant. In the winter Clarence

A peek of the carriage house past the pool. Courtesy of the Brooks family.

would occasionally drive the children to school. He would drop off the boys at St. Paul Academy, which at the time was a semi-military school, where boys wore uniforms and every morning spent forty-five minutes at compulsory drill sessions. Binky was driven to Summit Avenue, just west of Lexington, where she would get out and walk to Summit School. In the spring and fall the boys either used bicycles or walked to school."[1]

Binky waited years before telling this story, but then shared it freely. When she was twelve, she was alone at the house and decided to go for a drive. She was always petite, so I imagine she was quite small at the time. She drove her mother's silver convertible with the top up (hence a small back window) across the Lake Street bridge. She saw police lights behind her and pulled over. The officer approached the car warily.

"Have I done something wrong?" she asked with true innocence.

"How old are you?" he asked.

She replied that she was twelve. Binky explained to me that her father taught her to drive: "He taught me how to drive when I was ten, sitting on his lap. I felt perfectly confident. But we had a clutch in those days, so when I put on the brake the car lurched." I don't know if she explained all of that to the officer, but if she did, I imagine he was unimpressed.

"Where do you live?" he asked next. After she replied, he instructed her, "Go straight home and don't drive again until you are sixteen!" As he walked away, she could hear him muttering, "I couldn't see anyone in the car! I couldn't even see a head!" He thought the car was driving itself.

At the time when Conley and Marney Brooks were married, Conley was in the Army Air Corps, so after a brief honeymoon to Excelsior Springs, Missouri, the newlyweds lived in three different rooming houses near the airbases where Conley was stationed. They were preparing for Conley to be deployed overseas in August 1945. Suddenly the glorious news arrived that the war was over! Within a few weeks the entire contingent was discharged, and in September Conley and Marney were back in St. Paul. They moved into the apartment over the Eastcliff carriage house. Markell helped the young couple furnish the apartment, which Marney remembered as cozy and attractive. Binky called the apartment the "Brook Nook." Marney's later remembrances give us a view into those days:

> During our months of living in the Eastcliff enclave, we saw a lot of Edward and Markell. Markell's influence was everywhere. She was an artist in every way; her dress, her decor, her entertaining, her garden and flower-arranging, her gift-giving and exquisite packaging, all proclaimed the artist in her. She created an atmosphere of peace and beauty, both at home and at Gull Lake, and was extremely generous in sharing her largess: lots of entertaining, large parties, as well as small get-togethers around the pool late in the afternoon.[2]
>
> Just going to bed was an experience at Eastcliff; monogrammed satin-like percale sheets, and monogramed blanket covers enveloped the bed. In the bathroom thick towels embroidered with flowers and leaves encircling the inevitable MCB were piled up in coordinated colors awaiting the lucky guest. This pursuit of beauty and elegance was new and dazzling to me and I ate it up. So did all of Markell's friends who were treated to the same experiences.[3]

There are many beautiful tributes to Markell, but what about Edward? Marney wrote, in *Turning the Leaves*, "I remember being terrified one day in 1945 when we were living in the Eastcliff garage apartment. He told me that I could use the '60 Special,' a long, gray Cadillac, and on backing out of the garage, I scraped and dented the right rear fender. I agonized all afternoon waiting for him to return from the office, but when I confessed to this dreadful deed, he put his arm around me reassuringly and said not to worry. Whether he would have been so understanding with one of his sons is anybody's guess."[4] My guess is that he would not have been. From all I have read, Edward, as one of three sons of a demanding father, was a demanding father to his three sons. His beloved daughter was different. Since there were many fewer opportunities for women in those times, I wonder if he felt less obligation to prepare his daughter for the future. He could also enjoy a relationship with his daughter-in-law without complication, as Marney wrote, "My relationship with my father-in-law was an easy one: I knew Edward loved me." Edward's father, Dwight, had had a similar affection for his daughter-in-law Markell.

In 1945, there was an additional reason for Edward to love Marney. On November 11, two months after Conley and Marney moved into Eastcliff, they were joined by their first child, Conley Brooks Jr. With the expectant father sequestered in the waiting room, Marney counted the minutes between contractions until she entered the "second stage." She was then given "scopolamine and another drug" and was unconscious until a nurse woke her with news that she had a baby boy. New mothers then were confined to bed for six days, could sit in a chair on day seven, walk on day eight, and go home on day ten. Once home at Eastcliff, Marney had to be carried up the steep steps in the carriage house, as stairs were forbidden for three weeks.

As a mother myself, who worked all day Friday while in labor, had a baby that night (it was 1988, so "natural"—unmedicated—childbirth, of course), and went home from the hospital on Sunday morning (Eric didn't miss a minute from work), I found the story of the birth of Edward and Markell's first grandchild to be an interesting window into another age.

I don't know when Clarence, the Brooks family's caretaker and driver, moved out of the carriage house apartment, but obviously before Conley Brooks returned from the service. Other caretakers later lived in the apartment with their families through the end of the Brooks years at Eastcliff.

The carriage house was remodeled during the Wilson administration. Kathy and Grant Moos lived in the apartment late in the Moos administration. During the Magrath administration, a caretaker lived in the carriage house and took care of the grounds. Mark Anderson, a recent University graduate, was the first caretaker. When he started law school, he was replaced by graduate student Neil Dylla. Neil and his wife lived in the carriage house apartment, and their son, Ryan, was born while they lived there. Neil took care of the gardening, fireplaces, and setting up tables for events. The

1980 Eastcliff docent manual said that Neil could be reached by finding him on the grounds, by phone, or by a buzzer in the first floor back hall. Neil and his son continued living in the carriage house for about ten years, into the Hasselmo administration. They moved out in 1990, but Neil continued as caretaker after that time.[5]

At some point, a change in fire codes deemed the upstairs of the carriage house uninhabitable due to the lack of a second egress. The space is currently used as storage, and the family cars are parked in the garage.[6]

When the Wilson and the Moos families lived in Eastcliff, the presidents each had a University-supplied car and driver. The carriage house was a livable apartment, but no one lived there. The University-supplied car ended in the Bruininks administration. The University had an airplane for a while, too, but those days are long gone.

Eastcliff's Menagerie

When Kathy Moos "left" for college at Macalester College in St. Paul, she moved into the Eastcliff carriage house. The carriage house was convenient and likely closer to her campus than the residences of many students. It proved a bit lonely, however, so brother Grant moved across the driveway as well.

Kathy and Grant both vividly recall Kathy's pet at the time. Kathy had a friend who raised doves and another who raised pigeons. While neither Kathy nor Grant recall the provenance of Kathy's pigeon, Hawthorne, they agree that it is more likely that the bird came from Kathy's friend Lisa than that the bird was captured from the wild. Hawthorne lived briefly as an indoor pet, roosting in a box, until Grant decided that was no life for a pigeon. Hawthorne was given free access to the Eastcliff grounds. (A bird with free access can actually go anywhere, but Hawthorne—smart bird—confined himself to Eastcliff.) Hawthorne spent a lot of time on the top of the stone wall that divides the Eastcliff back parking area from the back lawn and connects to the main house. He would strut along the wall, then fly up to the carriage house window and watch Kathy while she studied.

There have been various other animals at Eastcliff, some invited, others not. We were awakened at dawn several mornings by an alarm triggered in the front yard. Hoof prints explained the intruder. The deer did little destruction; each spring they might eat the first tulips, but little else. We turned off the alarm in that part of the yard.

We saw eagles soaring overhead, and I once saw a flock of wild turkeys in the side yard along Dayton Avenue.

Chipmunks ate each and every cherry off all four trees in one July afternoon; they fortunately stopped doing this of their own accord after two years. Squirrels ate the fall pumpkin decorations; the year we displayed all the winners of a pumpkin-carving contest we also had a lot of very fat squirrels.

Rabbits were plentiful and obliterated the barberry bushes one winter, but it was a hard winter with little to eat so we didn't blame them. The rabbits left calling cards throughout the yard at night but stayed hidden on the periphery of the lawn during the day—until we moved out. Our dogs had been gone only a week when I went back to get some final items and saw that several rabbits were already relaxing on the lawn close to the house.

During several springs, after the pool was opened, a mallard drake and hen would visit and go for a swim. One day the hen and a flock of darling ducklings were swimming in the pool. It was a clever spot for a swimming lesson, safe from predators, and they swam very happily, until the mama duck hopped out of the pool and quacked like crazy as the ducklings swam in circles, unable to get out. The hen got back in and swam around some more, not seeming to understand that a shallow spot would not be found. My friend Lizzy and I made a little ramp for them and left them alone. When we checked back, they had escaped.

When I hosted Neighborhood Night Out, the police officers who stopped by neighborhoods enjoyed coming to Eastcliff in bad weather because they could come inside. One year, McGruff the Crime Dog came, but the next year was a bigger hit: a mounted police officer brought a very large horse into the backyard. I don't know who liked seeing the horse more—me or three-year-old Frank from across Otis Avenue. I discovered later that having a horse visit was anticlimactic compared to the cow.

During Nils Hasselmo's last year in office, he and Pat were honored at forty farewell receptions. Nils said, "The events have run the gamut from the sublime to the bovine." The most memorable event was likely the University of Minnesota Alumni Association's annual meeting and farewell tribute in Northrop Auditorium. Garrison Keillor, a University alum of *Prairie Home Companion* fame, wrote a show, "Our University—Our Times," and performed it in collaboration with University faculty and students for an audience of 1,500. For the grand finale, Keillor said the University had a gift for Nils, and a 1,700-pound Holstein cow entered stage left, carefully climbing a specially built ramp. The cow was named Bovine #1525. Keillor challenged Nils to name her after a beautiful woman. Nils quickly named her "Odhumla," after the mythological Scandinavian cow who helped create the first human. That seemed like a good end to the joke, but in a continuation that you can probably see coming, Keillor had the cow delivered to Eastcliff. Nils and Pat awoke the next morning to find Odhumla grazing contentedly in the backyard.[7]

THE TERRACE

The original terrace was made of New York bluestone and ran the length of the house outside the living room. In 1923, a swimming pool was added to the yard. In 1926, the south porch was expanded to the east into the area of the patio. In 1930, a new, larger pool was added farther back in the yard.

While the terrace has undergone many changes, the harboring arms of the L-shaped house have remained to make it a secluded oasis. It feels that way even when crowded with more than a hundred guests. The terrace is a lovely place for events, and a lovely place for a family. The Brooks family had a large round table on the terrace, with the base made from the trunk of a tree. Binky recalled many wonderful conversations around that table.

Nils Hasselmo wrote a note to a friend in 1989: "Pat and Anna just completed the move from Arizona, and the boxes are stacked everywhere. Our first family dinner on the patio was highlighted by locking ourselves out of the house and using the car phone to make a sheepish call to the University Police. It's a good way to enforce humility."[8]

The terrace was our favorite space at Eastcliff. On rare, quiet Sunday mornings, Eric and I would sit in the sun with our cups of coffee, two dogs, and three newspapers. We would throw a tennis ball from the terrace across the lawn for the dogs to chase. I imagined that our bashful dogs thought their fondest dreams had come true and Eastcliff belonged to just the four of us.

Examining a 1960 floor plan, I was surprised to see that there was a swallow pool, likely filled with water lilies and goldfish, outside along the dining

room wall. I saw further evidence of this pool when reading articles from the 1988 media blitz over the 1980s Eastcliff renovation. Ken Keller said the only specific request he made was for the old goldfish pond to be filled in, which caused me to wonder how many guests had inadvertently stepped into that old pond.

The plans for a 1987 terrace renovation called for the removal and disposal of that concrete pool and brick edging. After the pond was removed, a brick terrace was installed in place of the flagstone near the house, surrounded by a large circular brick patio two steps down. The flagstones were saved and reused in a patio that extended farther into the lawn, and therefore more suitable for entertaining larger groups. The plans specified that a thirty-inch-diameter oak tree was to be retained and protected.[9]

The Garden Parties

Very large groups were entertained beautifully on the 1987 terrace. After the controversy over those 1980s renovations, Friends of Eastcliff was formed as a donor group to support the work of the house. The Friends of Eastcliff Garden Party began in 1995 as an annual event to thank Eastcliff donors and solicit more support. The party has continued annually ever since, typically on a Sunday afternoon in June. The gardens are particularly beautiful that time of year, currently with the help of University of Minnesota Landcare. Every year, someone would tell me that the gardens were the most beautiful they had ever been.

At the 1996 party, there were garden displays, music by University students, tours of Eastcliff, and an "unveiling of new plans to restore guest quarters for visiting scholars" in the carriage house. Five years

The original terrace in 1923.
Courtesy of the Brooks family.

later, the party celebrated the completion of the carriage house project as an exterior renovation rather than as living quarters.

According to the notes from the fifth annual party, in 1999, committee member Cay Shea Hellervick was to talk "about financial goals of the committee for the coming year and ask guests for their help: go over wish list." The wish list included table settings of china, flatware, and glasses; improvements to the tennis court; refurbishing the swimming pool; and a large screen television for the amusement room.

The late 1990s renovation, headed by Judy Yudof, was accomplished with donations to the Eastcliff Legacy Fund, headed by Pat Hasselmo. At the 2001 party, Mark Yudof's remarks included: "So much has been accomplished with this house, and all with an eye to its historic significance. You'll hear about our latest improvements from a person who has spent much of her lifetime trying to improve me. Needless to say, she has done a much better job on the house." The theme of the 2002 party, the Yudofs' last year at Eastcliff, was "Hats Off to Thee: Mark and Judy Yudof."

The invitations for the first eleven parties included a picture of Eastcliff and themes such as "The Heritage of Eastcliff: Restoring the Past, Nurturing the Future" and "Come Home to Eastcliff: Share the history; continue the tradition." Guests at the tenth annual garden party in 2004 were invited to "celebrate the upcoming ground-breaking for the new dining terrace and garden walkways made possible by generous donations from the Friends of Eastcliff Legacy Fund."

The large oak tree that was preserved in 1987, with a flagstone terrace encircling it, had grown during the next fifteen years so that its roots made the patio uneven and unsafe. The tree was leaning precariously close to the house; photographs from a garden party show the tree at a frightening angle. During the Bruininks administration, the tree had to be removed. A log twenty feet long was saved from the grand old tree and made into mirror frames and furniture for the house.[10]

The large, flat brick terrace includes steps and an accessible ramp to brick walkways that extend parallel to each wing of the house. Along the north–south wing, there are beech trees, hydrangea bushes, and, near the house, the first daffodils to bloom each year. Along the west–east wing, there is a planting area next to the house that has been there many years. It contains pink peonies, allium, and bluebells. Next to that bed are two brick walkways that include three planting areas. The center one is called the Rogers Rose Garden in appreciation of Jim and Leeann Rogers, who supported the patio project. This garden is planted with *Summer Waltz* roses.[11] The two outer beds each had a pine tree, pink echinacea, and blue salvia. The flowers are all pollinator friendly.[12]

The 2005 garden party celebrated the new brick terrace, as well as another accomplishment from the 1999 wish list. With many donations, and the help of committee member Jolee Suskovik securing a discount from J. B. Hudson Jewelers, eighty-four place settings of new china were purchased. These are beautiful dishes with maroon and gold trim, and each place setting includes seven pieces: dinner plate, salad plate, soup bowl, cup, saucer with maroon and gold trim, gold-rimmed bread and butter plate with "Eastcliff" in the middle, and a lovely gold dessert bowl.

The Friends committee helped plan the garden parties and the themes.[13] Working with Susan Hagstrum, the party expanded to themes relevant to Eastcliff that are also areas of expertise at the University, and we followed that pattern throughout our eight years.[14] The 2006 invitation included a detail of Swedish American artist B. J. O. Nordfeldt painting *Flower with Shell,* now in the University art collection, and welcomed guests to enjoy the new sculpture garden. The 2007 invitation included a lady's slipper botanical illustration from Andersen Horticultural Library, and at the event, Deb Brown of University Extension discussed gardening. Other speakers included Mark Seeley on Minnesota weather in 2008; Kathy Zuzek on *Summer Waltz* roses in 2012; Karen Oberhauser on monarch butterflies in 2015; Deb Swackhamer on water and the Mississippi River in 2016; Matt Clark on Minnesota grape breeding in 2017; Lisa Von Drasek on children's literature in 2018; and Trevor Ames on the human/animal bond (and research) in 2019.

The 2010 theme was a midsummer afternoon's garden party with performances by University of Minnesota opera theater and orchestral students. The 2014 theme was "Birds and Bees, Flowers and Trees" featuring the University's Raptor Center, the Bee Lab, Eastcliff's gardens, and experts on horticulture and forestry. Invitations for four of the garden parties we hosted were designed by students in the University's College of Design (as were other invitations and many of our winter greeting cards).

As the day of the garden party is often sunny, the 1998 invitation stated, "garden hats encouraged." In 2005, the invitations began stating, "Please wear a hat!" We continued with "please wear a hat" in 2012, and several people mentioned that they had to go buy a hat. We left it off the next invitation, and I heard "I miss the hats" and "Can't I wear a hat?" I thought those who wanted to wear hats would do so without permission. After that, we included a line of fine print: "Hats admired but not required."

One of our more memorable garden parties occurred when a fallen tree knocked out the power to the block early on the morning of the event. The event team bought lanterns and called The Deco Catering and asked them to pre-prepare any food that needed cooking and to bring coolers. In my remarks, I quoted my friend Tracy Moos's theory on memorable events: once something big goes wrong, everyone relaxes and has a good time because they are together in an adventure. And I was quite happy to wear a hat that year, since with no electricity, I couldn't dry or style my hair.

The Friends of Eastcliff Garden Party is always a great time, no matter the weather, as it brings together people who care about Eastcliff and understand that donor support is vital for the upkeep of this Minnesota treasure.

Halftime Entertainment with Eddie Vedder

In 2011, shortly after moving back to Minnesota, I toured the University's children's hospital with Nancy Lindahl and Elizabeth Patty.[15] I happened to meet Dr. John Wagner, who told me about the work the University was doing with the care of patients and seeking a cure for epidermolysis bullosa (EB). I had read previously about EB, a rare genetic connective tissue disorder that causes, among other complications, skin to be as fragile as butterfly wings, leading to severe blistering. This chance meeting was memorable for several reasons. John Wagner told me he is from Delaware and graduated from Newark High School, as did both of our sons. (I have an honorary diploma from the school, in recognition of my volunteer work.) A few months after this visit, I began volunteering in the neonatal intensive care unit at the hospital (now named the University of Minnesota Masonic Children's Hospital). I started working with Elizabeth Patty on the FashionFest committee to support the hospital and continued that for eight years, as well as attending WineFest each year. Our daughter-in-law Lisa gave birth to our beautiful granddaughter, Ophelia, in the hospital in 2017.

I researched the University's work on EB and learned about the Jackson Gabriel Silver Foundation. Jackson Silver was just four years old at that time, and it really struck me that in his toddler photographs he looked a lot like our son Charlie at the same age. It brought home the fact that my own child could be born with this horrific condition. Jackson's parents described how they discovered their newborn had EB: "Jackson had a routine heel prick, and the nurse placed a band-aid on his heel. When the band-aid was removed the next day, all the skin on his tiny foot tore off with it."

Eric and I met Jackson, and his wonderful parents, Alex and Jamie, and have visited with them and Jackson's little sisters, Michaela and Charley, in New York. When I told Jamie that Jackson looked like our son, she said our son must look like Alex. Over the time that we have become friends, our Charlie looks more and more like Alex, and Jackson has become an intelligent, charming young man who deals with his medical challenges with a grace that should inspire us all.

Eric and I were happy to hear that Alex would be visiting Minnesota on October 18 and 19, 2014. He and Jamie were merging their foundation with another family foundation, and another couple who would help bring awareness to EB were joining as cofounders of EB Research Partnership. We were eager to see Alex and meet the two new cofounders. We were, however, leaving town for a meeting early Sunday morning, and we had the Gopher homecoming football game on Saturday afternoon. We arranged to meet at Eastcliff after the game.

The game turned out to be quite exciting. The Gophers came from behind to beat Purdue 39–38. This was the sixth win of the season, making them bowl eligible (they played in the Citrus Bowl at the end of the season). And it was Homecoming! There were lots of celebrations after the game. We left the after-game celebrations early to get home to see Alex.

I knew the other cofounders were Jill and Eddie Vedder—yes, *the* Eddie Vedder, activist and front man of Pearl Jam. What I didn't know was what wonderful people Eddie and Jill are. They really care about making a positive difference in the world, and they care about the children suffering from EB. We had a lovely afternoon sitting on the Eastcliff terrace. Elizabeth Patty and Jakub Tolar were there as well, after giving Eddie and Jill a tour of the hospital. Eddie loved the circular reading room in the hospital library; he said the acoustics were great and he would love to return and play his ukulele for patients.

Elizabeth brought a fruit and cheese tray. Eric and I brought out some—and then some more—Ladera wine from our personal collection. We visited throughout the late afternoon, and longer. Years later, Elizabeth remembers it as I do: "It was a magical evening."

After an hour or more, I heard a loud "¡Hola!" Our son Sam and girlfriend, Lizzy, had arrived back after the game. I encouraged them to join us on the terrace and meet our guests. Lizzy was her charming self, telling Jakub about her recent experience as a bone marrow donor, telling Alex about her close relationship with her father, telling—well, telling everyone everything. I had failed to consider that Lizzy was now a graduate back on campus for homecoming. The celebration started early and had continued long after we left the game. While we had all been drinking wine on the terrace, we had not kept up with Sam and Lizzy's level of homecoming celebration. I offered, "Sweetie, would you like a cookie?" hoping a snack might help.

Eric texted Sam, who was sitting across the table from him: "Time to go." Sam lifted Lizzy from her chair and took her into the house for a nap. After they left, Eddie graciously thanked us for the "halftime entertainment."

We then enjoyed hearing stories about the adventures of a superstar on the road, tales that relieved any embarrassment we might have felt.

The next day at the Pearl Jam concert, Eddie invited Dr. Jakub Tolar on stage at Xcel Energy Center, saying he and a bandmate had been given a tour of the hospital, so they wanted to give Jakub a tour of "their facility," which included the stage and all the band members. Onstage, Jakub said of Eddie, "What we both do is give people hope."

Eric and I were quite sorry to miss that concert. When we visited the Silver family several years later in New York, they told us that Jill and Eddie Vedder still say, "Sweetie, would you like a cookie?"

THE FRONT AND BACK YARDS

"Until recent years, the main entrance to the property, with its elaborate gates, was on the River Boulevard, not on Dayton Avenue," wrote Ted Brooks. "Moreover, there used to be a thick row of hedges, always carefully manicured, between the front fence and the Boulevard itself, and extending the entire width of the property from Dayton to our original neighbors on the south, the Herbert Benz family."[16]

Binky described the backyard of her childhood as a lawn, with a garden on the side, then a woods. "Oh yes, you've civilized the whole thing," she said to me while looking out the window. "You've put grass all the way over to the neighbors. See, that never used to be grass—the woods were dense." She continued, "Change is the name of the game. I guess we can be grateful for change."

One thing hasn't changed: it is a wonderful large yard, and particularly so for children. One night in the early 1930s, it may have seemed a bit *too* large. Conley and Ted had vivid memories of a night when they were in their pajamas and their father offered them twenty cents each if they would run completely around the house barefoot. Conley said, "It was about ten below zero or something. Very cold. Well, we jumped at that, and we went flying out the front door. It's a pretty long ways—you go way down the front, around the back." The boys ran out the front door, along the length of the house, then to the back between the tennis court and pool. At this point, I imagine they were rethinking their decision, but it seemed easier to continue. They ran across the front of the summer house—perhaps the veranda roof offered a few feet without snow—and onward in front of the carriage house. The driveway down the east–west wing likely seemed longer

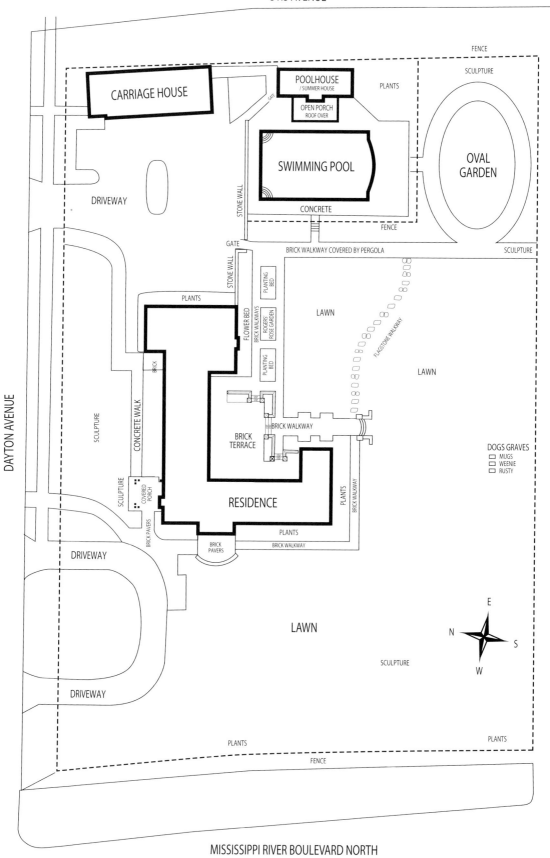

The grounds, 2020.

than they remembered, then finally they turned left and went back in the front door. Conley recalled that when they arrived back inside, their feet were numb, and their father was in hysterics laughing. Ted said, "I can still feel the cold."[17]

The boys were more properly clad for a winter activity that Ted described with fonder remembrance: "While we children were still very young, my Father built a toboggan slide (perhaps fourteen feet high) at the east end of the wooded area adjacent to the tennis court. This structure was in constant use through the winter months, and each year there was a lively competition among the Brooks children and their numerous local friends to see who could make it on his toboggan (or sled) all the way to the front fence without stopping. I recall that Howie Wilcox was the winner year after year; I think I once came within six feet of the goal."[18] This toboggan slide was made from leftover pine boards from house construction. The slide was likely stored in the carriage house basement in the warm months, as there is room there. It is a testament both to Ted's competitiveness and to his

Front yard. Courtesy of the Brooks family.

magnanimous nature that he recalls how close he came to the goal and also the name of the victor, giving Howie Wilcox[19] credit.

On Saturday afternoons in the fall, after a morning Gopher football game, Ted would get a bag of flour from the kitchen and sprinkle flour for sidelines and yard lines in Eastcliff's big front yard. Then he would gather "a gang of young fellows from the neighborhood" and regularly had enough for two eight-boy teams.

Decades later, the expansive lawn was the scene of Conley Brooks's granddaughter's wedding: Markell Kiefer is a playwright and founder of TigerLion Arts. She has created walking plays, including *The Buddha Prince* and *Nature*. When she married actor Tyson Forbes, they co-created *Tying the Knot* as their wedding ceremony, progressing throughout the Eastcliff lawn.

The Trees of Eastcliff

Conley Brooks Jr. recalled that the Eastcliff lawn from his boyhood remained heavily wooded. Photographs from the 1920s and 1930s show many high-canopy trees; the house was fully visible from the street, with only tall trunks interrupting the view.

A landscape plan from 1961 shows many trees, most of them elms. In the mid-1970s, Sandra Magrath described Eastcliff as "surrounded by a spacious lawn, large (but doomed!) elms, oaks and pines, with shrubbery and flower borders, all enclosed within a tall, white picket fence."[20] By 1985, the elms were indeed all gone. After Dutch elm disease hit the Twin Cities, many boulevard trees were replanted with ash trees. Now that the emerald ash borer is decimating those trees, we have learned the great value of diversity, even among trees.

A few old oak trees remain on the property. Near one of the giant oaks are raspberry bushes that have been on the property for many years.[21] When visiting Eastcliff, former presidents Peter Magrath and Nils Hasselmo mentioned the raspberries from the 1970s and 1990s. A landscape plan from the 1980s showed a large vegetable garden between the raspberries and the tennis court.

Some of the newer trees are quite special. A tall, shapely tamarack is in the front yard. Three planting areas in the brick terrace include *Stately Manor* Kentucky coffee trees with leaves that look almost lacy as you look through the green leaves to a bright blue Minnesota summer sky, and the leaves are even more striking when bright yellow in the fall.[22] The three pine trees planted in the 2005 terrace renovation became overgrown and

The trees of Eastcliff, 1924. Courtesy of the Brooks family.

were replaced with six *Northstar* cherry trees, a University introduction, that bloom beautifully and are even more glorious when covered in cherries.

Other trees added during our tenure included two apple trees. There's a Haralred® apple tree in the front yard and a Honeycrisp (the University's most famous apple) tree outside the back fence. A 1987 landscape map shows a large apple tree in the backyard near the house, which I didn't know was there, so I'm glad apple trees have returned to Eastcliff.

Woodchuck USA, founded by University alumni Ben VandenWymelenberg and John Guenveur, designs and manufactures distinctive custom wood products. They are great supporters of the University's children's hospital. Their *Buy one. Plant one.*® motto has resulted in more than one million trees planted. Their one millionth tree, a ginkgo, was planted at Eastcliff.

A most special new tree was planted in 2019 in honor of President Joan Gabel's inauguration. Her three children, Grace, Jack, and Luke, had a serviceberry tree planted as a housewarming gift to their mother.

THE POOL AND SUMMER HOUSE

The Eastcliff pool was a major source of entertainment—even before it was built. The first pool was built when Con and Ted were toddlers in 1923. In 1930, they were old enough that they, and their friends, found the excavation of the new larger pool to be exciting. "It was fascinating to watch," Ted said, "quite an event. Life was simple in those days. There wasn't much variety, but we had a lot of fun."[23]

A Daily Family Ritual

All the children must have started swimming when quite young, as Binky was four and Dwight only two when this description was written in 1931:

> The swimming pool is unusually large and is built so that there is a constant flow of fresh water. And if you think this pool is merely a thing of beauty, you should see the tiny four-year-old of the family executing all the intricate aquatic feats of a little mermaid, and watch the little gathering of four eager youngsters awaiting the daily appearance of their father for their regular mid-day swim. "Yes, we do it every day until the weather gets unbearably chilly," said Mr. Brooks.[24]

Just short of "unbearably chilly" sounds much colder than I could bear, particularly on days when the midday swim was moved to early morning. As Binky described it as an adult:

The first pool. Courtesy of the Brooks family.

The Brooks family, 1951. Courtesy of the Brooks family.

> Every spring we were just dying to get out in that swimming pool, which wasn't filled. We didn't keep it filled all the time because there was no filtering system or heat, or anything like that. My father said, "If I fill the pool, you will have to use it. You'll have to take a dip before breakfast every day." And that was enforced for everybody except Mother. She didn't have to do it, but we filled it in April . . . I can remember going out when there was frost on the grass.

Ted inserted, "I think it was slightly snowing one time when Father started going into the pool." Binky laughed and agreed, then continued:

> We just jumped across the corner. We'd just get in and be paralyzed— and hopefully get out.[25]

While the Brooks children loved the pool, and described using it "almost without intermission," there were a few less enjoyable activities associated with it. Ted described polishing the brass railing on the ladder at the deep end to earn his father's approval. The boys recalled that they polished the rail daily.

Although Edward was particular about the boys keeping the pool rails gleaming, Frannie Underwood recalled that he was less particular when the children were very small. As the first Eastcliff pool was close to the house, people would walk with wet feet right into the living room, to Markell's

Bathhouse and pool. Courtesy of the Brooks family.

dismay. Edward said, "We are not going to have any kind of rugs that we can't walk on and we're gonna walk on them and you are not going to tell them not to."[26]

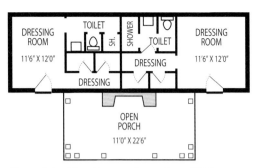

The original bathhouse floor plan, 1930. Drawn by the author from the C. H. Johnston original.

As the Brooks sons got older, throughout later childhood and adolescence, they were required not just to jump in but to swim laps every morning in the interests of health and vigor. They began the first week in May and continued until mid-October, unless the ice arrived first. Recall that the pool was *not* heated in those days, and breakfast was at 7:30 a.m. Ted wrote, "I can't say I'm any the worse for it, though this was emphatically not my sentiment at the time!"[27]

A bathhouse was constructed when the original pool was added in 1923. It was expanded to double its size (to thirteen by forty-one feet) in 1930. It backs onto Otis Avenue at the east edge of the property. The architectural plan from February 1930 labeled the structure a "playhouse," which may have been a fit description before the expansion, but the March 1930 "bathhouse" plan was adult oriented. It included separate entrances for men and women with a dressing room with cork floors and a bathroom with a shower and toilet on each side. The right (women's) side also included a room of dressing booths. The most striking feature of the building is the white-columned veranda with a big, open fireplace centered in the wall. This was designed for entertaining. Markell would host get-togethers by the pool in the late afternoons.

The fireplace in the bathhouse occasionally served a second purpose: it was a target for the Brooks boys during the 1940s. As the family told the story:

> As teenagers, Con and Ted played a lot of touch football on the lawn. They tried to kick the football across the swimming pool and into the fireplace. The games became quite competitive, and Ted, who was good at kicking, was sometimes able to hit the target three times. Once he kicked the football too high and broke a hexagonal Chinese lantern that hung from the ceiling; the glass shattered. The boys turned the lantern so that the broken pane didn't show and waited for their father

to be in a good mood before confessing. The inevitable confrontation with Edward followed.[28]

The placekicking practice came in handy later. Ted played football for Harvard University's Leverett House in the fall of 1942. The highlight of the season was their victory over Yale's Pierson College, thanks to Ted kicking a field goal from the fifteen-yard line at a side angle.

The 1930 Eastcliff pool had a drain and was refilled with fresh water as needed throughout the season. At some point the chlorine system was added. A heater was added in 1961, early in the Wilson administration. The pool was relined and new piping was added in 1974, at the end of the Moos administration.

One of the "wonderful conversations" Binky recalled on the Eastcliff terrace was with Piet Kolthoff and involved the Eastcliff pool. Izaak Maurits "Piet" Kolthoff was a professor of chemistry at the University from 1927 until 1962. He is considered the "father of modern analytical chemistry." As Binky described the conversation to me:

> Piet Kolthoff was at the University of Minnesota, and I used to go horseback riding with him. One night he was here having dinner on the terrace and my father looked at him and said, "You know a lot about chemistry—how much salt is there in the ocean?"
>
> He was riveted on making our pool salt water, and he was trying to find out how much salt to put in! He kept asking Piet Kolthoff, but I don't think he got a satisfactory answer. Then he used the encyclopedia.

In another conversation with her brothers,[29] Binky had elaborated: "He thought salt water was healing. My father wanted to convert our swimming pool water into an ocean. He looked it up in the encyclopedia: how much salt is there in the ocean? Of course, we know that it varies, it isn't always the same, but anyway, he picked some figure, and then based on that he ordered these barrels of salt to be delivered. Do you think there were two? At least two barrels."

"Oh, more than that," interjected her brothers. "There were a bunch of fifty-five-gallon (big) barrels."

"They came in the afternoon and then the boys came home from school," Binky continued. "It was all a very serious thing. They were corralled, told to go out to the pool right away. Get their suits on and bring their friends. And then they tipped over these big barrels of salt into the pool. The boys had to get in and kick to try and get it mixed in. And there was no perceptible difference at all. The ratio wasn't right." Binky said the boys kicked like crazy and got plenty of exercise, but the water didn't even taste salty.

Saltwater pools are now quite popular, so Edward was ahead of his time. The swimming pools actually have much lower concentrations of salt than ocean water. The problem was more likely that the salt didn't dissolve, rather than the ratio.

When they next drained the pool, it was very, very slow to drain. As Ted said, "It finally did it, at long last, and then the boys were put to work shoveling all this salt back out of the pool again. His experiment was an utter failure."

Edward was not necessarily dissuaded. Ted continued, "I can imagine Dad at our summer home on Gull Lake, looking out at the lake and thinking, 'I wonder . . .'"

Pool Parties

When I lived at Eastcliff, an event guest looked at me with a twinkle in her eyes and said, "Would you believe I was last here fifty years ago?" I replied, "I bet you were here in the swimming pool with the Wilson teenagers." Among the six Wilson children, there were two or three teens in the house throughout the Wilson presidency (1960–67), and the teens loved the Eastcliff pool. I had heard from others who still had happy memories from those times. I also heard that sneaking into neighborhood pools was a popular form of misbehavior during those days, and Eastcliff was a prime target. I found records stating that a "non-climbable twisted wire" (chain-link fence) was installed around the back of the pool in 1961, but an older gentleman told me he "knew where the hole was under the fence, and it's still there!" The entire fence was replaced with a wooden fence (without holes) in the 1980s.

The Moos children made frequent use of the pool. Monette Magrath learned to swim in the Eastcliff pool and enjoyed having girlfriends over for swim parties. Jesse Keller loved the pool, and his preschool class came for an end of year party. The Keller/Sindelirs hosted potluck pool parties for the president's office staff.

In July 1988, Interim President Richard Sauer may have had the largest non-teenager pool party at Eastcliff. He and his wife, Betty, held a party for sixty-three members of their family. The invitation read:

Join us for a day of fun fun
tennis, swimming, lounging in the sun
Touring of Eastcliff is allowed,
Visiting and laughter won't get too loud (maybe!).

The Hasselmos made use of the pool when their sons' families would join them for summer vacations. The Yudofs hosted deans and/or president's office staff each year for swimming, lawn games, and a cookout with Texas beef brisket or burgers and chicken. The Bruininks/Hagstrums and the Kalers continued having pool parties for the Morrill Hall staff each summer.

At the 2003 garden party, Susan Hagstrum spoke about the need to restore and preserve the bathhouse, as the pool house began to be called. Friends of Eastcliff sought donations to "protect and secure the structure, make certain the roof is sound, and repair holes in the eaves. This will include encouraging several of our furry friends to take up residence elsewhere." By 2008, the pool deck also required attention. The flagstone pavers, having lasted since 1930 and reset in the late 1990s, had become dangerously uneven. Renovation plans specified resetting the flagstone from the original pool surround into a concrete slab. With this plan, the flagstone appearance would remain, while making the surface flat and safe to use. This plan was likely too expensive, as a 2010 renovation replaced the flagstones with concrete. The swimming pool surface was also restored, and the diving board was removed. The bathhouse was renovated to be more in keeping as a venue for large, indoor/outdoor events rather than a place for family swimming. The two changing rooms with two bathrooms and showers were replaced with an open area and kitchenette for events, one handicap-accessible half bath, and one handicap-accessible shower.

During 2010 renovation, a sign reading "C. H. Johnston, Architects" was discovered. It currently hangs in the Eastcliff bathhouse.

The last event we had at Eastcliff was a wonderful pool party. It was during the time of the Brooks family annual meeting, which alternates between Minnesota and Oregon. Binky Brooks and some of Edward and Markell's grandchildren, great-grandchildren, and great-great-grandchildren came over to swim in the family pool.

THE TENNIS COURT

The tennis court was in the southeast corner of the property, nestled between the pool and the south edge of the property, with an east–west orientation. A tall (approximately twelve-foot) wire fence surrounded the court on three sides. At the east end (the back of the property next to Otis Avenue) was a practice wall, approximately ten feet tall, which also offered privacy. Over time, the fences were covered with vines.

> Almost every Saturday afternoon during the spring and early fall, the Tennis Club gathered at Eastcliff. It was a great day, and it included tennis and lunch at the pool. The games went on all afternoon. Late in the afternoon guests would go home to change, then return for dinner, this time dressed more formally for the evening. Hours and hours of dancing followed dinner. The music and laughter could be heard by the children, whose rooms were on the second floor. They frequently came out of their rooms onto the landing to watch the activities. Edward and Markell were known as outstanding hosts. Everyone loved a party at Eastcliff.[30]

Don't you wish you could have been there? The tennis court included a high judge's stand—I don't know if that is an indication that the tennis was serious, or if the stand was intended to add to the charm of the court. I suspect the latter.

Returning in the evening dressed for dinner seems particularly delightful. Ted said that, although Edward wasn't musical like Markell, he did love to dance. He particularly loved the tennis party dances.[31]

The Brooks children mentioned that it took two of them an hour and a half, three times a week, to roll the gravel court. The children didn't say they played tennis themselves.

In 1960, the tennis court had lines for both tennis and badminton. The court must not have been in good condition, because reconstruction began in August 1960, six months before the Wilson family moved in, and wasn't completed until May 1962.[32] The Wilson family moved in in February, and the two younger girls began sliding around on the frozen swimming pool. President Wilson suggested he might flood the tennis court the following winter to use as a skating rink. There is no written account of whether that happened.

The Moos children and their friends would play tennis regularly, then cool off with a swim. They have distinctly different memories of the tennis and pool parties: Kathy remembers eating cucumber sandwiches and talking about Kierkegaard, whereas Grant recalls a naked friend jumping off the roof of the pool house into the pool. The tennis court was used as an outdoor dining room on at least one occasion, when Tracy Moos hosted newspaper reporters for lunch.

Sandra Magrath described the tennis court as "somewhat sad-looking from lack of use."[33] If the tennis court had an emotional life, it was happy that the next president was a tennis player.

When accepting the position as president, Ken Keller was said to have joked, "Since I play tennis, I wouldn't have taken the job if the house hadn't had a court."[34] He may have been kidding on the square.

Ken and Bonita played tennis on the Eastcliff court and occasionally had guests over to play. One of the tennis-playing guests was former Gopher basketball coach George Hanson. After tennis, they had refreshments by the pool. According to Bonita, "George passed a plate to Jesse and said, 'Would you like some sausage?' Young Jesse's response: 'That's not sausage; that's paté.' Jesse learned to play tennis on that court (his mother patiently retrieving balls) and went on to play varsity tennis in school and to teach in the St. Paul Urban Tennis program."

Jesse also learned to ice skate at Eastcliff during December 1986 when his parents created a rink in the backyard. Jesse would have been barely four years old; he learned to ice skate holding onto a chair on the ice. Unlike tennis, this lesson was less formative, as only his sister (born after the Keller's Eastcliff years) became a hockey player.

The Hasselmo family made excellent use of the Eastcliff resort-like property when sons Peter and Michael and their families visited for summer vacations. They would all enjoy long days by the pool and walks across the Lake Street bridge to the nearby Dairy Queen. They set up a basketball hoop on the tennis court.

After Anna and Jim Williams married, they regularly joined Nils and Pat for Sunday evenings of tennis at Eastcliff or golf at the nearby Town and Country Club. Pat and Jim were both competitive in their tennis play. Pat would relish hitting the ball along the line to send Jim running.

Besides playing golf with the family, Pat played with her friend and neighbor Kaye Lillehei. The Town and Country Club hires a lot of college students; Anna knew a worker who shared that the golf cart with Mrs. Hasselmo and Mrs. Lillehei (Kaye doubtlessly wearing one of her famous hats) was always a popular sight at the club.

THE OVAL GARDEN

Although I have never lived in a home with a tennis court, I feel confident in saying that tennis courts, like swimming pools, need to be cared for or removed. After the turn of the twenty-first century, the tennis court deteriorated to the point that it was unusable. It was not only unsightly and would be expensive to refurbish, it was also causing drainage problems at Eastcliff and for the neighboring homes. With support from Friends of Eastcliff donors, particularly Robert and Deanna Sparboe, the area became a garden and event space.

In 2005, after the renovation of the terrace and addition of brick walkways, the dilapidated tennis court was removed and replaced with what was first planned as a literary walk but is now a sculpture garden. Bob Bruininks and Susan Hagstrum put up with heavy construction equipment and a dirt path through the front yard and around to the back for months. The beautiful end result was ready for the 2006 garden party.

The garden that replaced the tennis court contains a large oval brick walkway. The southwest corner has a large concrete sculpture by Charles Biederman. Outside the center of the oval to the south is a small semi-circular pool with a Haddenstone lion head fountain (similar to the now non-working fountain inside in the garden room). A brick wall with a trellis covered in nugget hops surrounds the fountain. In the back (east) center of the area is a sculpture by John Rood, backed by another brick wall covered by hops.

The rectangular outline of the former tennis court is retained by the fence on the south and east edges of the property and by hedges along the north and west edges of the former court. The pool fence with an arbor gate is behind the north hedge line. The tall hedge along the west edge became overgrown and full of dead branches and was replaced with a lower hedge of ninebark shrubs during our tenure.

Art and Romance in the Garden

All the sculptures at Eastcliff are on loan from the University's Weisman Art Museum. Their placement was supported by Friends of Eastcliff donations. The welded steel sculpture in the oval garden, *Landscape with Lakes,* by John Rood, was first installed at Eastcliff in 1996 in a different location, along with two other Rood sculptures and one by Katherine Nash.

John Rood, *Seated Figure*. Photograph by Patrick O'Leary. Courtesy of University Photographer records, University of Minnesota Archives.

Artist John Rood (1902–1974) didn't begin sculpting until 1933 but had his first solo exhibition at the Argent Gallery in New York in 1937, gaining a favorable review in the *New York Times*. In 1944, he was offered, by telegram, a position teaching sculpture at the University of Minnesota. He accepted immediately. He taught at the University for twenty years; after leaving, he exhibited in Milan and Rome. John Rood established a fund at what was then the University Gallery (now the Weisman Art Museum) for the purchase of sculpture by emerging artists. Several pieces acquired with that fund are now very important artworks of the museum's collection. In addition to the piece in the sculpture garden, Rood's sculpture *The Moon*, made of Indiana limestone, is in the Eastcliff north side yard, across from the dining room window. His *Seated Figure*, made of Alabama limestone, is by the porte co-chère door. Both were carved in 1949.

Katherine E. Nash's large stainless steel sculpture *Continuum* is in the Eastcliff front yard. Nash (1910–1982) was considered a feminist artist in the 1950s, and she established large-scale sculpture (welded steel and cast concrete) as a medium for women artists as well as men. She was a professor of sculpture at the University from 1963 to 1976. The Katherine E. Nash Gallery on the University's West Bank was named in her honor in 1979.

After success in New York and Chicago, artist Charles Biederman moved to Red Wing, Minnesota, in 1941. Weisman Art Museum director Lyndel King said that Biederman observed nature every day in Red Wing, and his intellectual abstract work was "revealing the structure of nature, and that's what he believed all art was about." Biederman was at Eastcliff for a dinner in his honor on December 27, 1991. The dinner, for thirty people, celebrated Biederman's bequest to the University Art Museum. Biederman was eighty-five at the time of the dinner, but fortunately he kept living—and working—for years afterward. Charles Biederman died in 2004 at age ninety-eight, and the work he retained in his own collection came to the University that year, including the piece at Eastcliff.

The sculptures at Eastcliff, particularly those by Biederman and Nash, are large—too large for a typical home—but they are smaller in scale than would be appropriate for the larger campus. At Eastcliff they are just right.

The oval garden is such a lovely setting, it could inspire romantic notions.

In March 2016, our younger son, Sam, asked Lizzy Shay to walk with him in the garden. They walked halfway around the oval, then he got down on one knee and proposed marriage.

There had been a "spark" between Sam and Lizzy when I introduced them at Eric's inauguration in September 2011. Lizzy, as Minnesota Student Association president, was supposed to be invited to lunch after the inauguration ceremony but had not received the invitation. When I saw her after the ceremony, I asked her if she was coming to lunch, and she politely deflected my question. I then introduced her to our son Sam, then to our son Charlie and his girlfriend (and future wife), Lisa Smith—but Lizzy's eyes never left Sam. Lizzy kindly offered to walk us over to the lunch location at the Carlson School.[35] Recognizing then that she had probably been invited to the luncheon, despite the waylaid invitation, she stayed for lunch and then by Sam's side the rest of the day.

The next day, Lizzy and two other student leaders gave speeches at Eric's portrait unveiling on the plaza in front of the student union. I noticed her scanning the crowd and told my mother, "That girl is looking for Sam. I think she really likes him." After that ceremony, Lizzy offered to give my mother a ride over to Morrill Hall. In a show of female solidarity, my mother asked, "Lizzy, do you have a boyfriend? My grandson Sam doesn't have a girlfriend, and he might be moving to Minnesota." The next day, Lizzy managed to find Sam in the Gopher football stadium, with a little help from

Sam's aunt Gail. Sam and Lizzy went out after the game with Sam's cousin Will and his future wife, Courtney.

Eric and I knew about all the family shenanigans of inauguration weekend. But Lizzy and Sam were discreet, and we didn't know how much they were seeing each other over the winter while Sam taught children to ski in Utah.[36] In the spring, after Lizzy finished her term as president and Sam found out he would be moving to South Dakota with his new job, we learned they were both dismayed that they would continue to live in separate states, so we understood the relationship had moved forward. Two years later, Sam transferred to a project in the Twin Cities.

In September 2015, Charlie and Lisa married in a beautiful ceremony by Lake Garda in Italy. Lisa's mother, Emilia, is from nearby Vincenza. Charlie and Lisa moved from California to St. Paul three months later. They were both at Eastcliff the day Sam proposed. When Lizzy came in from the oval garden wearing a diamond ring, Eric was the only one who was surprised. He was judged by the family as unable to keep the secret.

Lizzy loves and appreciates Eastcliff like I do, so I told her the story about Marney Brooks calling her mother from the Eastcliff phone room. She called her grandparents, Jon and Maricarol Wallace, who are alumni of the University, from the tiny room, albeit calling on her cell phone. While I don't know if Marney actually *did* call her mother from the phone room, I know for certain that Marney and Conley had a big party at Eastcliff the night before their wedding; Lizzy and Sam did the same.

Marney and Conley had about twenty-five guests in the living room on March 17, 1944; Lizzy and Sam had more than a hundred people in the Eastcliff backyard on July 21, 2017. The setting was beautiful, the weather was perfect, and, as the saying goes, a good time was had by all.

THE SIDE YARD

Dogs of Eastcliff

Near the south border of the property, even with the terrace walkway, there are two rows of raspberry bushes. Between the raspberries and the fence are three wooden headstones of the last three Brooks dogs at Eastcliff; the painted names read Rusty 1946–1959, Weenie 1936–1946, and Mugs 1930–1945. I had heard that one of the conditions for the gift of the house was that the dogs' graves were not to be disturbed. This condition is not mentioned anywhere in the gift agreement, or anywhere in writing. Rusty, in fact, died after the house was gifted but while Markell Brooks was still residing in Eastcliff.

The Brooks family had many dogs through the years. "We had two dachshunds, Weenie and Deacon," Binky told me. "Weenie was brown. The male was Deacon, he was a beautiful dog: black with this coral or orange fur down the center of his front. He was a wonderful dog, very noble. Something like *The* Deacon. They weren't allowed in the dining room, but they'd sit outside. They would sit up these *looong* bodies and beg at the entrance, just quietly sitting there. Mugs was an English springer spaniel. Rusty was an Irish water spaniel. He was just a wonderful dog." Mrs. Brooks had other Irish water spaniels after Rusty. Weenie and Mugs are in Brooks family portraits from the 1940s, and Rusty is in a family portrait from the 1950s.

The Brooks children with their dogs, circa 1935. Courtesy of the Brooks family.

Many other dogs, a few cats, and one pet pigeon have enjoyed the Eastcliff lawn. Our dogs loved the yard but were anxious around people they didn't know. While Spanish water dogs are known as swimmers, they were bred to herd sheep. Our two often

Dogs' graves on the Eastcliff grounds.

barked as if everyone they already knew, especially family members, were sheep and they suspected any stranger, particularly any tall man, of being a wolf.

When we first moved in, several University staff members were coming over to meet with us in the backyard. They were people I didn't know at the time but whom I came to admire over the years for their excellent care of Eastcliff, as well as other University facilities. It was my first opportunity to see if the dogs could overcome their inherent shyness and begin getting used to people they might see later. We had three dogs with us at the time, our two as well as our son's dog. We got Mo (short for Erasmo) as a puppy when we lived in a house on four acres in Delaware, not expecting we would be moving several times during his life. A friend met our sweet Mo and wanted a dog just like him. Her husband was not like-minded and named the dog Salida, meaning "exit" in Spanish. Six weeks later, we got Salida, whom we called Lida; I said we got our puppy a puppy. Two years later, Sam got Illi.

Mo and Lida. Courtesy of the Kaler family.

In the summer of 2011, Sam was in a study-abroad program, and we had Illi for the summer. Illi and Lida are half sisters; they share the same mother, who was named Reina ("queen" in Spanish) for her bossy attitude. There was sibling rivalry. They would get along happily until the wrong one walked through the door first, then there was a dogfight.

Back to the Eastcliff meeting: I walked out to join everyone with all three dogs on leashes. So far, so good.

Eric offered to take a leash, but unfortunately the leash he took was attached to Illi. Lida, the older sister, took offense at the special attention her little sister was receiving and snarled. Illi, the younger sister, did not take kindly to criticism and snapped back. In a split second, we had a full-blown dogfight on the ends of the leashes, with both dogs rearing up on their hind legs and going at each other full steam. Eric and I dragged the dogs apart.

I was still holding both Mo and Lida, so Mo decided to scold Lida in the way that dogs do to display dominance. Yes, he hopped right on top of her and started humping vigorously. I pulled those two apart, then grabbed Illi's leash and rushed the three dogs down the sidewalk and quickly back into the house. As I hurried away, I could hear Eric remark, "Entertainment at the Kalers. We feature both sex *and* violence."

That was the first and last time I introduced the dogs to a group of strangers. Shortly after this incident, I hired a behaviorist to see what could be done. (We joked that Mo kept the University's excellent Vet Med program in business. Following the behaviorist, and in addition to regular care, he saw a urologist, orthopedist, neurologist, oncologist, and acupuncturist.) From the behaviorist, I learned that Mo had too much anxiety to ever enjoy being around strangers. Many people behave in a way that is threatening to dogs. "How would you feel," she explained, "if a large stranger bent over you, stuck his fist in your face, and said 'Hello, sweetie'?"

Since we couldn't train strangers to ignore the dogs, and we couldn't train the dogs to ignore strangers, we kept our pets locked away in a large closet upstairs when we had guests. I hung framed photographs of the dogs in a first-floor half bath so that those interested could see what they looked like.

The beautiful front staircase at Eastcliff is open to the upstairs, so sound travels. To appease my own need for privacy, I would pretend that workers couldn't hear me shushing the dogs and couldn't hear me walking down the hall. It was hard to pretend they couldn't hear the dogs running down the hall, as the two of them could manage to sound like a herd of buffalo. I'll admit that on one or two or, well, maybe ten occasions at most, we used that to our advantage. Every so often, a few guests would linger long past the end of an event. Eric and I would finally say goodnight and head upstairs, but the servers hired for the event couldn't finish cleaning and go home if the guests didn't depart. Eric would let the dogs out of their confinement, and the thundering paws and excited yelps would send lingering guests out the door.

I've made it a point to list the names of family pets throughout the book. While our eight years at Eastcliff were a wonderful, significant portion of our lives, those eight years were the majority of our dogs' lives. Mo died a few months after we moved out of Eastcliff, shortly before his fourteenth birthday. Lida slowed down without her companion but made it to almost sixteen before she died in Cleveland in 2021.

The first Eastcliff story I heard was about Rusty, and I have saved that story for last. Susan Hagstrum was the first to tell me about the infamous Brooks family dog, and then I was regularly either told the story by others or asked to tell it myself. For example, when I was asked to speak at an event for the University Retirees Volunteer Center, I asked on what topic. "Just tell the story about Rusty" was the reply. That happened again and again.

The story, as it evolved over the times I heard it, is this: Mrs. Brooks had a dog named Rusty. (Some might include the detail that he was a golden retriever—although he wasn't.) Rusty would escape the yard and go swimming in the nearby St. Thomas College pool. Mrs. Brooks was trying to decide what to do with Eastcliff: Should she donate it to the University of Minnesota? Or to St. Thomas? One morning she said to herself, "Today is the day I shall decide!" Then the phone rang. It was a priest from St. Thomas, and he yelled at her that Rusty was in the pool again. That did it. The University of Minnesota got Eastcliff!

While people loved that story, it didn't ring true to me. I had come to greatly admire Markell Brooks from all I knew to be true of her. I couldn't picture her being so frivolous as to make an important decision on the spur of the moment. The family had connections to the University of Minnesota: Edward Brooks's brother had graduated from the University, as had both of Marney's parents. Ted was a big fan of University of Minnesota football in the 1930s and 40s, and later got his PhD from the University. One of the Brooks grandsons had lifesaving heart surgery at the University—pioneering surgery in 1958 by Dr. Walton Lillehei, who lived nearby on Otis Avenue.

At the time, St. Thomas College, which later became St. Thomas University, allowed only priests as presidents, so the president wouldn't have the family that Mrs. Brooks envisioned in Eastcliff. Brooks family members were Unitarian, Congregationalist (later UCC), Presbyterian, and Buddhist,

Rusty. Courtesy of the Brooks family.

but not Catholic.[37] And I didn't really think a priest would call and yell at Mrs. Brooks.

Searching for Rusty's story introduced me to other Eastcliff stories and led to further research.

Conley Jr. told me that after the Brooks family had donated Eastcliff to the University of Minnesota, but prior to moving out, Mrs. Brooks had a dinner party attended by the St. Thomas president. Mrs. Brooks joked to him that if Rusty had stayed on the swim team, she might have given the house to the College of St. Thomas.

I learned from a videotape interview with Judy Yudof where the wider legend began. Judy asked about "the dog with the swishy tail."

Conley began, "Ted told the story in front of the Regents at the twenty-fifth anniversary of the University receiving the house. I think you're the one that ought to tell the story, Ted." Ted complied.

Well, it involved an Irish water spaniel named Rusty, a wonderful dog. My father just adored him—we all did.

It became Rusty's habit to wander up to St. Thomas—what was St. Thomas College then, on Summit and Cretin—and find his way to the swimming pool. That, of course, is where the St. Thomas swimming team practiced, and Rusty became a fast friend of the St. Thomas College swimming team.

I guess he was actually *lured* into the water on more than one occasion. He did a fifty-yard dash in record time. This practice went on— too long.

The monsignor called my mother one day on the phone and said, "Mrs. Brooks, you know, we have always enjoyed wonderful relations with the Brookses, but, uh, um, I must mention a situation that is frankly becoming intolerable. It involves Rusty. We're going to, I'm afraid, have to ask that you not allow Rusty to come on to the St. Thomas College premises anymore—because he disrupts swimming practice and the coach gets very mad."

I made the observation after telling that to the Regents, "Geez, you know if the Monsignor had been nicer about it, they might have gotten Eastcliff instead of the University of Minnesota."

There you have it. The true story.

When asked why they gave the house to the University, Binky said her mother considered an orphanage, a school, and other possibilities over several months, but the University seemed the best option. Ted added that he believed that Edward's close friendship with Dr. Arthur Strachauer was a factor. There was a "feeling of reverence, almost, for the medical establishment at the University."

"The University of Minnesota was an entity that would agree to keeping it as a president's house," Conley added. "There was no problem to sell the house, because they could tear the house down and it was a beautiful piece of property. But she wasn't going to do that. And she wasn't going to sell the house to someone who would cut it up into apartments or something like that. Her feeling was if she couldn't find the ideal place to give it, she would tear it down."

On December 8, 1983, Peter and Diane Magrath hosted "A Celebration of Eastcliff" in honor of the twenty-fifth anniversary of the gift of Eastcliff by the Brooks family. This is the event where Ted told Rusty's story. The invitation to that event, along with a certificate of appreciation from the University, are included among the curated papers in the Brooks archive at the Minnesota Historical Society.[38]

I was touched that the family saved the invitation, literally for posterity. I interpret that as the Brookses valuing the ongoing relationship between their family, Eastcliff, and the presidential families as much as we do. The certificate of appreciation reads, in part:

> Eastcliff, as a gift of goodwill, has helped to humanize the University, welcome—with open arms—all those who care about the institution, and at the same time has provided a unique retreat for each President's family. High atop the east cliff of the mighty Mississippi, Eastcliff stands tall and proud as a symbol of the generous spirit of a remarkable Minnesota family for the good of a great University and all people.

Epilogue
STILL GOOD STORIES

LIKE MANY OTHERS, I have delighted in the stories about Rusty, the Brooks family dog. A couple of years after I had begun research for this book, our beautiful granddaughter, Ophelia, was born. While rocking her, I felt compelled to write Rusty's story as a children's book. I titled it *Rusty Goes Swimming* and gave copies to special Friends of Eastcliff.

One couple told me they loved the book. "But why," the husband asked, "didn't you tell the part about the priest yelling at Mrs. Brooks, and that's why the University got the house?"

I replied, "Well, because it's not really true."

"Yes," he agreed, "but it's a good story!"

"It *is* a good story, but I think the truth is a *better* story."

When I was a little girl, before I knew better, I would correct my father when he, a talented Southern storyteller, would change the details of a story as I knew them. "Karen," he would say, "you shouldn't let the facts get in the way of a good story." I was intrigued by many good stories about Eastcliff, but in this book I endeavored to present facts.

Even though the peacock room was a powder room, not a Prohibition bar (I was eager to believe that myth), isn't it charming that Edward Brooks took such delight in, and spent so much money creating, a room for women to enjoy at Eastcliff events?

There really were gangsters nearby, including John Dillinger and Ma Barker, who was portrayed as a criminal mastermind. The legends about Ma Barker likely began because it was unseemly for an elderly lady to die of multiple FBI-inflicted gunshot wounds, with no evidence to support her being a genius of any kind.

Marney Brooks didn't call her mother from the telephone at Eastcliff to announce her engagement, because her mother and Markell arranged the engagement, then

Edward jumped the gun announcing it in the newspaper. In this case, I think the true story is more charming than the legend.

Clarence Howard Johnston Sr. did not design Eastcliff, but his son did while working in his architectural firm, so it is correct to say that C. H. Johnston Sr. was the architect of record as he was head of the firm.

Eastcliff has nine fireplaces, but the wealthy Brooks family did not need to burn scrap lumber for heat.

Katharine Hepburn didn't spend the night at Eastcliff, with or without Clark Gable, but she did visit Eastcliff and made real connections with its residents. Clark Gable likely did too.

There aren't holes in the fence that allowed unrestricted swimming for trespassers during the past seventy years, but friends of the Wilson teens had good times and made good memories at the Eastcliff pool.

Tracy Moos didn't panel the basement with wood recovered from an old pig barn, but she convinced a lot of people that she did.

Ken Keller didn't spend $600,000 on a kitchen, but Keller-era renovations enhanced University events for many years—and more years to come.

Markell Brooks didn't give Eastcliff to the University of Minnesota because a priest yelled at her, but Rusty did love to swim.

Chronology of Eastcliff

1920 Edward Brooks and Markell Conley are married on April 5.

1921 Edward and Markell Brooks buy land at 176 North River Boulevard on May 20. Clarence Howard Johnston Jr. creates the architectural drawings of the house that will become Eastcliff (plans dated August 1921; revised September 12). Construction begins.

Conley Brooks is born on September 16.

1922 The Edward Brooks House is finished, and the young family moves in.

Edward "Ted" Brooks Jr. is born on November 8.

1923 A swimming pool (north–south orientation) and bathhouse are built.

1926 The first addition to the house (with plans drawn by Johnston) is an expansion of the south porch to the east and, above it, a second floor sleeping porch.

Anna Markell "Binky" Brooks is born on October 23.

1929 Dwight Frederick Brooks II is born on April 23.

1930 A major structural remodel (with plans drawn by Johnston) includes a peacock-design powder room replacing the telephone room; a new telephone room replacing a hallway that connected the front entry hall to the den; an expansion of the two second floor maids' rooms and bath into two guest rooms, a larger bath, and a half bath; an addition of a sunroom near the guest rooms; a remodel of the attached garage into three bedrooms for maids; an addition of a two-story (plus basement) carriage house (five-stall garage on ground level, three-bedroom apartment above); an enlargement of the pool house; and a new larger swimming pool is added further back on the property (east–west orientation).

1934	The master bathroom is remodeled.
1935	More work is completed from the 1930 plans, including paneling and bookshelves in two bedrooms. The second floor of the garage is furnished as family quarters. Edward's screen porch is remodeled into a bedroom/sitting room.
1936	Built-in bookcases are added to the living room.
1937	C. H. Johnston Jr. creates architectural drawings to expand the dining room (this extension was never built). Built-in bookshelves are added to one bedroom, and paneling is added to another bedroom.
1938	The sunroom is refinished.
1944	Conley Brooks and Margaret "Marney" Brown's pre-wedding dinner is held at Eastcliff on March 17; they marry the next day.
1945	Conley Brooks Jr. is born on November 11. His first home is the Eastcliff carriage house.
1954	Binky Brooks and John Krafchuk marry on April 18, followed by a reception at Eastcliff.
	Edward Brooks dies at Eastcliff on December 8.
1958	Markell Brooks donates Eastcliff to the University of Minnesota.
1960	Markell Brooks moves to Long Lake, Minnesota.
1960–61	Eastcliff is renovated to be the official residence of the president of the University. Renovations include a kitchen remodel with new electric appliances, a vinyl floor, a double refrigerator, and a double freezer; a sauna with a shower and dressing room in the basement; Goodyear rubber tile in the bathroom between two bedrooms upstairs; and new paint and carpet (off-white) throughout the house.
	O. Meredith Wilson, the University's ninth president, and family move into Eastcliff in February.
1961–64	Renovations during the first years of the Wilson administration include a new roof on the carriage house; a new pool heater and a "non-climbable twisted wire" (chain-link fence) around the back of the pool; reconstruction of the tennis court; a humidifier, single and double boiler installation, and a hot water heater; and a new heating system in the carriage house.
1965	Constance (Connie) Wilson and David Bennion marry at Eastcliff on December 27.

1967   Mary Ann Wilson and John Hansen marry on June 24, followed by a reception at Eastcliff.

The Wilson family moves out. The family of Malcolm Moos, the University's tenth president, moves in.

The amusement room fireplace in the basement is surfaced with hand-split fieldstone.

1968   The amusement room walls are paneled with wood. Plans are drawn for a large addition to Eastcliff, principally a dining room extending into the back yard. A construction loan is secured for $70,000, but the addition is never built.

1970   The first-floor powder room is remodeled. The second-floor bathroom and the closets between two bedrooms upstairs are remodeled into two full bathrooms.

1974   The swimming pool receives new piping and is relined inside.

The Moos family moves out.

C. Peter Magrath, the University's eleventh president, and Sandra Magrath move in.

1977   Peter and Sandra Magrath divorce.

1978   C. Peter Magrath and Diane Faye Skomars marry on March 25 at Eastcliff. Diane and daughter, Monette, move in.

1983   The bathroom between two bedrooms upstairs (formerly called the boys' bathroom) is renovated.

1984   A task force recommends that Eastcliff be renovated, including an enlarged dining room and catering kitchen, an upgraded electrical system, and air conditioning. A security system is installed.

The Magrath family moves out in November.

1985   The family of Kenneth H. Keller, the University's twelfth president, moves in in July.

Dining room expansion plans are drawn by Leonard Parker Associates in October.

1986   A new chiller and ceiling air ducts are added for air conditioning.

1987   Renovations include the addition of a catering kitchen, a dining room expansion, a terrace renovation, and exterior cleaning and painting.

1988   The Keller/Sindelir family moves out.

1989   Nils Hasselmo, the University's thirteenth president, moves in, joined a few months later by spouse, Patricia, and daughter, Anna Hasselmo.

1990	Mississippi River Boulevard is rerouted immediately south of the Lake Street/Marshall Avenue bridge. The driveway entrance to Eastcliff moves to Dayton Avenue.
1991	The first-floor bathroom by the dining room is remodeled to be wheelchair accessible.
1992	One hundred Eastcliff windows are replaced, providing better insulation.
1994	Acoustical improvements (new noise-absorbing ceiling tiles) are added in the dining room. A carriage house renovation feasibility study is completed.
1996	Anna Hasselmo and Jim Williams marry on April 20, followed by a reception at Eastcliff.
	The driveway along the east–west wing of the house is removed and replaced with a horseshoe driveway off Dayton Avenue in the front, a sidewalk, plants, trees, and a wheelchair accessible entryway.
	Sculptures by Katherine Nash and John Rood are installed on the grounds.
1997	The Hasselmo family moves out.
	Eastcliff is renovated, including adding wallpaper to the entry, the dining room, two guestrooms, and all bathrooms except the first-floor powder room; replacing light fixtures and furniture in the living room and garden room; refinishing all wood floors; adding a washer and dryer to a second-floor closet; adding a bookcase to the master bedroom sitting room/office (Edward's room); replacing the roof and gutter; and painting the exterior.
	Mark G. Yudof, the University's fourteenth president, and spouse, Judy Yudof, move in.
1998	Fire detection and alarm systems are upgraded; fire damage is repaired in the attic, the Waller suite, and the office below. The basement is renovated with oak benches and bookshelves, and a powder room replaces the bar. The fireplace is returned to its original design. The guestroom half bath is replaced with a small kitchenette with a sink and mini refrigerator.
1999	A new roof of fireproof cedar shingles, attic insulation, and a new irrigation system in the yard are added.
2000	Eastcliff is added to the National Register of Historic Places.
2001	An elevator and a perimeter (grounds) security system are added.
2002	The Yudof family moves out.
	Robert H. Bruininks, the University's fifteenth president, and spouse, Susan Hagstrum, move in.
2004	A new brick terrace, including walkways and a rose garden, is installed.

2005–6   The tennis court is removed and replaced with an oval sculpture garden. A sculpture by Charles Biederman is added to the grounds.

2007   HVAC and mechanical systems are improved.

2008   Plans are made for the renovation of the swimming pool and bathhouse.

2011   The swimming pool, pool patio, and bathhouse are renovated. The Bruininks/Hagstrum family moves out. A bedroom upstairs is converted into a family kitchen.

Eric W. Kaler, the University's sixteenth president, and spouse, Karen F. Kaler, move in.

2012   The shingles on the roof of the house and the carriage house are replaced.

2016   The Eastcliff chiller is replaced.

2017   Samuel Kaler and Elizabeth "Lizzy" Shay's pre-wedding party is held at Eastcliff on July 21; they marry the next day.

2018   An electrical transfer switch is installed, which allows the use of a generator for emergency power.

2019   The Kaler family moves out.

Eastcliff's heating and electrical systems are updated, replacing two gas-fired boilers from the 1960s. Cloth-insulated wiring, including some from the original 1920s construction, is replaced. The event lawn is refurbished, and the home's sound system is upgraded.

Joan T. A. Gabel, the University's seventeenth president, moves in, joined a few months later by spouse, Gary, and sons, Jack and Luke Gabel.

2020   Eastcliff is closed for events beginning in March due to the coronavirus pandemic.

2022   Eastcliff celebrates its centennial year.

Eastcliff Guest List

Many special guests have visited Eastcliff, perhaps including you! This list is not exhaustive, but it seems better to risk leaving someone out rather than not include a list at all. Guests marked with an asterisk are alumni of the University of Minnesota.

EDDIE ALBERT* Best known for his leading performance in television's *Green Acres*, Eddie Albert received two Academy Award nominations for best supporting actor and had a very successful career on stage and screen. He was at Eastcliff when Ken Keller and Bonita Sindelir hosted a small dinner for six on September 22, 1986. Albert and actress Ann Sothern were both in the class of 1926 at Minneapolis Central High School. Albert studied business, not acting, at the University of Minnesota. News journalist and author Eric Sevareid graduated from Minneapolis Central and the University of Minnesota four years after Albert did. The musician Prince is the most famous recent graduate (1976) of Minneapolis Central. The school closed in 1982.

ANN-MARGRET Anna Hasselmo remembers internationally famous Swedish-born actress Ann-Margret visiting Eastcliff, as well as visits of many other well-known Swedes during Nils Hasselmo's presidency. From February through April 1993, the actress was in Minnesota filming with Walter Matthau and Jack Lemmon. Ann-Margret toured the American Swedish Institute and spoke Swedish with some of its guests.

DOMINICK ARGENTO Dominick Argento was a renowned composer of operatic and choral music who taught music theory and composition in the University's music department for many years. He received a Grammy Award in 2004 and the Pulitzer Prize for music in 1975. He attended an event at Eastcliff in 2004 to celebrate the publication of his memoir, *Catalogue Raisonné As Memoir*. Soprano Maria Jette performed in the living room at Eastcliff during the event.

EARL BAKKEN* Earl Bakken founded Medtronic and invented the portable pacemaker. He visited Eastcliff several times. At an Eastcliff event in 1997, Dr. Bakken and Dr. Walt Lillehei were honored together on the fortieth anniversary of the pacemaker.

LOU BELLAMY* Director, actor, and founder of Penumbra Theatre Company, Lou Bellamy visited Eastcliff in 1993.

Charles Biederman Artist Charles Biederman was at Eastcliff for a dinner in his honor in 1991.

Norman Borlaug* Norman Borlaug, who received his BS, MS, and PhD from the University of Minnesota, was an agronomist whose advances in agriculture created the Green Revolution. He was credited with saving more than a billion people from starvation worldwide, and he won the Nobel Peace Prize in 1970. He attended a dinner at Eastcliff hosted by Nils and Pat Hasselmo in his honor in 1992, with leaders in the Twin Cities food industry, including executives from General Mills, Green Giant, Pillsbury, Minneapolis Grain Exchange, Cargill, and Northrup King. A statue of Dr. Borlaug on the St. Paul campus, facing the Borlaug building in Siehl Plaza, is a casting of the statue in Statuary Hall in the U.S. Capitol Building. Although the statue represents Iowa, it includes Borlaug's University of Minnesota ring. (University of Minnesota Professor Maria Sanford is one of the two statues there representing Minnesota.)

Herb Brooks The head coach of the 1980 gold-medal U.S. Olympic hockey team was a guest at Eastcliff.

Phillip Brunelle* Conductor and founder of VocalEssence, Phillip Brunelle visited Eastcliff in 1999.

Carol Channing American actress, singer, dancer, and comedian, Carol Channing is best known for her performance in the 1964 Broadway musical *Hello, Dolly!*, for which she won a Tony Award.

Noel Coward Englishman Noel Coward was considered the world's most successful living playwright in the 1930s. His plays are still performed today, ninety years later. He was also an actor, director, composer, and singer, and he had a reputation for being exceptionally charming. He visited Edward and Markell Brooks at Eastcliff.

Seymour Cray* Seymour Cray, known as "the father of supercomputing," attended an event at Eastcliff in 1987.

Dalai Lama *See* **Tenzin Gyatso.**

Agnes de Mille Dancer and choreographer Agnes de Mille was a guest of Nils and Pat Hasselmo at Eastcliff.

Edo de Waart Dutch conductor Edo de Waart has been with the New York Philharmonic, the Netherlands Wind Ensemble and Rotterdam Philharmonic Orchestra, the San Francisco Symphony, and the Sydney Symphony Orchestra. He was music director of the Minnesota Orchestra when he visited Eastcliff in 1987.

William Dickey Baseball player Bill Dickey was a catcher for the New York Yankees for nineteen seasons, and he was player/coach during his last season in 1946. He played from 1928 to 1943, then served in the U.S. Navy in World War II. He was named an All-Star in eleven seasons. He was a guest of Edward and Markell Brooks in the early 1930s.

VIGDÍS FINNBOGADÓTTIR President Finnbogadóttir of Iceland visited Eastcliff during her presidency. Ms. Finnbogadóttir was the world's first directly democratically elected female president and served as president of Iceland from 1980 to 1996. She visited the Magraths at Eastcliff while she was president, and she visited the Yudofs at Eastcliff in 2002. (When Eric and Karen Kaler met her in Reykjavik in 2017, Ms. Finnbogadóttir spoke of her lovely visits at Eastcliff.)

FLOYD OF ROSEDALE This ninety-eight-pound bronze pig football rivalry trophy was a special guest at an agricultural leaders' breakfast shortly after Floyd's 2014 return to Minnesota. With the University Meat Lab's delicious Gopher Gold bacon on the menu, and Floyd in attendance, the Minnesota Pork Producers Association, the Minnesota Pork Board, and Minnesota Pork had every right to be proud. Before the Iowa–Minnesota football game in 1935, Minnesota Governor Floyd Olson sent Governor Herring of Iowa a telegram in which he proposed the bet of a Minnesota prize hog against an Iowa prize hog: the loser must deliver the hog in person to the winner. The Gophers won thirteen to six, and Governor Herring got a live pig from Rosedale Farms and walked the pig into Governor Olson's carpeted office. The pig was sent to live peacefully on a farm. Governor Olson commissioned a bronze sculpture in Floyd's likeness, and the football teams fight for the right to Floyd each year. So far, the Gophers lead overall, 62-51-2.

CLARK GABLE "King of Hollywood" Clark Gable was a leading man in more than sixty movies, and he won an Academy Award for best actor in *It Happened One Night* in 1934. He is arguably best known for playing Rhett Butler in *Gone with the Wind* in 1939. He visited Edward and Markell Brooks at Eastcliff.

ALEXANDER BORISOVICH GODUNOV Alexander Godunov was the premier dancer with the Bolshoi Ballet. In 1979, he defected to the United States and joined the American Ballet Theatre (ABT). He visited Eastcliff with the ABT as a guest of Peter and Diane Magrath.

PETER GRAVES* Actor Peter Graves, best known for the television series *Mission Impossible* and the movies *Airplane!* and *Airplane II*, visited Eastcliff for lunch in 1979 and for a dinner in his honor in 1982.

TENZIN GYATSO The Fourteenth Dalai Lama, Tenzin Gyatso, visited Eastcliff in 2001, and again in 2011.

KATHARINE HEPBURN An actress whose career spanned sixty years, Katharine Hepburn won a record four Academy Awards for lead acting performances. She visited the Brooks family at Eastcliff in 1940.

THEODORE HESBURGH Father Theodore Hesburgh was the president of the University of Notre Dame for thirty-five years and was considered one of the leading educators in the United States. Diane Skomars Magrath fondly recalls a dinner at Eastcliff when she was seated next to Father Hesburgh and was inspired by him and his belief that the world was still a place where kindness could prevail.

PRINCE HITACHI Prince Hitachi of Japan visited Eastcliff in April 2001. He received an honorary degree from the University for his work as a research associate of the Japanese Foundation for Cancer Research. One of the requirements for a princely visit was a private waiting room with restroom, which was achieved in the walnut den. The prince spoke in the living room.

STANLEY S. HUBBARD* Chairman and CEO of Hubbard Broadcasting, and founder of United States Satellite Broadcasting, Stanley Hubbard and his wife, Karen, are good friends of the University of Minnesota and of Eastcliff.

HUBERT H. HUMPHREY JR.* Hubert H. Humphrey was the mayor of Minneapolis (1945–48), a U.S. Senator from Minnesota (1949–64; 1971–78), the thirty-eighth vice president of the United States (1965–69), and the Democratic Party's nominee for president in 1968. He visited his college friend Malcolm Moos and joined the Moos family at a Gopher football game while he was running for president in 1968. Humphrey later taught at the University.

LOUIS IGNARRO* Nobel Laureate Louis J. Ignarro attended a breakfast in his honor at Eastcliff in 1998, very soon after he won the Nobel Prize in Physiology/Medicine. Dr. Ignarro holds a doctorate in pharmacology from the University of Minnesota.

GARRISON KEILLOR* Author and radio personality Garrison Keillor attended several events at Eastcliff.

HELEN A. KELLER Helen Keller was the first blind and deaf person to earn a college undergraduate degree (at Radcliffe College of Harvard University). She became an author, lecturer, and political activist. She visited the Brooks family at Eastcliff.

AMY KLOBUCHAR U.S. Senator from Minnesota, Amy Klobuchar was a guest of Eric and Karen Kaler at a winter celebration party at Eastcliff. Ms. Klobuchar campaigned for the Democratic nomination for U.S. president in 2020. Her memoir is titled *The Senator Next Door.*

IZAAK MAURITS (PIET) KOLTHOFF Piet Kolthoff, the "father of modern analytical chemistry," was a professor of chemistry at the University from 1927 until 1962. He visited the Brooks family at Eastcliff.

BRUNO KREISKY Austrian Chancellor Bruno Kreisky joined the Magraths for dinner at Eastcliff in 1977, during his thirteen-year tenure as the leader of Austria. Chancellor Kreisky was visiting the University to donate a million dollars for a Center for Austrian Studies. The University was selected in a competition for the award.

ERIKA LEE Professor Lee is director of the Immigration History Research Center at the University of Minnesota. Her book *America for Americans: A History of Xenophobia in the United States* becomes increasingly timely.

C. WALTON LILLEHEI, MD* The renowned heart surgeon known as "the father of open-heart surgery," Walt Lillehei lived a short walk from Eastcliff on Otis Lane. He had four degrees from the University of Minnesota and was a faculty member. He visited Eastcliff many times, and his wife, Kaye Lillehei, was a faithful docent; she volunteered at Eastcliff dozens of times and was a close friend to Pat Hasselmo. (During the Magrath, Hasselmo, and Bruininks administrations, docents gave tours of the house and grounds and assisted guests at events.)

John* and Nancy* Lindahl   The Lindahls (known widely by just "John and Nancy") are loyal alumni and wonderful friends to the University. John's mother was on staff at the University's Institute of Child Development; Nancy's parents, Ralph and Betty Miller, were both on faculty when they met in Northrop Auditorium. Nancy's mother was so honored to attend events at Eastcliff that she saved all of the invitations she had received through the years and tied them together with a ribbon. John and Nancy are frequent guests at Eastcliff.

Harvey Mackay*   Best-selling author, motivational speaker, business coach, and business owner Harvey Mackay and his wife, Carol Ann, are good friends of the University. He most notably visited Eastcliff in celebration of his University of Minnesota Outstanding Achievement Award in 2008.

Warren MacKenzie   University of Minnesota art professor Warren MacKenzie has been described as one of America's greatest potters. While he always insisted he was making "everyday pots" to use in daily life, his work is now in many major museums throughout the world.

Rhonda Fleming Mann   Rhonda Fleming was an actress and singer. She acted in more than forty films, mostly in the 1940s and 1950s, and also had guest-starring roles on television in the 1950s and 1960s. She was known as one of the most glamorous actresses of her day. She was married to University alumnus Ted Mann for twenty-four years until his death in 2001.

Ted Mann*   Businessman and theater owner Ted Mann began "collecting" theaters while still a student at the University. In 1993, a beautiful campus music building was named the Ted Mann Concert Hall in his honor. At an Eastcliff dinner to celebrate the dedication, he and his wife, actress and singer Rhonda Fleming Mann, joined Nils and Pat Hasselmo. Among the other guests were Governor and Mrs. Elmer Andersen, Curtis and Arleen Carlson, John and Sage Cowles, Thomas and Ellie Crosby, Skip and Barbie Gage, Stanley and Karen Hubbard, Joan Kroc, Charles Lowe and actress Carol Channing, Robert and Polly McCrea, Morton and Pauline Phillips (known as Abigail Van Buren, author of "Dear Abby"), George and Sally Pillsbury, Carl and Eloise Pohlad, John and Rosemary Raitt, Vern and Phyllis Sutton, and Mann's grandchildren, John Brendan and Blythe Brendan. Blythe, who is a good friend of the University and particularly its children's hospital, remembers that the dedication was especially meaningful to her as she heard her grandfather sing with his wife. John Raitt also sang, but Blythe recalls that even Raitt said that Mann sang better.

Ann Masten   University of Minnesota professor Ann Masten in the Institute of Child Development researched resilience in highly mobile children and developed strategies to help children facing trauma and adversity. She is the author of *Ordinary Magic: Resilience in Development*.

DAVID MCCULLOUGH Author David McCullough came to a dinner party in his honor hosted by the Bruininks/Hagstrums in 2003, the night before he gave the Guy Stanton Ford Memorial Lecture on campus. At that time McCullough had already received the Pulitzer Prize twice for his books *John Adams* and *Truman,* and he was then working on a book about the American Revolution, which became *1776.* In 2006, he was awarded the Presidential Medal of Freedom.

DANIEL MCFADDEN* Dan McFadden, who received his BS in physics and PhD in economics at the University, visited Eastcliff several times with his wife, Beverlee. He won the Nobel Memorial Prize in Economic Sciences in 2000.

KATE MILLETT* Author and feminist pioneer Kate Millett, whose influential book *Sexual Politics* began as her doctoral thesis, was awarded an honorary doctorate at Eastcliff in 2014.

MINNESOTA TWINS A luncheon and press conference for the Danny Thompson Memorial Research Fund for leukemia research (and the associated golf tournament) was hosted by Nils and Pat Hasselmo at Eastcliff on November 1, 1996. Harmon Killebrew, who established the fund, was unable to attend, but other Minnesota Twins greats including Rod Carew, Kirby Puckett, and Paul Molitor* attended. Kirby Puckett had been at Eastcliff seventeen months prior for a luncheon with Puckett Scholars; Kirby and Tonya Puckett were the benefactors for this scholarship. Paul Molitor returned in 2005 when he received an Outstanding Achievement Award.

DIMITRI MITROPOULOS Greek conductor and composer Dimitri Mitropoulos achieved international fame. He was principal conductor of the Minneapolis Symphony Orchestra from 1937 to 1949 before he moved to the New York Philharmonic. He was a guest of Edward and Markell Brooks at Eastcliff.

WALTER F. "FRITZ" MONDALE* Walter Mondale was a lawyer, a diplomat, a U.S. Senator from Minnesota (1964–76), the forty-second vice president of the United States (1977–81), and the Democratic Party's nominee for president in 1984. He visited Eastcliff multiple times as a wonderful, and humble, University citizen.

CHESTER MORRIS Chester Morris was nominated for an Academy Award for best actor for his 1929 film debut in *Alibi.* He is best known for starring in fourteen "Boston Blackie" films in the 1940s. He was a guest of Edward and Markell Brooks at Eastcliff.

LOU NANNE* Gopher great hockey player, coach, and businessman Lou Nanne was awarded an Outstanding Achievement Award at Eastcliff in 2008 at an event hosted by Bob Bruininks and Susan Hagstrum. Louie and his wife Francine are good friends of the University.

PATRICIA NEAL Academy Award–winning actress Patricia Neal visited Eastcliff in 1979. She was in Minneapolis as international chair of the membership drive for Aid to Adoption of Special Kids. Ms. Neal was recognized as much for her grace and tenacity in overcoming obstacles as for her acting (even though she also received a Tony Award). She and her husband, writer Roald Dahl, had a son, Theo, who suffered brain damage after his baby carriage was hit by a taxi; as he recovered, their daughter, Olivia, died of measles encephalitis. Ms. Neal suffered three burst cerebral aneurysms while pregnant in 1965. She eventually was able to work again, becoming a model of recovery for stroke victims.

MARILYN CARLSON NELSON One of the greatest achievements of highly accomplished businesswoman Marilyn Carlson Nelson, CEO of Carlson Companies, resulted in her being presented the "Presidential Award for Extraordinary Efforts to Combat Trafficking in Persons" from the White House. She and her husband, Glen Nelson, MD*, visited Eastcliff many times.

FIONNUALA NÍ AOLÁIN University of Minnesota law professor Ní Aoláin is one of the world's leading scholars on conflict resolution and gender-based violence in conflict. She is a special rapporteur for the United Nations Human Rights Council. Her book *The Politics of Force* is about the conflict in Northern Ireland.

EUGENE ORMANDY Conductor Eugene Ormandy was with the Minneapolis Symphony Orchestra from 1931 to 1936, then spent forty-four years with the Philadelphia Orchestra. He was a guest of Edward and Markell Brooks at Eastcliff.

MICHAEL OSTERHOLM University of Minnesota public health professor Michael Osterholm has been encouraging preparation for a global pandemic throughout his entire career. Never has a researcher been so sorry to be so right.

PAULINE PHILLIPS Pauline Phillips, a.k.a. Abigail Van Buren, the famous advice columnist of "Dear Abby," visited Eastcliff in 1993. "Dear Abby" was the most widely syndicated newspaper column in the world, with syndication in 1,400 newspapers reaching 110 million readers. Her husband, Morton Phillips,* was a student at the University of Minnesota when they met on campus.

JOHN RAITT John Raitt was an actor and singer known for his stage roles in musicals and in the film *The Pajama Game* with Doris Day. He is the father of singer Bonnie Raitt. He visited Eastcliff in 1993.

EINOJUHANI RAUTAVAARA Finnish composer Einojuhani Rautavaara visited Eastcliff in 1999.

JAMES "SCOTTY" RESTON James Reston (known as "Scotty" because he immigrated from Scotland at age eleven) was associated with the *New York Times* for fifty years, advancing from reporter to Washington correspondent and executive editor. Considered one of the most influential journalists of his time, he won his second Pulitzer Prize in 1957 for a five-part analysis of President Eisenhower's fitness for office after his heart attack in 1955. Malcolm Moos went to work for the Eisenhower White House in 1957, and Moos, the speechwriter, and Reston, the journalist, became friends through their connections to the Eisenhower White House. Reston would visit his friend Malcolm Moos at Eastcliff—while working, smoking cigars, and having fun, according to Grant Moos.

JAMES ROSENQUIST* Internationally acclaimed artist James Rosenquist attended a luncheon in his honor at Eastcliff in March 1993.

THOMAS J. SARGENT Tom Sargent was a professor of economics at the University of Minnesota (1971–87). Together with his colleague Chris Sims, he won the Nobel Memorial Prize in Economic Sciences in 2011. He visited Eastcliff several times.

MISCHA SCHNEIDER Cellist Mischa Schneider and other members of the Budapest String Quartet visited the Brooks family at Eastcliff.

PAT SCHROEDER* Alumna Pat Schroeder, the first female U.S. representative to Congress elected in Colorado, briefly ran for president in 1987. She visited Eastcliff in 1997, at an event hosted by the Hasselmos to thank participants in a University of Minnesota radio ad campaign. Other guests were also outstanding alumni, including Kiaora Bohlool, Barbara Carlson, Margaret Carlson, Stan and Luella Goldberg, Steve Goldstein, Stanley S. Hubbard, Libby Larson, Kevin McHale, Dave Mona, Alan Page, Tom Swain, and Mike Wright. Journalist and author Jim Klobuchar, the father of Senator Amy Klobuchar, was also there. Twelve-term Representative Schroeder wrote a memoir about her years in Congress, *24 Years of House Work . . . and the Place Is Still a Mess*.

CHRISTOPHER A. SIMS Chris Sims was a professor of economics at the University of Minnesota (1968–90). Together with colleague Thomas Sargent, he won the Nobel Memorial Prize in Economic Sciences in 2011. He visited Eastcliff several times.

CORNELIA OTIS SKINNER Actress and author Cornelia Skinner was active on the stage and screen from the 1920s to the 1960s. She was a guest of Edward and Markell Brooks at Eastcliff.

GALE SONDERGAARD* Actress Gale Sondergaard, the first winner of the Academy Award for best actress in a supporting role for the 1936 film *Anthony Adverse*, was hosted by Tracy Moos at Eastcliff in 1968.

GERALD F. SPIESS* Schoolteacher Gerry Spiess is best known for single-handedly sailing his ten-foot sailboat *Yankee Girl* across the Atlantic Ocean in 1979 and across the Pacific Ocean in 1981. He visited Eastcliff not long after his Pacific crossing.

MARLA SPIVAK University of Minnesota professor Marla Spivak is a world-renowned entomologist, a MacArthur Fellow, and leader of the Spivak Honey Bee Lab. Her home and beehives are close enough to Eastcliff that both she and the bees have visited.

RISË STEVENS Mezzo soprano Risë Stevens was a leading singer of the Metropolitan Opera from 1938 until 1961. She was best known for her performance as the title character in *Carmen*. She visited Eastcliff in 1981 while she was serving as a consultant and director of auditions for the Metropolitan Opera Council.

ARTHUR STRACHAUER* Dr. Arthur Strachauer was a professor of surgery and Owen Wangensteen's predecessor as chief of surgery at the University of Minnesota. He was a close friend of Edward Brooks.

JOAN SUTHERLAND Famous coloratura soprano Joan Sutherland visited Eastcliff for an after-opera gathering. Dame Sutherland performed with the Metropolitan Opera from 1961 through 1989, winning a Grammy Award in 1962.

Tom Swain* In 1998, Mark Yudof hosted a farewell dinner for University icon Tom Swain, who was then serving as interim vice president; Tom was back as interim vice president in 2004. He served the University tirelessly for most of his life, beginning in the athletic ticket office before 1940, and he attended many events at Eastcliff after that first farewell. Tom's continued vigor was evident when he was elected mayor of Lilydale, Minnesota, at age eighty-five. Tom was born on July 4, 1921, and celebrated his 100th birthday by championing climate change research at the University. His memoir is titled *Citizen Swain*.

Anna Bell Thomas A relative of Edward Brooks, Anna Bell Thomas stayed with the Brooks children while Edward and Markell traveled. In 1944, Miss Thomas became the first female principal of Minneapolis Central High School.

Christopher Uggen University of Minnesota professor Christopher Uggen studies crime, law, and justice, "firm in the belief that sound research can help build a more just and peaceful world." He wrote *Locked Out: Felon Disenfranchisement and American Democracy* with coauthor Jeff Manza.

Eddie Vedder Eddie Vedder is an activist and front man of Pearl Jam. He visited Eastcliff in 2014 in his role as cofounder of EB Research Partnership.

David Winfield* Dave Winfield attended a reception at Eastcliff in his honor in 1980. Winfield played baseball and basketball for the University and was drafted into four professional leagues: the MLB, where he had a long, successful baseball career; both the NBA and ABA for basketball; and by the Minnesota Vikings in the NFL, even though he never played college football. He was elected to the Baseball Hall of Fame, along with Twins great Kirby Puckett, in 2001, his first year of eligibility.

Marlene Zuk The books of University of Minnesota professor Marlene Zuk have been quite successful at entertaining readers and informing them about ecology and evolution. They include *Sex on Six Legs: Lessons on Life, Love, and Language from the Insect World*; *Paleofantasy: What Evolution Really Tells Us about Sex, Diet, and How We Live*; and *Dancing Cockatoos and the Dead Man Test: How Behavior Evolves and Why It Matters*.

Writing about Eastcliff

Eastcliff has inspired writers through the years. Following is some of their work.

EASTCLIFF

Barbara Austin Foote

This is the house where gentleness abides;
Builded upon the mutual love of years.
It stands serenely firm against the tides
Of shifting fates—impregnable to fears.

Here is a light which darkness cannot quench,
Flame of a love outlasting all desire;
And here are bonds which only Time may wrench,
Welded within the heart of that white fire.

Here is a way of living touched with grace;
Life is an honored guest within these walls.
And peace dwells here in every quiet space,
While softly from all corners Beauty calls.

Here the weary guest will find surcease from strife
And new love for living in this house of life.

Edward and Markell Brooks met Edwin and Marion Austin on a cruise in 1933, and the couples became lifelong friends. Mr. Austin, a prominent Chicago attorney and close friend to Edward, became closely involved with Brooks–Scanlon, the Brooks family business, as well as their family affairs.

Edwin and Marion's daughter, Barbara, became a close friend of the family and visited Eastcliff regularly. Barbara was president of the Junior League of Chicago and the national board of the Association of Junior Leagues, chairwoman of the executive committee of the Chicago Community Trust, and a trustee of Vassar College. After Edwin Austin retired, Barbara's husband, Robert Foote, became legal counsel to Brooks–Scanlon.

In 1948, Barbara self-published a small book of her poetry titled *The Falconer*. The dedication reads: "To Markell and Marion and their namesakes." Barbara and her husband had named the oldest of their three daughters, born in 1944, Markell. They had two more daughters, Marion and Helen. Markell Foote Kaiser named her oldest child Brooks.

Edwin and Marion sent *The Falconer* to their friends with "every good wish for the holiday season." The copy I found was signed "For Naomi, with affectionate regard and deep respect. Barbara, November, 1960." Knowing that the Austins spent time with the Brooks at Gull Lake, I was attracted to the poem on page 81 written in September 1945, right after the end of World War II:

> Too long away, we have returned to Gull
> To live with wind, pine-spiced air;
> My mind and heart are hungry for this lull,
> I am wearied beyond words of city fare.
>
> The sun is my companion as I lie
> Outstretched in pagan peace upon the sand;
> I hear the "Sea-Hag" strain her buoy nearby,
> Impatient for your steady tiller hand.
>
> From dad's beloved boat I scan the skies,
> Nearer and vaster here—to find my peace;
> Sunset and starlight soothe my jaded eye,
> And in the sum of these is my release.
>
> Too long away, we have returned to Gull;
> How mind and heart are strengthened by this lull.

EASTCLIFF

Marlow Brooks

I sat on top of the soft armrest in my grandmother's low green sedan, my small feet resting on the seat next to her—entranced by the scent of her lily-of-the-valley perfume. We were on our way to Eastcliff, my grandmother's house, and I was already a queen—I was in her magic land and was about to enter her elegant palace on the banks of the Mississippi River. When we arrived, the aroma of lilacs wafted around us in the damp, heavy air and, as I walked through the door and smelled the sweet, pungent, slightly musty scent of her home, I knew I'd found peace, safety, and the promise of an exquisite experience to come.

"Darlings!" She announced in her low melodic voice, "Proceed to the closet upstairs and choose your gowns—tonight is very special—the Empress Eugenie is having a ball and we are her special guests!" My little sister Sky and I rushed up the spiral staircase and opened a closet brimming with sumptuous gowns smelling faintly of gardenia. They rustled between our fingers as we moved through the textures of soft velvet, shiny silk, and crinkly chiffon to find our dress of the evening. We wrestled, trying not to be too eager, through the stiff, soft, silky fabrics as we wiggled our toes in the smooth gray carpet under our feet. It felt like an island of pleasure. I chose the red velvet with delicate lace because I was a queen and Sky chose the yellow chiffon with dainty trim and a puffy gauze skirt that scratched on the floor when we teetered on our high heels. We carefully descended the staircase, clinging to the smooth mahogany banister, so we wouldn't trip—past the dark pink azaleas, soft pink cyclamen, and forest green ferns that graced the landing, down to the Victrola closet at the foot of the stairs where our grandmother, Markell, waited in her elegant lavender gown. Her silver hair was brushed up like a cloud that hovered around her face and her smile swept us into a complete subservience to her beauty. Markell then carefully placed a black vinyl record on the turntable of the Victrola and proclaimed, like the grand dame she was, "Welcome to the ball! Ladies! And now we will waltz!" As the Viennese waltz music drifted through, we lifted our skirts and danced and whirled and swished our long dresses in circles around the stately living room and with each stanza entered deeper and deeper into the magic and mystery of Markell's world. Markell danced with us, her rhythm smooth and satisfied—her eyes flashing with delight. I felt transported—lifted out of the chaotic world of my family life and dropped down into a mystical realm I never wanted to leave. My tummy was already dreaming of the sweet sugary dessert that followed our dinner but I swallowed my hunger and kept dancing until Markell announced, "Now, ladies!

When we finish this dance we will proceed to the drawbridge of our grand ocean liner, the *Queen Elizabeth,* and set sail for Europe where we will meet the Empress Eugenie!"

We mounted the stairs and found that a table was set at the landing—overlooking the banister—laden with sparkly silver, embroidered linens, and fine china. As we nestled in our seats, Markell looked in wonder into the distance, sighed, and purred, "Isn't the ocean magnificent tonight? . . . look how it reflects the light of the moon—it glistens like silver!"

Sky and I gazed out over the railing at the vast blue-green ocean, listened to the gentle lapping of the waves against the ship, and remarked in our most queenly fashion, "Ahhhhh, yes! isn't it absolutely divine!"

Then Markell's housekeeper joined the fun and appeared in a starched white cap and apron with a silver basket of fresh buns, sweet butter, and raspberry jam—my mouth watered and I gingerly picked one—truly feeling we were sailing on a grand ship, dining in elegance, crossing the smooth shiny waters of the Atlantic to Paris—a city of palaces, glittering lights, and live music so dramatic and powerful we'd never be the same.

We ate our dinner overlooking the ocean and landed in Europe. The ancient buildings loomed golden and were decorated with all manner of swirls and curls and fancy facades—we marveled at the grand avenues and majestic statues and knew we were in fairyland far different from the neat rows of conventional houses so common in our land. We were in a place where anything could happen; crystal chandeliers hung over our heads, an orchestra played romantic waltz music, and we delicately held canapés of chestnuts wrapped in salty bacon, cheese puffs that melted in our mouths, and salty crackers with smoked sturgeon as we watched the lavishly dressed guests whirl around. We were in heaven. I never wanted it to end—this was the place my heart longed for—a place where the atmosphere was sweet with elegance.

The soft tinkle of the empress's jewelry alerted us to the Grand Dame's entrance and our skirts rustled and rubbed together as we backed aside so she could pass. The Empress was grand—she was kind, her voice smooth, and words ran from her mouth like a flowing river. I tried to contain the excited beat of my heart that sounded so loud I thought people could hear. I was alive—the "ouuu's and ahhh's" echoed around the room and mixed with the luscious aroma of myriad perfumes. The fragrance of bliss. I was home.

EASTCLIFF 1978–1984

Diane Skomars Magrath

Among the gifts of age is the ability to look back on life from the vantage point of lessons learned, experiences added, and truths revealed. My Eastcliff years, in truth, were magical. I grew up in Duluth, Minnesota, third child and only daughter of a mechanical engineer/photographer father and an artist mother. A graduate of UMD (University of Minnesota Duluth), I was/am a Bulldog to the core. I worked in administration for many years at UMD, and later at the U of M Twin Cities, and have always held the university dear to my heart. So when President C. Peter Magrath and I married at Eastcliff in 1978, I considered it my privilege and duty to open the doors wide to the citizens of the state, my Minnesota. I believed a public house as grand as Eastcliff had to be shared.

By welcoming three to four thousand people to Eastcliff each year, it would be easy to focus on the role of President's Spouse as a host, advisor, house manager, speaker, and University friend/fund raiser. But what I recall most are the special events that featured a Nobel Prize winner, Regents Professors, Hollywood film stars, noted alumni athletes and artists, American Ballet Theatre dancers, opera performers, student leaders, and the outstanding faculty and staff. Coming from a background in student affairs, I especially loved inviting the student government representatives to meet with the President for breakfast at the house.

During Scandinavia Today we hosted a reception out-of-doors and a dinner inside Eastcliff for the President of Iceland, Vigdís Finnbogadóttir. She was the world's first democratically directly elected female president. It was an honor! A couple years later, I recall hosting a football brunch in the atrium of the School of Architecture. As Vice President Nils Hasselmo delivered a fascinating lecture on Icelandic literature, a huge Viking ice sculpture I had ordered keeled over with a crash! (Not my finest hour.) Nils was, as always, gracious about the interruption.

Peter and I tried to create as normal a family life as possible in a home that contained six bedrooms; a tennis court and swimming pool; and rooms with names such as the Peacock Bar, the Red Den, the Black Bathroom, the Barn Room. For our young daughter Monette, we created the Pillow Room and the Puppet Theatre on the landing of the back staircase. Many a production took place in that special theatre. I can still hear Monette's Girl Scout troop whooping through the house playing hide and go seek. I remember her school class coming to Eastcliff for a tour, a history lesson, and a dance around the May pole in the back yard. At every formal dinner, Monette came down clad in pajamas to get goodnight kisses and hugs. A tour of the entire house was offered to every visitor, causing Monette to utter her famous line, "Why are all these people coming to see me?" I insisted that the upstairs be open to all, and that we had to keep our private space "visitor ready"—probably a dumb idea in retrospect.

Although the work was exhausting, and I struggled to find the right balance between all the demands, Eastcliff made the time magical. It is a beautiful, celebrated house and a warm and welcoming home. Many rooms are sunny and cheerful, and the location of the house near the cliffs of the Mighty Mississippi endows it with an air of permanence and grandeur. It was no surprise to me to learn that the architect of both Eastcliff and Duluth's Glensheen Estate was Clarence H. Johnston Sr. Both homes have housed families and entertained royalty with equal charm and success. I thanked the Brooks family every day for giving this valued family treasure to the University. My Eastcliff years were a happy time for me.

EASTCLIFF

Monette Magrath

I was fortunate enough to live at Eastcliff from 3½ to 10½ years old. As my mother shared in her words here, it was a magical time in an incredible house.

One of my very earliest memories of childhood was during my mother's wedding to then President Peter Magrath. I was 3½ and had run upstairs to my new room in tears, for some reason that I don't recall; it may have had to do with a teddy bear losing his eye during the festivities? I think it was my mother who put a sprig of baby's breath where the eye had been, and Peter came up and carried me down the stairs as I dearly clutched the repaired bear. That sweeping staircase winding around the stunning crystal chandelier will never leave my mind. I remember being fascinated when it had to be cleaned!

Equally important was the back staircase, whose landing held my puppet theater. My parents smartly strung a curtain across the nook there, and I put on many shows for willing visitors. Adjacent to that back staircase on the upstairs level was a beautiful room with two walls of windows that became my playroom. My mother covered about two dozen oversized pillows with brightly patterned fabrics and placed them there instead of furniture. Those pillows became my forts, my secret castles, and my soft place to land. I remember specifically having a play date there with a little boy when I was probably five or six and knowing for certain that I was absolutely in love with him. Ah, the certainty of youth!

Outside the "Pillow Room" and to the right was the Moroccan room. I know that some of the rooms at Eastcliff were named before us, but I think my mother added a few. I loved the Moroccan room because it held the most beautiful turquoise rug that my parents actually brought home from Morocco (hence the name). Turquoise has always been my favorite color, and I suspect that rug is why. Lucky for me, it now sits in my dining room for my daughter to gaze upon. I recall there were other exotic and beautiful items in that room. A brass table, a tea set of some kind, and a coffee table book about Princess Grace. I remember sitting in that Moroccan room of exotic beauty and reading about a real-life princess. Heady stuff for a little girl, indeed.

Down the long upstairs hall were guest rooms and a small den that held a TV. It had the most comfortable, soft couch and a low stool that would spin. I remember watching *Charlie's Angels* on that little TV and lying on my stomach on that small leather stool, extending my arms and legs out to the side while I spun around as fast as I could.

I also remember that that room had a black telephone, which was rotary, I think, if one can imagine that in this day and age. I remember that our telephone number was typed out and enclosed in a little plastic sleeve on the face of the phone. It was a big deal to memorize your phone number when you were little, and I used to practice dialing it over and over on that sturdy phone.

Next to that den, as I recall, was my bedroom. It was large for a child. My mother had let me get bunkbeds, but they were not ordinary! Each one was a tube, covered in a yellow leather-like material. Very mod, actually. On the side of each tube was an oval opening through which you got into bed. On the end of the bed were circular steps to get up to top tube. I always slept on the bottom, and friends who would sleep over got the top. Peter read to me most nights, and I specifically remember him reading *The Diary of Anne Frank* in its entirety, one chapter a night. Besides books, my other form of entertainment in that room was a small record player. It may have actually been a Mickey Mouse record player now that I'm thinking of it, with the needle extending down from his plastic, white-gloved hand. I remember listening to the cast album of the musical *Annie* on that record player. When we moved away, I hid a wooden dog toy in a secret cabinet in that room. I've been back to the house only once, when I was in college, and we retrieved the dog, but he was hidden for quite a while. Children always do find the nooks and crannies of a place.

The rest of the upstairs was devoted to my parents' rooms. Their bedroom, of course, with beautiful furniture from Mexico and a quilt that was made for them when they married. The three of us used to play the board game Clue on the floor in front of the fireplace at the foot of the bed. My mother had a wonderfully large bathroom off the master that definitely spoiled me for all future bathroom expectations.

Across the landing, Peter had a bathroom and closet area and then there was a large family room with a fireplace and a bigger television set. I spent an increasing amount of time in that room as I grew older, particularly the summer that I was seven. Every day that summer I would play outside in the morning on the beautiful grounds and then make a can of Campbell's chicken noodle soup with herbs shaken in to make it "home-made," and I would watch a video tape that I had recorded of the television broadcast of the movie musical *Grease*. I memorized every single word of that movie, with the exception of those that were edited out for broadcast. We also had a piano there and, during the brief time that I took lessons, I practiced on it with great reluctance. Not my favorite activity! My mother played, and it was always lovely to hear that piano brought to life. Around the corner from the family room was a beautiful though quite adult feeling sitting area with lovely windows that I rarely went into and Peter's office, which always seemed so very mysterious to me.

In the downstairs more public portion of the house, my favorite rooms were the peacock bar, where I practiced ballet staring into the reflection from the gorgeous gold glass, and the black bathroom—so very exotic. The kitchen was not fancy, but it held some sweet memories. My mom used to wash my hair in the sink, with me lying down on the counter and her gently spraying the water through my hair. Also, I recall waking early to watch the wedding of Prince Charles and Princess Diana on the tiny black-and-white television that we had set on the counter in the corner. More royalty—you see what children attach to! I think because the kitchen appliances were very large and meant for catering, it never seemed like a kitchen in which I should touch very much. It intimidated me, and I did not learn much about cooking until later in my life.

Out of those kitchen windows was the enormous, peaceful backyard. The lawn seemed endless to me as a child. I had a black metal swingset with a wooden seat, and I specifically remember my grandfather pushing me on that swing. My grandfather also helped me carve pumpkins on the patio just off the lawn. There were lilac bushes, and berries to pick in the summer. And of course, the gorgeous swimming pool! I'm not exactly sure when, but I got tired of not knowing how to swim, so one summer I taught myself in that pool. I remember that I had a Wonder Woman bathing suit (surely a help in conquering any fears of the water!). I remember many pool parties with giddy girl-friends. For all the formality of the property, there certainly was a tremendous amount of splashing and more than one cannon ball.

When I was asked to write about my memories at Eastcliff, I wasn't sure at first what to say. I don't have the greatest memory, but it's funny . . . thinking through a house can lead you back. The reason I share these things with you is to say, for me, this was not an official residence. For me, it was my childhood. Beautiful, unseen things occurred in those fantastically named rooms, not just visiting dignitaries and prize winners: imagination and joy and innocence and learning and laughter. I'm very grateful that I was given a place to live that inspired so much for me. In writing this, I recognize what a gift that truly was. When we moved away when I was 10½, I entered a different chapter of childhood, one where innocence begins to give way.

So Eastcliff remains like a dream. The walls hold giggles and pinky swears. The grand stairs hold barefoot, nightgowned tiptoed steps, down to kiss my parents as they dined by glittering candlelight with long tables of guests. Somewhere that great lawn holds impressions made in winter, as countless snow angels flew. Life got harder after we left Eastcliff. It does that. How lucky I was for that season of sweetness in that beautiful place.

CONLEY BROOKS'S NOTE TO HIS SIBLINGS, MARCH 1988

You may wonder, as I did, how the Brooks family felt about Eastcliff being so heavily in the news (in a negative way) during the 1980s renovation. Conley Brooks Sr. wrote a note to his three siblings on March 9, 1988, a few days before Ken Keller resigned. Dwight and Binky were then living in California.

With thirty years' perspective and access to much more information, I still couldn't distill the information as concisely and accurately as Conley did in this note to his beloved siblings. One of the family members added a copy of this typewritten note to the Brooks file box in the Minnesota Historical Society, purposely making it available to the public.

Date: 9 March 1988
To: TED—BINK—DWIGHT
From: CB

Dear all of you,

I sent some clippings to Bink and Dwight about Eastcliff because Ted & Ginny had undoubtedly seen them. Dwight wonders why I commented that it was "too bad." The way I look at it, the media has made a huge public event out of cost overruns on the renovation of Eastcliff and the President's office. Opponents of the University in general have used the incident as a means of attacking other University projects such as the President's Focus Program. The way I look at it (and others obviously do not agree) is that while the accounting for the renovation was, at best, sloppy, it was not the horrifying event as the press made it out to be. I think that the repercussions on the University are and will be profound and that the incident will do substantial, meaningful damage to a great University. This is not to excuse the cost overruns or the failure to keep the Regents informed.

I think Ken Keller is an outstanding new head of the University, and I fear greatly that he may be seriously (if not mortally) wounded by this incident. Dave Lilly is one of the most canny people I know, and I have felt that the University has been fortunate to have a businessman dealing with the DFL legislature on behalf of the University.

They ran into a lot of unpredictable things which could easily have been overlooked in the beginning. For example, I understand that the State made them collect all of the old paint chippings (some 10 coats) and put them in steel barrels which were then sealed and then sent to Illinois due to the lead content. This little event cost something like $200,000.

The enclosed additional clipping takes a much more moderate view of the whole thing.

There's no question but what Eastcliff had gotten run down because of other priority uses of the funds in the past inflationary times (same problem we have at Carleton and that I saw so clearly at Yale last week when I was in New Haven).

> Best to all of you,
> [*Signed by Conley*]
> CB:bk
> Enc.

STEFAN, THE EASTCLIFF CAT

Nils Hasselmo

with assistance of children and grandchildren
who at one time enjoyed Eastcliff

We did not have a dog when we lived at Eastcliff, but we did have a cat, a cat named Stefan. She—yes, it was a she with a male name—she was actually named for the Swedish tennis star Stefan Edberg, at one time #1 in the world and a two-time Wimbledon champion. Our daughter Anna, then in her teens, admired Stefan Edberg very much (she may even have had some kind of teenage crush on him)—Anna insisted that our cat had to be named after her idol.

Stefan's, that is Cat Stefan's, favorite spot was in the windowsill of one of the windows in the Eastcliff dining room. She would sit there by the hour. Why? Well, Stefan had a good view of everything that was going on in the garden of Eastcliff! We don't think she cared for people in the garden but, as we learned, the garden was full of other forms of life. Stefan would get very excited by all the squirrels running up and down the trunks of the old trees and leaping from one branch to the other. You could see her excitement because her ears would be perked, every hair in her fur would stand on end, and her tail would be wagging. Stefan would also get excited by the birds that were singing out there. We didn't think she appreciated their singing: she was just aching to get out there to catch them. And, if a rabbit came jumping across the garden, well, Stefan behaved as if she wanted to break the glass of the window to get at this tempting prey! Our daughter Anna and Karen, our oldest granddaughter, called Stefan "The Hiss Machine!"

One day—as a matter of fact, it was the day after Garrison Keillor had given us—well, you may not believe this, but it is true—it was the day after Garrison Keillor had given us a—yes, this is true—a cow! A real milking cow! He had presented it to us at a gathering in Northrop Hall, on the stage of this venerable building. There is actually a door at the back of the stage big enough to accommodate a cow. The architect must have anticipated that at some point there would be a need to admit a cow to Northrop.

But, back to Stefan! The day after the gathering at Northrop, we woke up to insistent mooing in the garden of Eastcliff. Well, there was the cow! Garrison Keillor's gift cow! Grazing contentedly, except for some mooing breaks. Well, you would think that this big, mooing animal would really catch Stefan's attention. The cow would, obviously, be so much more exciting than a squirrel or a bird, yes, even more exciting than a rabbit. All Stefan's hairs would stand on end, her ears would be perked, and her tail would really wag.

But here was Stefan, inscrutable as only a cat can be, here she was lying in the windowsill, yawning now and then, looking very bored, as if cows would appear in the garden of Eastcliff every day. And then, instead of getting all excited by this big, new denizen of the Eastcliff garden, well, what did this inscrutable cat do? She jumped down from the windowsill and, after sharpening her claws on the rug, leisurely walked over to the baby carriage in the breakfast nook. This was where our second-oldest granddaughter, now married but then just Baby Christina, was taking her morning nap. After taking careful aim. Stefan leapt into the baby carriage and snuggled into the blanket next to the sleeping baby. If you listened carefully, you could hear her purring contentedly. As if cows would be grazing in the Eastcliff garden every day!

Well, go figure, Stefan, the Eastcliff Cat!

Recipes from Eastcliff

MARKELL BROOKS'S RECIPES

These recipes are from Food of My Friends, *by Virginia Safford (Minneapolis: University of Minnesota Press, 1944), pages 201–5. (I've made them all and particularly recommend the nut puffs.)*

Chicken with White Grapes

two 4- to 5-pound
    roasting chickens
¼ pound butter
½ teaspoon curry powder
1 small glass cognac

3 cups thick cream
3 or 4 small onions
salt and pepper
seedless green grapes,
    peeled and halved

Cut chicken into serving pieces. Put in large frying pan with melted butter. Add onions, sliced very thin, and salt and pepper. Cover and cook slowly until chicken is tender and golden brown. Add cognac and curry powder, then stir in cream. Simmer for 5 minutes. Remove to serving dish, add grapes, and serve very hot.

Accompanying this dish will be tiny new potatoes—boiled in their jackets except for one narrow strip cut from around the center, and served under a napkin—and a purée of peas and lima beans, which has an unusual and delicious flavor.

Puree of Peas and Lima Beans

1 package frozen lima beans
2 packages frozen peas
2 small onions

1 cup cream
butter
seasonings

Cook peas and beans until done, following directions. Cut up onions, add to cream in double boiler, and heat. Put cooked peas and beans through a sieve, then put in a pan with a large lump of butter. Heat and add hot cream to which onions have been strained. Beat while the cream is being added. Season. Watch for the right consistency when adding cream—not too thin or too thick.

French Dressing

Markell said she got this recipe from the chef at the Café de la Paix in Paris.

6 tablespoons olive oil
1 tablespoon tarragon vinegar
1 tablespoon cider vinegar
¼ teaspoon Worchester sauce

½ teaspoon salt
¼ teaspoon freshly ground
    black pepper
1 small clove garlic, minced finely

Pour oil in bowl, whip with a fork. Add vinegar slowly. Then add other ingredients and beat thoroughly.

Vegetable Soup

3 or 4 carrots
1 stalk celery
1 large bunch parsley
1 pound spinach
tomato juice

sugar
celery salt
chili sauce
freshly ground pepper
sour cream

Wash and prepare vegetables and put through a food grinder into the pan in which they are to be cooked. Add 1 quart boiling water and simmer very slowly for 15 minutes. Cool and put stock in refrigerator until ready to use. Measure vegetable stock and add it to an equal amount of tomato juice, seasoned with sugar, celery salt, chili sauce, and freshly ground pepper. Heat and serve piping hot, with a topping of sour cream. This soup is also good when served very cold.

Frozen Eggnog

3 egg yolks
½ cup sugar
⅓ cup brandy

⅓ cup rum
1 quart cream
grated nutmeg

Beat egg yolks with sugar until lemon color. Add nutmeg and cream. Freeze in ice-cream freezer until partially frozen, then beat in brandy and rum. Return to freezer and complete freezing. Serve with a dusting of nutmeg.

Nut Puffs

1 cup butter
4 tablespoons granulated sugar
½ teaspoon vanilla
2 cups flour, sifted once

1½ cups ground pecans
or almonds
Powdered sugar

Mix together with hands. Roll into little balls and flatten on top. Bake in a greased cookie shcet in slow oven for 20 minutes. Roll in powdered sugar while still hot.

Thin Chocolate Cookies

½ cup butter
1 cup cake flour
¼ cup powdered sugar

2 tablespoons cocoa
½ teaspoon vanilla

Mix with hands. Roll into small balls, and flatten very thin, ⅛ inch or less. Bake in a slow oven. These cookies are hard to manage but very delicious.

MARIAN WILSON'S RECIPE

This pot roast recipe is from Marian Wilson was prepared by Mae McBroom for a dinner for student government leaders. It was served with homemade rolls.

Italian Pot Roast

Brown one five-pound boned and rolled rump roast (or any pot roast), which has been fitted with garlic inserts, salted, and peppered. Pour in one cup water and cook slowly for an hour. Add two cans tomato paste and about one quart of water, but don't fill pan more than half full.

Add two onions that have been sliced and sautéed, celery leaves, oregano, sweet basil, parsley, salt, and pepper. Cool. Slice roast when cool and return slices to sauce after removing garlic cloves. Cook one more hour.

Serve hot from chafing dish over slices of French bread, or cool and serve in buns with a small amount of sauce.

MAGRATH ADMINISTRATION RECIPES

Diane Skomars Magrath contributed these recipes to Minnesota's Greatest and Best Recipes: A University of Minnesota Cookbook. *The book was a fundraiser for the David Winfield Development Fund for recreational sports at the University. The paté and chicken marsala were mentioned as favorites from Eastcliff menus and were served at a reception for Peter Graves after he filmed the third season of* Matrix. *Diane's strawberry cake recipe was also in the cookbook (and in the newspaper) and was said to be one of Peter Magrath's favorites.*

Chicken Liver–Mushroom Paté

¾ cup butter
1 pound chicken livers
½ pound fresh mushrooms

⅓ cup green onions,
    finely chopped
1 teaspoon garlic salt
1 teaspoon paprika

⅓ cup dry white wine
dash of dill weed

3 drops Tabasco sauce
salt to taste

Melt ¼ cup butter in skillet; cook and stir chicken livers, mushrooms, onion, garlic salt, and paprika in the butter for five minutes. Stir in wine, dill weed, and Tabasco sauce. Cover and cook over low heat for 5 to 10 minutes. Cool mixture; place in blender and blend until smooth. Blend in ½ cup of softened butter; add salt to taste. Pack mixture in serving dish. Chill several hours or overnight. Makes 3 cups.

Chicken Marsala

1½ pounds chicken breasts, split, boned, and skin removed
flour
freshly ground pepper

¼ cup butter
marsala
½ cup chicken stock
½ pound fresh mushrooms, sliced

Flatten chicken breasts to about ⅜ inch thick. Dredge in flour and pepper. Put butter in skillet and heat. Brown breasts and put in baking pan. Add marsala and chicken stock to skillet and boil liquid one to two minutes until slightly thickened. Loosen all browned fragments that cling to pan. Put fresh mushrooms over chicken and pour marsala mixture over all. Put in 350 degree oven and bake for 20 to 25 minutes. Baste once or twice during baking with juices in the pan. Serves 4.

Strawberry Cake

1 package white cake mix
1 small package strawberry flavored gelatin
½ cup water
3 tablespoons flour
1 cup oil

4 eggs
1 package (10 ounces) frozen strawberries
1 pound powdered sugar
1 stick of butter, softened

Mix and beat first six ingredients together. Add half of the package of berries, slightly thawed. When well mixed, pour into two 8-inch layer cake pans, well-greased and floured. Bake 30 minutes at 350 degrees.

For frosting, mix powdered sugar and butter together. Add the rest of the package of berries, and beat to spreading consistency. Makes 8 servings.

KAREN KALER'S RECIPE

When I was a young girl in Nashville in the 1960s, our next-door neighbor Willa Ogilvie made this fudge every year. She shared it with us when we visited her on Christmas Eve. I've never had better. This is not "never-fail" fudge—you have to follow the recipe carefully. The almond flavoring and the directions are my additions to Mrs. Ogilvie's original recipe. I made pounds of this fudge each December for the UMWC tea, the faculty/staff open house, and the December regents' dinner.

Fudge

12 ounces evaporated milk

4½ cups sugar

18 ounces dark chocolate (good quality semi-sweet chips or chopped dark chocolate, but not milk chocolate)

1 cup (2 sticks) butter

1 tablespoon vanilla

1 teaspoon almond flavoring

Mix evaporated milk and sugar in a large pot. Heat, stirring regularly, until it begins to a boil, then stir constantly. When the mixture begins to boil, set a timer to boil for exactly seven minutes.

Have cold butter and chocolate ready in a large bowl. Pour milk mixture into bowl and beat by hand for about five minutes, until butter is completely melted and mixture is very smooth. Stir in vanilla and almond flavorings. Pour into a buttered pan. Lining the pan with parchment paper is optional, but will make it easier to lift out and cut nicely. Refrigerate before cutting into squares (or diamonds). The fudge keeps best stored in the refrigerator (or on a cold enclosed porch) but bring it to room temperature before serving.

Notes

1. Welcome to Eastcliff

1 Conley Brooks, Marney Brown Brooks, Edward Brooks Jr., Virginia Dahleen Brooks, Markell Brooks, and Dwight F. Brooks, *Turning the Leaves: The Brooks Family Tree* (privately printed, 1995), 135.

2 Ibid., 141.

3 Several books have been written about Glensheen, and in 2015 there was even a musical titled *Glensheen*. Glensheen has notoriety not only as a large mansion but also because two murders were committed there. In 1977, someone broke into Glensheen and bludgeoned nurse Velma Pietila with a candlestick and then smothered heiress Elizabeth Congdon with a satin pillow.

4 C. Howard Johnston (1888–1959) began working for his father's firm in 1906. He left the firm for a course in architecture at Columbia University (1908–10) and to serve in World War I (1917–18) but otherwise remained with the firm until retirement in 1956. In 1936, he became president of the firm, renamed C. H. Johnston, Architects–Engineers.

5 When we first moved into Eastcliff, written descriptions of the house listed the architect as Clarence Johnston Sr. When I read about the Johnston firm in Paul Clifford Larson's book *Minnesota Architect: The Life and Work of Clarence H. Johnston* (Afton: Afton Historical Society Press, 1996), it stated that in the 1920s son Howard (CHJ Junior) was handling almost all the residential work for the firm. It is apparently technically correct to refer to a building's architect as the firm's head, rather than the actual architect who did the design, but it became important to me to give credit to the correct person. The application for the National Register of Historic Places from May 2000 referenced CHJ Senior as the architect in 1921 and CHJ Junior as the architect of the 1930 addition. Binky Brooks told me that she knew her father hired his good friend as the architect for Eastcliff. It made sense to me that he

would be more likely to be close friends with a man his same age than a man thirty years older. Diane Skomars Magrath developed a Docents' Manual for Eastcliff in the 1980s that credited CHJ Junior as the architect. The proof that the architect was CHJ Junior came when I found a copy of an original signed architectural rendering of the house in the archives of the Minnesota Historical Society. Those drawings are signed by Clarence H. Johnston Junior.

6 The costs for the additions were about $8,000 for the garage; $12,000 for the bathhouse and pool; and $15,000 for alterations to the main house. The value of $35,000 in 1930 would be more than $540,000 in 2020. Other expenditures in the 1930s included $2,392 for master bath changes in 1934; $1,560 for paneling in the two older boys' rooms; $2,496 for a renovation to Edward's screen porch den in 1935; and $4,245 for remodeling the two younger children's rooms in 1937.

7 Jeffrey A. Hess and Paul Clifford Larson, *St. Paul's Architecture: A History* (Minneapolis: University of Minnesota Press, 2006), 124.

8 Ibid., 123.

9 The transfer of the property had three restrictions (as paraphrased): 1. Mrs. Brooks would maintain the premises, pay the real estate taxes, and lease the property until December 31, 1959, with the option to renew for no more than two additional years to conclude arrangements for another residence. 2. The University would not use the premises for any purpose other than the residence of the president of the University until January 1, 1979 (twenty years later) and would keep the property in good condition. 3. The Board of Regents would not use the premises for any purpose objectionable to any living donor, nor would it sell or dispose of the property without giving right of first refusal to any living donor. The letter was signed by Markell Brooks and

her four children, Conley Brooks, Edward Brooks Jr., Markell Brooks Krafchuk, and Dwight F. Brooks. The letter was accepted and approved by President J. L. Morrill and University Secretary W. T. Middlebrook.

10 Markell Brooks died in 1971. Mary Haldeman Dayton bought Longshadows in 1975. While she updated the kitchen, enclosed a porch, and added a heated swimming pool, she left most of the house as it was. Her son, David Dayton, said, "She felt it was a treasure to be preserved. She thought it was gorgeous the way it was." After Ms. Dayton's death in 2008, Longshadows was sold in 2010. According to architect James Dayton's website, his firm was hired to update the house and add bedrooms for the client's children "while enhancing the masterful design of the original house. Taking cues from Rapson's palette and the wonderful, intimate scale of the house, the renovation is at once a dramatic refresh of the original and a sensitive addition to the composition."

11 While it was rumored that the donation of the house was contingent on preserving the graves, the gift agreement does not include this stipulation.

12 The May 6 event at Eastcliff was the welcome event. May 7 events included a press conference, a several-hour gathering with the Twin Cities Tibetan community, then an invitation-only gathering with mainland Chinese students, including a panel discussion. The Dalai Lama was awarded an honorary degree from the University of Minnesota, the doctorate of humane letters, on May 8 at Mariucci Arena (renamed 3M Arena at Mariucci in 2017), after which he gave a public address titled "Peace through Inner Peace." From May 6 through May 22, the Tibetan Institute for Performing Arts (an institute set up by the Dalai Lama in Dharamshala, India) collaborated with local playwright Markell Kiefer, of TigerLion Arts, and local performers on a production called *KIPO!* Markell Kiefer, Edward and Markell Brooks's granddaughter who was then just twenty-seven years old, directed *The Buddha Prince* in coordination with the Dalai Lama's visit in 2001.

13 Marian Wilson was interviewed by Ann Pflaum on February 23, 2000. This interview, along with many others used in this book, was part of an oral history project by Clarke A. Chambers, a member of the history faculty since 1951. He began the project in 1986 with sixteen to eighteen interviews, then revived the project in 1994 after he retired, at the encouragement of Nils Hasselmo. The interviews were intended to, and did, help inform the sequel to James Gray's centennial history of the University, *University of Minnesota, 1851–1951,* which was Stanford Lehmberg and Ann Pflaum's *The University of Minnesota, 1945–2000.* Professor Chambers had completed 130 interviews by 1998, when he "interviewed" himself to explain the project. Ann Pflaum conducted additional interviews beginning in 1998.

14 Who owned this land before 1887? Prior to 1837, all land that is now Minnesota was "Indian country" and not legally open to other settlement. In 1837, a delegation of twenty-six eastern Dakota leaders signed a treaty giving rights to five million acres of land east of the Mississippi River to the U.S. federal government. The sad history of those treaties is the subject of other books. In 1850, 1,294 people lived in St. Paul; the population increased to 10,401 by 1860. Land west of the Mississippi was "purchased" by treaty in 1851. Minnesota became a state in 1858. Edward Brooks's grandfather, Sheldon, moved to Minneiska, Minnesota, between those last two events.

15 Dayton Avenue was named in 1854 for Lyman Dayton, a St. Paul real estate speculator (not the more famous Minnesota Dayton family). Nearby Marshall Avenue was developed in 1855. One of the developers was real estate speculator William Marshall, who founded the *Pioneer Press* and was elected governor of Minnesota in 1866.

16 Otis Avenue was named in 1887 for George Otis, mayor of St. Paul in the 1860s.

17 Edward Brooks Jr.'s letter to Mrs. G. A. Godfrey, director of the University of Minnesota Department of University Relations, March 25, 1972.

18 The University's original Old Main was on the site of the current Chute Park in St. Anthony Main. The Ard Godfrey house is now on the site, but that house, built in 1849 on the ox cart trail at Main and Second, was moved to its current location in 1909.

19 Folwell wrote this evocative description on July 10, 1869. Solon W. Buck, *W. W. Folwell: Autobiography and Letters of a Pioneer of Culture* (Minneapolis: University of Minnesota Press, 1933), 178.

20 "Executive Mansion," *Minneapolis Star,* December 15, 1958.

2. Gangsters, Weddings, and Celebrities

[1] Marney Brown Brooks wrote and published *A Pioneer Legacy: The Story of Sheldon Brooks* in 1981. She explains in the preface that Markell Conley Brooks had collected historical family material and desired that the histories be preserved. After Markell's death in 1971, Ted's wife, Virginia Dahleen Brooks, began working on Markell's family history, and Marney was "assigned the Brooks family." She then "became fascinated with the man and his times" and wrote an excellent biography, informed by Sheldon's diaries and letters. *Turning the Leaves,* a great resource to me in writing this book, was a natural extension of *A Pioneer Legacy.*

[2] On January 30, 1901, the *Minnesota Journal* article "Build New Lumber Mill: A Scanlon–Brooks Co. Move" stated that "The new Brooks–Scanlon Lumber company is planning the erection of a big saw mill at Cloquet, one of the best equipped in the west." The article ends: "The Brooks–Scanlon company incorporated yesterday with capital stock of $500,000." Eleven months later, on December 30, 1901, the location of the mill, just east of Cloquet and eighteen miles southwest of Duluth, was incorporated as the city of Scanlon. The mill closed in 1909, after having cut 700,000,000 feet of timber, and exhausting the supply.

[3] On December 7, 1923, the first event in the Gates Mansion during the Brooks ownership was the first formal activity of the newly formed Minneapolis Junior League. While a November 27 article in the *Minneapolis Morning Tribune,* titled "Newly Formed Junior League to Give Ball at Gates Mansion," said 300 guests were expected in the ballroom, a story the day after the event ("Former Gates Mansion Is Scene of Junior Leaguers Yule Party," December 8, 1923) said that 600 guests attended the event given for the benefit of the Children's Protective Society. Game tables for bridge and Mah-Jongg were set up in the anterooms for those who did not wish to dance in the ballroom.

[4] While some Eastcliff brochures have incorrectly stated that artist Gustav Krollman painted the peacock room, Edward Brooks's careful ledger shows that he paid Frank Post for the work. Gustav Krollman painted bird and plant murals on silver-leaf walls in the dining room around the same time. Those murals are no longer in Eastcliff.

[5] Edith D. Williams, "The Home of the Month," *Amateur Golfer and Sportsman,* November 1931, 36–37.

[6] Alvin Karpis with Bill Trent, *The Alvin Karpis Story* (New York: Coward, McCann, and Geoghegan, 1971), 100.

[7] Quoted in Paul Maccabee, *John Dillinger Slept Here: A Crook's Tour of Crime and Corruption in St. Paul, 1920–1936* (St. Paul: Minnesota Historical Society Press, 1995), 8.

[8] Conley Brooks, Marney Brown Brooks, Edward Brooks Jr., Virginia Dahleen Brooks, Markell Brooks, and Dwight F. Brooks, *Turning the Leaves: The Brooks Family Tree* (privately printed, 1995), 146.

[9] Maccabee, *John Dillinger Slept Here,* 198.

[10] Ibid., 251.

[11] FBI Law Enforcement Bulletin, June 1936, 7. The quotation continues: "True, they are dressed as we are dressed. They live as we live and often upon a better scale owing to the rich rewards of their so-called profession but their standards of life are those of pigs in a wallow, their outlook that of vultures regurgitating their filth."

[12] "Guide Jane Borchert said one man told her he had often gone to the house during the Prohibition era, long before it was university property. He was especially glad to see the Peacock Room: 'He said he learned to drink in that room.'" Chuck Haga, "Lavish wasn't the word for what the public saw at Eastcliff," *Star Tribune,* September 20, 1989.

[13] Maccabee, *John Dillinger Slept Here,* 197.

[14] Former Governor Elmer L. Andersen stated with hindsight: "The highlight of Malcolm Moos' Administration was his relationship and empathy with students and their concerns and their objections to things. He was at his best when he was dealing with students and kind of understanding them enough so they didn't feel they had to have such outbursts as occurred in some campuses." Elmer L. Andersen was interviewed by Clarke Chambers on October 2, 1995.

[15] Marian Wilson was interviewed by Ann Pflaum on February 23, 2000.

[16] The issue ended in a "two bowl" plan, offering students a choice of union or nonunion produce. This plan also kept the issue before the community.

[17] Diane Fay Skomars, *Have I Taught You Everything I Know?* (Minneapolis: Mill City Press, 2014), 307.

[18] Edith D. Williams, "The Home of the Month," *Amateur Golfer and Sportsman,* November 1931, 37.

[19] Conley Brooks, *Turning the Leaves,* 169.

[20] Marney Brown Brooks, *Turning the Leaves,* 205.

21 Ibid., 207.

22 Ibid. Marney wrote in her memoirs that Markell also bought her "going-away outfit (a black suit with frilly blouse and bolero jacket and a hat with bows)."

23 Marney Brown Brooks, "Marney's Memoirs" (unpublished, 2004–7).

24 Ibid.

25 Dwight had married Carol Summerfelt in Nagoya, Japan, in 1953. Ted married Virginia (Ginny) Dahleen in 1957 at House of Hope Presbyterian Church in St. Paul, followed by a small reception at St. Paul College Club.

26 Descriptions of the living room and entry hall are from the November 1931 issue of *The Amateur Golfer and Sportsman* magazine, in which Eastcliff was featured in "The Home of the Month," an article by Edith D. Williams.

27 Dallas Bohnsack had been the regent chair of the Friends of Eastcliff Committee and was a strong supporter of Eastcliff.

28 Members of the Brooks family were interviewed by Judy Yudof in 1998.

29 *Turning the Leaves,* 155.

30 Members of the Brooks family were interviewed by Judy Yudof in 1998.

31 Members of the Brooks family were interviewed by Judy Yudof in 1998.

32 Sandra Magrath, "Notes from Eastcliff," *Alumni News,* November 1976.

33 Frannie Underwood was interviewed by Conley and Marney Brooks on September 22, 1990.

34 Edward Brooks Jr.'s letter to Mrs. G. A. Godfrey, director of the University of Minnesota Department of University Relations, March 25, 1972.

35 Claire "Shorty" Long was an All-American quarterback on the Gopher football team in 1916 while in law school. In 1917, Shorty Long, like Edward Brooks, was serving for the United States in World War I in France. Around the time of this visit to Eastcliff (in 1931), Shorty Long was in the quarterfinals of the golf championship at the Minikahda Golf Club. Fellow Gopher alum Les Bolstad won the tournament. Bolstad won Big Ten golf titles playing golf for the Gophers in 1927 and 1929. After his playing career, he coached Gopher golf from 1947 to 1976. The University's golf course is named in his honor.

36 I found documentation of Miss Keller's visits to Minnesota for speaking engagements in 1914, 1915, 1921, 1922, and 1925. In January 1925, according to the *Minneapolis Star,* she met with "outstanding social leaders" and stayed a week. It is most likely that she came to know Edward and Markell during that time. She was at the Mayo Clinic in Rochester in 1937 and 1938, the probable dates for the visit that Binky recalled.

37 Binky told me this story in 2014. I asked about Miss Keller's speaking voice. Binky said it was "kind of monotonous. It wasn't a loud voice, but it was clear once you got used to the intonation."

38 Since hearing this, I have smelled every fuchsia I have seen. I have a strong sense of smell, and they have little to no scent to me. Everything that Helen Keller experienced with the plant was through touch. In a speech in New York in 1913, Miss Keller said, "The belief that the loss of one sense increases the power of others is a fallacy. The habit of patience is the only thing that helps one to bear the limitation." In a *Winona Republican–Herald* article in 1949, the writer said that Miss Keller served as gardener to her beautiful rose garden and knew every rose by its name from the different aromas and the feel of their petals.

39 George Sparth, "Helen Keller Cheerful but Admits Missing Joys of Family Life," *The Minneapolis Sunday Tribune,* October 10, 1937.

40 "Helen Keller Visits Deaf at Rochester," *The Minneapolis Tribune,* October 8, 1938.

41 Miss Keller was also in Minnesota in 1943, 1945, and 1948, so it is possible that visit Binky recalled was in 1943 rather than 1938.

42 Elsa Mannheimer (1881–1972) also made pieces for Mrs. James Ward (Narcissa) Thorne, whose rooms are on display at the Art Institute of Chicago.

43 The finished dollhouse was displayed in the upstairs sunroom at Eastcliff while Mrs. Brooks lived in the home. In 1974, it was in an exhibit at the Minnetonka Center of Arts and Education.

44 The L-shaped house is represented in a single wing by placing the dining room where the walnut den is in the real house and putting the walnut den in place of the garden room on the first floor. The boys' bedrooms are represented by furniture and various pieces arranged in the attic.

3. What's for Dinner?

1 Gustav Krollman was born in Vienna in 1888, studied at the Academy of Fine Arts in Vienna, and immigrated to the United States in 1923. He settled in St. Paul, which was the headquarters of the Northern Pacific and Great Northern railways, and is most known for his paintings for posters of scenic places along the railroad route. He was also known for magazine illustrations, portraits, and murals in public buildings.

2 Marney Brown Brooks, *Turning the Leaves: The Brooks Family Tree* (privately printed, 1995), 211.

3 Marney Brown Brooks, "Marney's Memoirs" (unpublished, 2006).

4 Conley Brooks, Marney Brown Brooks, Edward Brooks Jr., Virginia Dahleen Brooks, Markell Brooks, and Dwight F. Brooks, *Turning the Leaves: The Brooks Family Tree* (privately printed, 1995), 147.

5 *Minneapolis Tribune,* January 25, 1902.

6 Barbara Foote was interviewed by Conley and Marney Brooks on September 22, 1990, in Wausaukee, Wisconsin, as background for *Turning the Leaves.* Frannie Underwood was interviewed there on the same day.

7 I discovered the 1937 architectural drawing of the dining room expansion in the University's engineering archives. I had never heard or read of it elsewhere.

8 The table from the Pillsbury mansion has also been referred to as a Hemplewhite reproduction.

9 Barbara Flanagan, "Eastcliff: A look inside Yudof home," *Star Tribune,* July 5, 1999. Flanagan continued, "Three university presidents later, the Ken Keller administration planned and began work on the kitchen. (I thought the kitchen redo, which stirred up a world of trouble for Keller, was much needed.) And, finally, during the era of Nils and Pat Hasselmo, the kitchen was completed."

10 I searched for the 1968 architectural drawings, after finding the loan papers in an old file cabinet at Eastcliff. The drawings are in the University's engineering archives. The short paragraphs authorizing the drawings and the loan are in the archived minutes of the Board of Regents' meetings.

11 Elmer L. Andersen was interviewed at his home by Professor Clarke A. Chambers on October 2, 1995. The excerpt of the quotation is reproduced here as transcribed.

12 Barbara Foote was interviewed by Conley and Marney Brooks on September 22, 1990.

13 Margaret Morris, *Minneapolis Tribune,* October 13, 1974.

14 Sandra Magrath, "Notes from Eastcliff," *Alumni News,* September 1976.

15 "'U' president, wife agree on separation," *Minneapolis Tribune,* April 25, 1977.

16 Mary Jane Smetanka, "Magrath likes tension, pressure of 'U' presidency," *Minneapolis Tribune,* October 31, 1982.

17 Camille LeFevre, "This Old Eastcliff," *Minnesota, a Magazine of the University of Minnesota Alumni Association,* March–April 2000.

18 Conley Brooks, *Turning the Leaves,* 169.

19 Barbara Flanagan, "'U' Head's Family Is Settled," *Minneapolis Tribune,* February 14, 1961.

20 Margaret Crimmins, "First Family of 'U' Moves Into New Home," *St. Paul Pioneer Press,* February 19, 1961.

21 Invitations were mailed to 2,376 women—several times as many guests as could possibly fit.

22 Mae Ailene McBroom (1911–1998) was the third of ten children in her family and the only of the six sisters who seems to have never married. She worked her entire adult life as a professional cook. According to University records, Mae was hired on her forty-seventh birthday as "Cook—President's Residence—November 1, 1958 . . . at the [annual] rate of $3,000."

23 "Come Right on in . . . Meet the Wilsons," *Minneapolis Star,* January 20, 1960.

24 Marian Wilson was interviewed by Ann Pflaum on February 23, 2000.

25 *Minneapolis Tribune,* March 12, 1961.

26 Ann Burckhardt, "Garden Party," *Minneapolis Star,* May 30, 1973.

27 William Swanson, "Eastcliff: Diane and C. Peter Magrath Put Their Stamp on the University's Presidential Mansion," *Twin Cities,* May 1980.

28 Paul Dienhart, "The Public Education of Kenneth Keller," *Minnesota,* special issue, 1985.

29 The Board of Regents currently meets eight times a year, after two meetings were eliminated due to the effort and expense involved in meeting preparation.

30 Josie Johnson's book *Hope in the Struggle* (Minneapolis: University of Minnesota Press, 2019) has a chapter titled "The Eastcliff Gathering" about

calming a storm between the Black and Jewish communities after Louis Farrakhan was invited to speak on campus after making anti-Semitic remarks, and Kwame Ture (formerly known as Stokely Carmichael) spoke on campus and said, "Zionism should be destroyed." Josie and President Hasselmo sought to bring together members of the Black and Jewish communities in "a warm and cozy environment with refreshments." Josie described the 1990 meeting: "The winter sun streamed through the large windows of the beautiful living room as though blessing this event, the first ever meeting of the University of Minnesota's Black and Jewish communities. And as daylight turned to dusk, the lively discussion we had hoped for took place."

31 Hy Berman with Jay Weiner, *Professor Berman* (Minneapolis: University of Minnesota Press, 2019), 135.

32 Georgia's daughter, Antigoni, has taken over most of the catering now, and she is also wonderful.

33 *What Should I Be When I Grow Up? by Goldy Gopher* was published by Goldy's Locker Room and is available through its stores and online. Author proceeds go to the Goldy Scholarship fund.

34 Paul Dienhart, "Not So Private Lives," *Minnesota,* special issue, 1985.

35 The Eastcliff renovation is included in Stanford Lehmberg and Ann Pflaum, *The University of Minnesota 1945–2000* (Minneapolis: University of Minnesota Press, 2001). I skimmed that book, but I chose to use original source materials and interviews from the University's digital conservancy for this chapter. After I compiled my research, I read chapter 4 in the Lehmberg and Pflaum book more carefully and saw that I used many of the same quotations they had used. I searched for quotations from David Lebedoff, and I used their book as a source for his quotation, as that interview is locked with permission-only access in the digital conservancy.

36 Kenneth Keller was interviewed by Clarke A. Chambers on December 1, 3, and 8, 1997, on the University of Minnesota campus.

37 Ingrid Sundstrom, "University's Eastcliff getting put back into shape for official and family roles," *Minneapolis Star and Tribune,* November 9, 1985.

38 Ken recalled, regarding the estimated cost and approvals: "It came to the [Board of Regents] Physical Plant Committee meeting. Irv Goldfine chaired that committee and Irv accepted the information for information and said, 'I don't think there's any reason to vote on this because it's not state money,' or this or that. 'We just need to be informed about it. Keep us informed as the work goes along.' He reported that to the board the next day. Naive that

I was, I didn't think much about it and I said, 'It's all reported. We've had the media through. We've got the bids. Everybody knows the amount. Here it is. Irv said there's no need for a board vote on this.' We went merrily on our way and, of course, the work didn't get done, and we moved in, and the work continued for a full three years." (Keller interviewed by Clarke A. Chambers on December 1, 3, and 8, 1997.)

39 Kenneth Keller was interviewed by Clarke A. Chambers on October 23, 1995, and November 6, 1995, on the University of Minnesota campus.

40 As reported in "Six Weeks That Toppled a President," by Paul Dienhart in the *University of Minnesota UPDATE,* April 1988.

41 Mark Fischenich, "Eastcliff valued at about half the renovation cost," *Minnesota Daily,* February 4, 1988.

42 Doug Grow, "Ken Keller's kitchen: Focus mainly on status at remodeled Eastcliff," *Minneapolis Star Tribune,* February 7, 1988.

43 Marcia Fluer, "Déjà Vu All Over Again," *University of Minnesota UPDATE,* December 1989.

44 Kenneth Keller was interviewed by Clarke A. Chambers on December 1, 3, and 8, 1997, on the University of Minnesota campus.

45 "KELLER: 'Resignation not called for at this point,'" *Star Tribune,* February 29, 1988.

46 State legislative auditor Jim Nobles said, "Eastcliff really opened the door for this office to be more involved at the University." He went on to detail how he and his staff, as the article's author wrote, "keep busy identifying challenging problems for University administrators to resolve." Chuck Benda, "A Nobles Tradition," *Minnesota Alumni* magazine, May–June 1994.

47 The resolutions up for vote on March 11 included that the internal auditing division of the University would report directly to the Board of Regents; a committee would conduct a general management review of the University; a management study of the University's physical plant operations would be conducted; a committee would consider the concept of the establishment of an independent advisory commission that would make recommendations to the Board of Regents regarding the mission, financial support, maintenance, and renovation of Eastcliff; and, except where legally obligated or where the work has already been paid for, renovations of Eastcliff would cease until further action by the Board of Regents.

48 Ann Pflaum was interviewed by Clarke A. Chambers on August 16, 1995.

49 Speaking about this ten years later, Ken Keller said, "We moved in and things began to move more and more slowly and we discovered things that hadn't been anticipated, like the eleven coats of lead paint on the outside of the house that we needed to remove. We knew that was going to be expensive. I remember going to Dave Roe and saying, 'Dave, this is really expensive stuff and we can't afford to pay union painters thirty-five dollars an hour to scrape this paint off,' which, then, had to be shipped to Illinois in special casks because it was toxic. 'Couldn't we use students, Dave,' I said. 'Couldn't we hire students over the summer to do this?' He would have none of that. He didn't want that. He said, 'However, I'll arrange for the unions to do this for free.' It was a wonderful offer about which nothing was ever done. So, it didn't happen and we wound up scraping the paint and that, actually, was about $110,000 to remove the paint from the outside of the house." (Kenneth H. Keller was interviewed by Clarke A. Chambers on December 1, 3, and 8, 1997.)

50 Kenneth Keller was interviewed by Clarke A. Chambers on December 1, 3, and 8, 1997, on the University of Minnesota campus.

51 Ken Keller served as director of SAIS Europe in Bologna, Italy, from 2006 until 2014. Immediately after his resignation, Ken was offered a position working out of Princeton University as a consultant to the Council of Foreign Relations in New York. He returned to the Department of Chemical Engineering at the University of Minnesota for the spring semester in 1990 and was elected to the National Academy of Engineering in 2002.

52 Paul Dienhart, "48 Hours: Hasselmo presidency gets off to a flying start," *University of Minnesota UPDATE*, January February 1989.

According to what Nils Hasselmo learned later as president, some Regents, in opposition to their ethical responsibilities, were working against the best interest of the University. Nils said, "It, clearly, was a very complicated situation where some Regents were talking to the legislature and were really kind of setting legislators up to accuse the university of various things. I think that was a very unfortunate situation."

Nils also said, "Ken was treated grossly unfairly and that's what happened at Eastcliff. Yes, there probably were some mistakes but they were more a matter of the inadequacies of the university's financial accounting system. I suffer from that, too. Certainly, the accusation that there was a slush fund was grossly unfair because what had happened with Ken and David Lilly—bless him—had changed the university's investment strategy. Instead of sitting there and earning practically no interest, they had invested university funds much more aggressively and they had made significant monies on interest from those funds. They reported it to the Board of Regents but, of course, it was hidden in reports that nobody knew about. The Board of Regents, clearly, was not aware of the fact that these rather large amounts had accumulated in interest income and that they were being allocated by the president and the vice-presidents for very good strategic purposes.

"I still heard complaints at the time I was leaving as president that Physical Plant was not performing well. We have this army of janitors who go and, presumably, clean the place and it's very hard, apparently, to ride herd on the quality of what they do. Some do an excellent job and others, apparently, do not."

(Nils Hasselmo was interviewed by Clark A. Chambers on March 16, 18, and 19, 1998 in Tucson, Arizona.)

53 Vicki Stavig, "Eastcliff Revisited," *Minnesota, a University of Minnesota Alumni Association Publication*, July–August 1994.

54 Chuck Haga, "Lavish wasn't the word for what the public saw at Eastcliff," *Star Tribune*, September 20, 1989.

55 Mary Jane Smetanka, "Summer brings long overdue overhaul to 'U' mansion," *Star Tribune*, June 17, 1997.

56 Garrett Weber, "Keeping tabs on expenses at Eastcliff," *Minnesota Daily*, January 14, 1992.

57 Gregor W. Pinney, "Repairs, upgrades made at residence of 'U' president," *Star Tribune*, January 2, 1996.

58 Josh Linehan, "A vacant mansion," *Minnesota Daily*, October 24, 2002.

59 Mary Jane Smetanka, "They're spiffing up Eastcliff," *Star Tribune*, February 25, 2006.

60 Josh Verges, "UMN president's St. Paul mansion could get $970,000 upgrade," *Pioneer Press*, December 13, 2018.

61 Austin Macalus, "University's presidential residence to get $970,000 in repairs," *Minnesota Daily*, April 11, 2019.

62 Kenneth Keller was interviewed by Professor Clarke A. Chambers on December 1, 3, and 8, 1997.

63 Diane Magrath and C. Peter Magrath, "The Dear Peter, Dear Diane Letters," *AGB Reports* (Association of Governing Boards), March/April 1985.

64 We have a rule in our partners' council meetings: what is said here, stays here. We speak freely. I hesitated to share this second conversation, but I have left out all but the basic details, so I feel confident

no one can identify the person. Here's another story for those special people who read footnotes: My husband was honored to work for the University of Minnesota. He accepted the salary and the standard contract that the Board of Regents offered him. After discussions at partners' meetings, I heard what I thought was an apocryphal story and asked for one change to his contract: three months' notice to move out of Eastcliff. I heard, and later confirmed the story to be true, that a university president died in office. At his funeral, a member of the university's governing board asked the grieving widow how soon she could move out of the official residence, with the implication that it should be *very soon*.

[65] Karli Jo Webber, "Mrs. Wilson Proves . . . Wife's Smile Is Husband's Asset," *Minnesota Daily*, January 15, 1960.

[66] Ken Keller described Bonita's work, ten years later: "She continued her job in the university attorney's office but, in fact, had to pay a rather heavy price for all of that because there was no way to do what she was called on to do and work full time in the attorney's office. What she did was reduce her appointment to a half time appointment. But, of course, there's no way to do a half time job in the attorney's office; so, she was spending almost full time there but had cautiously sort of arranged it so that she was above reproach in what she was doing. She did take on not just the role of hostess but the role of president's spouse and some speaking in the things that she was interested in. The center of her professional life remained her legal career." (Kenneth H. Keller was interviewed by Clarke A. Chambers on December 1, 3, and 8, 1997.)

[67] With the mean age of male partners (62.8) being significantly higher than that of female partners (57.9), and fourteen percent of males being over seventy, it is likely many of the unemployed males were retired.

[68] Thirty-two percent reported being satisfied, thirty-six percent very satisfied, and sixteen percent extremely satisfied.

[69] Paul Venable Turner, *Campus: An American Planning Tradition* (Cambridge, Mass.: MIT Press, 1984).

4. Families Live Here

[1] Some Minnesotans took umbrage at this otherwise excellent play in that it did not give Hubert H. Humphrey proper respect and credit for his role in the passage of the 1964 Civil Rights Act.

[2] Grant Moos, "Before the renovation: when Eastcliff got that lived-in look," *Rochester Post-Bulletin, Minneapolis Star Tribune,* March 17, 1988.

[3] Marney Brown Brooks, *Turning the Leaves: The Brooks Family Tree* (privately printed, 1995), 213.

[4] The chairs (probably four) were listed at approximately $880, with an additional expense of $72.50. They would have been very nice chairs: $952.50 would be the equivalent of more than $16,000 in 2020.

[5] Edward Brooks Jr., *Turning the Leaves: The Brooks Family Tree* (privately printed, 1995), 147.

[6] There is a mid-1930s photograph of the Brooks children in costume. Marney wrote a description of the photo in 2007. Conley is dressed in black shirt with silk kerchief, green knickers and matching socks, and a brimmed hat with a feather. This costume was purchased in Italy. Ted is wearing a double-breasted suit. Binky is wearing an embroidered costume, likely from Mauretania. Dwight, only about seven years old, is dressed as a cowboy. The many costumes. from Austria, Egypt, Greece, Holland, Italy, Japan, Madeira, and others, were still (in 2007) in a closet in the Conley and Marney's basement.

[7] Tracy told me, as an example of Helen Grant's personality, that she had been gravely ill and told the family that either she was going to live or she would have to decide whom to haunt first.

[8] Dorothy Harmon, "On the Home Front," *Litchfield Independent Review,* week of October 23, 1972.

[9] While studying many Eastcliff architectural drawings in the engineering records office, I discovered that the installation of the barn wood wasn't as "do-it-yourself" as it had been portrayed. University plant services drew plans for the installation of hand-split fieldstone on the fireplace wall in October 1967. They drew plans for the installation of the wood paneling in March 1968 and drew revised plans in August 1968. Besides the paneling, there were benches along the walls (which would have held the "food troughs" Tracy described).

[10] Elmer L. Andersen was interviewed by Clarke Chambers on October 2, 1995.

[11] Minnesota's college bowl team won three national championships for the University in the 1980s.

[12] Margaret Morris, *The Minneapolis Tribune*, December 10, 1972.

[13] The UMWC began as the Faculty Women's Club more than one hundred years ago as a group for faculty wives. The organization has since expanded its membership to anyone with an interest in the

University. The group cohosted the new faculty receptions at Eastcliff for several years.

[14] Margaret Morris, "About People," *The Minneapolis Tribune,* December 17, 1969.

[15] Margaret Morris, *The Minneapolis Tribune,* December 13, 1972.

[16] Robert Burgett is the senior vice president of development at the University of Minnesota Foundation. We were also traveling with Molly Hayes from the president's office and Tim Wolf, director of international development (a great team), and we visited Guangzhou, Shenzhen, Hong Kong, Shanghai, and Beijing.

[17] While the tree on the stair landing was spectacular, Kristia and Bethany agreed that they missed the first-floor tree, and they placed a smaller, artificial tree in the corner of the dining room. I decorated that one with ornaments from all the campuses— Crookston, Duluth, Morris, Rochester, and Twin Cities—and Gopher ornaments. I had purchased football trophy ornaments only when we won those trophy games. I had Floyd the Pig (from the Minnesota–Iowa rivalry) and the Little Brown Jug (from Minnesota–Michigan competition). While we were in Hong Kong, the Gophers beat Wisconsin for Paul Bunyon's Axe, so I completed my ornament set.

[18] See Marlow Brooks's story about Eastcliff at the end of this book.

[19] No mention was made in the newspaper about the men's apparel, but it was noted that the groom's brother was six feet, four inches tall and played center on the Harvard basketball team.

[20] The gown in the wedding photograph of Connie Wilson Bennion was described as (and looks like) Bruges lace. The *Minneapolis Tribune* description of the same gown when Mary Ann wore it said it was Swedish lace. Swedish lace looks nothing like Bruges lace. The description of the "pale-pink floor-length" gowns the bridesmaids wore seems accurate, and lovely.

[21] I wasn't able to find information about the reception, but I learned that Mary Ann and John both received their undergraduate degrees from the University of Minnesota, where they likely met. They were both students at Stanford University when they married. She was studying for a master's in education, and he was in medical school. He later had a distinguished career at the Fred Hutchinson Cancer Research Center in Seattle. John and Mary Ann had three children, and she died of cancer, much too young, in 1993.

[22] William Swanson, "Eastcliff: Diane and C. Peter Magrath Put Their Stamp on the University's Presidential Mansion," *Twin Cities,* May 1980.

[23] Once, after an event, Eastcliff facilities manager Jim Bossert, to his discomfort, found a pair of Spanx tights under a coat rack in the walnut den. I imagine the owner removed them before a second visit to the buffet table.

[24] Tracy, Kathy, and Grant Moos all remembered Mrs. Brinkerhoff fondly, more than fifty years later. I considered anonymizing her name to "Mrs. B," but as she is without fault and was remembered so kindly, I have left her name intact.

5. The Private Life Upstairs

[1] They're married and interviewed us couple-to-couple.

[2] The only other time we invited the news media into Eastcliff was at the request of the family of Ken Brown. Ken was nearing the end of a terminal battle with ALS in March 2017 and didn't expect to live long enough to see his son, Collin, graduate from the University. The president's office (and particularly Laura Wegscheid) determined that the best wheelchair-accessible place to have an early ceremony for Collin would be in the Eastcliff living room. Ken and his wife, Patti, requested that members of the media be allowed to attend to raise awareness for ALS. It was a lovely event, and Ken lived long enough to see Collin's second, "real" graduation in May.

[3] *Ashes of roses* was a Victorian name for a shade of gray with a pinkish tint. Inexplicably, we had the room painted in a gray with a pinkish tint before we moved in. When the room next needed painting,

Joan Gabel chose "agreeable gray"—a shade of gray that seems to go agreeably with everything.

[4] Two more of Markell Brooks's fans were included in that exhibition, a white ostrich plume fan with diamond monogram that had belonged to Dowager Queen Mary, and a nineteenth-century valentine fan.

[5] Diane's description included more on the location of the drawer. I left that out in case a current or future resident finds and uses the hiding place. It must be well-hidden, as I never found it.

[6] Eastcliff is near mile marker twenty-one of the Twin Cities Marathon, not long before the slow climb up Summit Avenue, at a place where encouragement is needed. I was delighted to stand in front of my home with my nephew Clay and watch my brother, John Fults, run past on his way to a time that qualified

him for the Boston Marathon. (When *I* tried running along the river, I tripped over one of our dogs and ended up in an orthopedic boot for eight weeks. I'm better suited to walking.)

7 Edith D. Williams, "The Home of the Month," *Amateur Golfer and Sportsman,* November 1931. The chaise, or lounge, with its salmon-colored chintz, is faithfully reproduced in the dollhouse. It is the one piece that appears out of scale, so I asked Conley Brooks Jr. about it. He confirmed that it is an oversized piece of furniture, and that it is still owned by the family.

8 The rest of the house was air conditioned in 1985.

9 The clear implication here is that the phone always rang for the young people in the home, which may have been typically true. In this case, however, the reporter was present for a call for the cook, Mae MacBroom.

10 Diane Skomars Magrath, "Magraths are job and marriage partners," *St. Paul Sunday Pioneer Press,* November 18, 1979.

11 Diane Magrath and C. Peter Magrath, "The Dear Peter, Dear Diane Letters," *AGB Reports* (Association of Governing Boards), March/April 1985.

12 Jodi Compton and Max Rust, "Union to protest Eastcliff renovation," *Minneapolis Star Tribune,* July 11, 1997.

13 Liz Kohman, "Indians take telescope protest to U president's home turf," *St. Paul Pioneer Press,* January 24, 2002.

14 *The Native American Press/The Ojibwe News,* October 4, 2002. A front-page photograph showed a large banner hanging from a KSTP television tower on September 25, 2002, in protest of Hubbard Broadcasting donating five million dollars to buy time on the large binocular telescope at Arizona's Mount Graham International Observatory. The banner read "U of M / Hubbard—Mount Graham is sacred—No $ for desecration." At the time, Interim President Bruininks was recommending that the University buy time on the telescope. Opponents protested that Mount Graham, in Arizona's Pinaleño Mountains, was sacred to the tribes of the Western Apache nation, and the telescope would harm the environment of the Mount Graham red squirrel. Proponents argued that the telescope would be built in 2004 with or without the University's benefitting from the facility, and the telescope offered research opportunities not available anywhere else. The telescope was authorized by Congress in 1988. The San Carlos Apache Tribe passed a resolution in 1991 stating that Mount Graham is sacred to them. Ongoing monitoring has found that the squirrel population

rises and falls in relation to the conifer seed crop but seems unaffected by the telescope or telescope infrastructure.

15 A similar situation occurred during the Magrath administration. A man tried to force his way into Eastcliff and was thwarted by housekeeper Mae McBroom. He then took out a knife and slashed two screen doors.

16 An outstanding example of this was the work of Officer Kevin Randolph to support student Abby Honold, who experienced a horrific assault and is one of our personal heroes. Officer Randolph learned that Minneapolis police (at that time, at least) didn't work to prosecute rapists unless there were three or more known victims. Officer Randolph found and supported other women, two of whom agreed to go on record, and helped bring a violent serial rapist to justice. Abby Honold and Kevin Randolph are both heroes.

17 In the first few days, the community, our local elected officials, and the local news media were making clear distinctions between the peaceful protesters (the great majority, who care about justice) and the opportunists and rioters (who care about themselves or are intent on harm).

18 While the horrific, yet true, previous note about rapists wasn't common knowledge, there were multiple cell phone robberies that actually turned out to be orchestrated by a crime ring, sending cell phones to China. While the crimes occurred off-campus in Dinkytown, campus police broke the case. Campus police also used "find my computer" to track computer thieves when Minneapolis police were unavailable.

19 Audrey Kennedy, "Students stage 'die-in' at University of Minnesota police headquarters," *Minnesota Daily,* June 16, 2020.

20 Nat Jacobwith, "Episode 59: The George Floyd Protests: The history of police brutality in the Twin Cities," *Minnesota Daily,* "In the Know" audio story, June 11, 2020. The previous Wednesday, President Gabel announced that she was canceling contracts with the Minneapolis Police Department.

21 This was during a week when some peaceful protests evolved into violence and burned buildings. There was reason to feel anxious. The "safety" exchange reminded me of a student a few years earlier who told me she wanted a prominent campus visitor, with differing political beliefs from her own, banned from campus because some in the community might not feel safe. She went on to exclaim that this potential visitor should not feel safe anywhere, with no apparent recognition of her hypocrisy.

22 Mark A. Cohen, "Online Exclusive: Minnesota Law Students Flock to Aid George Floyd Protesters, Advocate for Change," *Minnesota Law,* Spring 2020.

23 All four hall bedrooms are sixteen feet, eight inches deep, with the first nineteen feet wide, the second two are thirteen feet, eight inches wide, and the fourth is twelve feet, eight inches wide. The third has a closet taking up a bit of space, so the second was a bit bigger than the third and fourth.

24 Paul Keller got his chemical engineering degree from his father's second alma mater. After receiving his liberal arts degree from Columbia, Ken Keller received a second undergraduate degree, his MSE, and his PhD in chemical engineering from Johns Hopkins University.

25 Markell Brooks, *Turning the Leaves: The Brooks Family Tree* (privately printed, 1995), 260.

26 I found a listing of the quartet playing at the University of Minnesota's Northrop Auditorium in February 1945, but Binky's remembered visit was likely later.

27 Conley Brooks, *Turning the Leaves,* 188–89.

28 Markell Brooks, *Turning the Leaves,* 159.

29 Ibid., 158.

30 Ibid., 279.

31 In 1966, Conley Brooks Sr. was awarded his delayed degree by completing fifteen credits at the University of Minnesota. He was eager to get his degree before his son, Conley Jr., graduated from Yale in 1968.

32 This Markell is Mrs. Brooks's granddaughter. Another Markell, Markell Kiefer, is Marlow's daughter (Mrs. Brooks's great granddaughter).

33 Edward Brooks Jr.'s letter to Mrs. G. A. Godfrey, director of the University of Minnesota Department of University Relations, March 25, 1972.

34 Bob Lundegaard, "Moos Is Friend of the Imprisoned—Including That Captive Coed," *Minneapolis Tribune,* July 3, 1967. The story title referred to when Malcolm Moos met Tracy Gager. She was supposed to be "campused"—restricted to campus for six weeks—for smoking in her room. She had to climb over rooftops to sneak back to her room after their dates.

35 I don't know the date of the puppies born in Grant's bedroom, but on Sunday, May 5, 1968, when Grant was twelve or thirteen, the Moos girls were in a *Minneapolis Tribune* newspaper photograph with golden retriever puppies. I mentioned a "male dog" that was wrestling with Grant, rather than calling him

by name, because Grant remembered the dog being Sandy, who was a later addition to the family. This date seems to correspond with the litter of puppies that would have been sired by Lord Boswell.

36 Brian Anderson, "Moos Addresses Dogs: Boning Up for Finals Provides Happy Tale," *Minneapolis Tribune,* June 21, 1968.

37 Sandra Magrath, "Notes from Eastcliff," *Alumni News,* September 1976.

38 Bonita Sindelir, article in the National Association of State Universities and Land-Grant Colleges (NASULGC) spouse/partner manual.

39 Diane Magrath and C. Peter Magrath, "The Dear Peter, Dear Diane Letters," *AGB Reports* (Association of Governing Boards), March/April 1985.

40 Mogadiscio is now more frequently referred to as Mogadishu.

41 Barbara Flanagan, "Their Vows Are Secret," *The Minneapolis Star,* March 21, 1978.

42 "Worth Noting," *The Minneapolis Star,* March 27, 1978.

43 "'U' President Magrath, Diane Skomars are married at St. Paul mansion," *Minneapolis Tribune,* March 26, 1978.

44 Later, Peter and Diane were able to combine University business in Morocco, Somalia, Kenya, Germany, and Finland with a four-day trip to Sápmi, in northern Scandinavia, formerly known as Lapland. This trip was described in a magazine article as their honeymoon, but Diane proofed these paragraphs and told me that the honeymoon's "secret location" that was mentioned in the press was Trinidad and Tobago.

45 Diane Fay Skomars, *Have I Taught You Everything I Know?* (Minneapolis: Mill City Press, 2014), 333.

46 Paul Dienhart, "48 Hours: Hasselmo presidency gets off to a flying start," *UPDATE for Alumni Faculty, and Staff,* January–February 1989.

47 The quotation, from Nils Hasselmo's interview with Clarke A. Clifford, March 16, 18, and 19, 1998, in Tucson, Arizona, is slightly paraphrased to correct for being used out of context. A postscript about the Hasselmo family: Nils retired from the University in 1997, then six months later was recruited to serve as president of the Association of American Universities (serving from 1998 to 2006). Patricia Hasselmo died of multiple myeloma in 2000. An Arizona obituary quoted the University of Arizona president who appointed Nils as provost saying that Pat "was one of the most admired and beloved people on campus," showing that those in Arizona

and in Minnesota had very similar opinions. In 2003, Nils married another wonderful woman, Ann Die, who is President Emerita of Hendrix College. The two former presidents lived together happily until Nils's death in 2019. Nils had expressed a wish for a service with jazz and martinis at the University of Minnesota. Eric and I were grateful that the family coordinated with us on a date when we could be in town and could have the entire family back at Eastcliff for dinner the night before the service. Besides the little swimmers and two next grandchildren listed above, Anna and Jim's children, Madeline and Eric, were there. They were then both students at the University, which partially makes up for Anna not being an official Gopher. Madeline graduated in May 2020 during the virtual celebrations due to coronavirus social distancing. She and her roommates made their own wonderful memories, walking across their Dinkytown living room in caps and gowns, presenting diplomas, and shaking hands. Anna continues to call Eastcliff "my house."

[48] Searching through old newspapers (digitally, thank goodness), I found 7,259 matches for Clark Gable in Minnesota between 1921 and 1954. Skimming through them I discovered that Clark Gable was frequently in Minnesota, albeit on the silver screen.

[49] Ruth Biery, "'I'm Not So Sure,' Says Clark Gable," *Photoplay* magazine, January 1932.

[50] Shevlin-Hixon also began in Minnesota, and the Shevlin family has interesting connections to the University of Minnesota. Thomas Henry Shevlin (1852–1912) began working for a lumber company at age fifteen, worked his way up, and moved to Minnesota in 1886 to establish North Star Lumber. He went into business with banker Frank Hixon to form Shevlin-Hixon in 1896. In 1906, Shevlin donated $60,000 to the University for construction of a new building on the former site of Old Main. (Old Main was destroyed by fire in 1904.) The building is named Alice Shevlin Hall, in honor of his wife, the former Alice A. Hall. (They wisely chose not to name the building Alice Hall Shevlin Hall.) Tom and Alice had three children: Thomas Leonard, Florence Hall, and Helen Alice. The younger Tom Shevlin was an exceptional athlete and three-time All-American as a Yale football player. While working as a millionaire lumberman, he was an assistant coach for the Golden Gophers football team where he developed the "Minnesota shift." His success in Minnesota caused his alma mater to recruit him as assistant coach in 1910. While coaching at Yale in 1915, he caught a cold that led to pneumonia, and he died that year at age thirty-two. Florence and her husband, David Tenney, were parents to three children, including Alice McNair Tenney Mitchell. Alice was an impressionist artist. Four of her works, all from the late 1930s, are in the collection of the Metropolitan Museum of Art in New York. We displayed one of her paintings from the University art collection at Eastcliff. Titled *Halloween*, it depicted her toddler son dressed as a little witch. That son, Robert Mitchell, became a civic leader, attorney, and mayor of Medina, Minnesota. Florence and David's daughters are Sally Tenney Lebedoff (her husband is triplet brother to former University Board of Regents chair David Lebedoff) and Ann Tenney Pflaum (Ann is University historian). I found no direct connection of Helen Tenney Beckwith McKnight to the University or Eastcliff, perhaps proving that not absolutely everyone in Minnesota connects to the University, but perhaps I just didn't find the connection.

[51] Frannie Underwood was interviewed by Conley and Marney Brooks on September 22, 1990.

[52] "Minneapolis Society Returns North After Winter Travels," *The Minneapolis Star*, March 28, 1925.

[53] "Mr., Mrs. Brooks to Visit Vancouver," *The Minneapolis Star*, April 17, 1933.

[54] *The Minneapolis Star*, March 20, 1934.

[55] Miss Anna Bell Thomas was the first female principal of Minneapolis Central High School, serving in that role from 1944 to 1946.

[56] I debated about how to present the UFO information. First, Binky stated that Dwight was the only one in the family who had seen a UFO. My worldview is that it is unusual for a family member to have seen a UFO, rather than unusual that *only one* member has had the experience. That is my limitation, not hers. Second, if I believe Binky, and I certainly do, am I wrong to share about the UFO since it was (or is) classified? It was well over sixty years ago, which seems long enough. On April 27, 2020, five years after I heard the story from Binky, the U.S. Pentagon released videos, from 2004 and 2015, of unidentified flying objects that seem to defy the laws of physics. Senator Harry Reid tweeted that "I'm glad the Pentagon is finally releasing the footage, but it only scratches the surface of research and material available." The news report said the U.S. government had been looking into "unidentified aerial phenomena since at least the 1950s" (*New York Times*, April 29, 2020). Dwight's sighting would have been in the 1950s. One of Dwight's "side hustles" as an adult was designing rubberized floor mats. One of them said "Welcome UFOs and crews."

[57] A brief shout out here to Laura Wegscheid and her daughter, Mikaela, who volunteered every single year.

[58] Harry's daughter Peggy was Binky's first friend, when they were three and four years old.

6. Go Outside to Play—and Party

[1] Conley Brooks, Marney Brown Brooks, Edward Brooks Jr., Virginia Dahleen Brooks, Markell Brooks, and Dwight F. Brooks, *Turning the Leaves: The Brooks Family Tree* (privately printed, 1995), 147.

[2] Marney Brown Brooks, *Turning the Leaves*, 210.

[3] Ibid., 211.

[4] Ibid., 212–13.

[5] The Eastcliff Technical Advisory Committee minutes of December 14, 1989, stated, "The live-in requirement for a caretaker is no longer necessary. Neil Dylla will continue in the caretaker position. He will vacate the carriage house by March 31, 1990. . . . There are currently no plans for the use of the apartment."

[6] In 1994, the Eastcliff Technical Advisory Committee asked for a plan to restore the carriage house. At the 1996 Friends of Eastcliff Garden Party, a new plan was unveiled to restore guest quarters for visiting scholars, seeking the support of donations. In 2001, the project was completed as an exterior restoration, without living space.

[7] Pat Hasselmo clearly appreciated the joke. In an article about Pat after her passing in 2001, her friend and chair of the University of Minnesota Board of Regents, Patricia Spence, was quoted as telling the rest of the story: "Later the cow was returned to its dairy barn. When about two hundred guests showed up for a garden party at Eastcliff a few days later, the cow reappeared. Without anyone's knowledge, Patricia Hasselmo had arranged for it to be grazing in the front yard before the party started." Mike Meyers, "Patricia Hasselmo, wife of former 'U' president, dies," *Star Tribune*, January 1, 2001.

[8] July 3, 1989, letter from Nils Hasselmo to Mel George, president of St. Olaf College, thanking him for service on the first Regent Candidate Advisory Council.

[9] During the 1980s terrace renovation, brick corners were also added at the end of the walkways. A chain-link fence in front of the swimming pool was removed and an arbor and new gate leading into the pool were added. A pergola was added over the full length of the walkway in front of the pool. Flagstones from the original terrace were used to repair the pool terrace and to create a walkway across the lawn toward the tennis court.

[10] The framed mirrors were made during the Bruininks administration and given to Brooks family members and each presidential family who lived at Eastcliff.

For University of Minnesota presidents seventeen through twenty-two, there is one for you in the attic.

[11] The *Summer Waltz* rose is a University of Minnesota introduction by Kathy Zuzek. It was still called Rosa 66 when the roses were planted at Eastcliff. These pink rose bushes with double blooms are winter hardy as well as blackspot tolerant, as required of University roses. They're also mildly fragrant and bloom all season long, from May until the blossoms are picturesquely covered with snow. More summer waltz roses are planted in the front yard, in memory of Barbara Bentson.

[12] When we first moved to Eastcliff, I had read about Professor Marla Spivak's research with honeybees and her efforts to solve colony collapse disorder. I hoped to meet Marla, and to keep a hive at Eastcliff to highlight her work. Although I was not allowed to keep bees at Eastcliff, Marla and I became good friends. My bees lived in her backyard, near enough to Eastcliff that I knew the bees visited regularly.

[13] I don't have reliable lists for all the Friends of Eastcliff board members. I apologize to all those whom I am leaving out, but here is a partial list of the community members who have served on the committee: Karen Bachman, Ruth Bachman, Kathy Beenan, Linda Berg, Cecilia Bolman, Conley Brooks Jr., Virginia "Ginny" Brooks, Gail Buuck, Vickie Courtney, Regent Emerita Elizabeth "Peggy" Craig, Dick Engebretson, Laurie Ward Gardner, Catherine "Cay" Shea Hellervick, Andrea Hjelm, Zehra Avsar Keye, Katherine "Kaye" Lillehei, Libby Lincoln, Ed Lindell, Nancy Lindahl, Lorraine Malkerson, Lois Maturi, Tom Meyer, Linda Mona, Susan Morrison, Susan Muscoplat, Sue Nelson, Patricia Newton, Peter Olin, Jevne Pennock, Linda Peterson Perlman, Kathleen Ridder, George Robb, Leanna Rogers, Nancy Rosenberg, Regent Emeritus Stanley Sahlstrom, Hugh Schilling, Jeff Sturkey, Jolee Suskovic, Ray Tarleton, and Joyce Wascoe. The committee has been chaired by Regent Patricia Spence, Regent Dave Metzen, Regent Dallas Bohnsack, and Regent Patty Simmons. Lyndel King, director of the University's art museum and chair of the Eastcliff Technical Advisory Committee from its beginning until her retirement in 2020, also served on the Friends committee as have representatives from the University of Minnesota Foundation and the president's office, as well as Patricia Hasselmo, Judy Yudof, Susan Hagstrum, and me.

[14] My understanding of the garden party was that it was primarily to thank donors. I didn't know what the previous programs were like until I moved out of Eastcliff and read the old files.

[15] Elizabeth Patty is associate vice president for development for children's health at the University of Minnesota Foundation.

[16] Edward Brooks Jr.'s letter to Mrs. G. A. Godfrey, director of the University of Minnesota Department of University Relations, March 25, 1972.

[17] Conley and Ted relayed this story in the 1998 interview with Judy Yudof.

[18] Edward Brooks Jr., *Turning the Leaves*, 227.

[19] Howard Albert "Howie" Wilcox was born on November 9, 1920 (less than a year older than Conley, two years older than Ted), studied at the University of Minnesota, and met his wife, Evelyn "Evie," in Minneapolis. While working as a teaching fellow at Harvard, he was recruited to work on the Manhattan Project at Los Alamos. Evie Wilcox also worked at Los Alamos as a machinist. I don't know if this is the Howie Wilcox who as a young boy won the toboggan slide races each year at Eastcliff, but that is a feat that fits a budding physicist. Physicist Howard A. Wilcox went with Enrico Fermi to the University of Chicago after the war. After earning his PhD in nuclear physics, he taught at the University of California, Berkeley. While searching to find a link from this professor to the Eastcliff toboggan slide (which I failed to do), I discovered that, in 1975, Howard A. Wilcox wrote a book titled *Hothouse Earth* that warned of a global heat disaster if humans didn't make changes to avoid climate change.

[20] Sandra Magrath, "Notes from Eastcliff," *Alumni News*, September 1976.

[21] I assume the red raspberries are the Latham variety, developed at the University. There are also golden raspberry plants that appear to be Fallgold or Honeyqueen.

[22] Since the Eastcliff trees were planted, the University has introduced True North™, which is a male Kentucky coffee tree with the benefit of having no pods to pick up.

[23] Vicki Stavig, "Eastcliff Revisited," *Minnesota* magazine, July/August 1994.

[24] Edith D. Williams, "The Home of the Month," *The Amateur Golfer and Sportsman*, November 1931.

[25] Brooks family members were interviewed by Judy Yudof in 1998.

[26] Frannie Underwood was interviewed by Conley and Marney Brooks on September 22, 1990.

[27] Edward Brooks Jr.'s letter to Mrs. G. A. Godfrey, director of the University of Minnesota Department of University Relations, March 25, 1972.

[28] Conley Brooks, Marney Brown Brooks, Edward Brooks Jr., Virginia Dahleen Brooks, Markell Brooks, and Dwight F. Brooks, *Turning the Leaves*, 148–49.

[29] Brooks family members were interviewed by Judy Yudof in 1998.

[30] Conley Brooks, Marney Brown Brooks, Edward Brooks Jr., Virginia Dahleen Brooks, Markell Brooks, and Dwight F. Brooks, *Turning the Leaves*, 150.

[31] Brooks family members were interviewed by Judy Yudof in 1998. When Binky met her second husband, she discovered that, although the two of them had never met before, his parents had played tennis with her parents at Eastcliff.

[32] The 1962 tennis court renovation cost $4,832.

[33] Sandra Magrath, "Notes from Eastcliff," *Alumni News*, September 1976.

[34] Ingrid Sundstrom, "University's Eastcliff getting put back into shape for official family roles," *Minneapolis Star and Tribune*, November 9, 1985.

[35] Lizzy was a finance major. The Carlson School is the University of Minnesota's school of management, named for Curtis Carlson.

[36] The romance developed chiefly in Park City, Utah. Sam had finished school and was teaching children to ski before beginning his "real" job with Mortenson Construction.

[37] A caveat: Markell's mother and Irish immigrant father had two weddings, a Protestant ceremony in Chicago and a Catholic ceremony in New York.

[38] The Edward and Markell Brooks archive at the Minnesota Historical Society includes the invitation to the twenty-fifth anniversary celebration of the Eastcliff gift, the Certificate of Appreciation, and a letter written by Conley to his siblings regarding the publicity over the 1980s renovation (that letter is reprinted at the end of this book). These items would have been added by the family after Mrs. Brooks passed away. Among the papers that seem to be directly from Markell are a stack of letters to her cousin, Helena Ann "Quail" Hawkins, in Washington State. Quail Hawkins was a bookseller in the 1920s and became a successful author of children's books in the 1940s. The Brooks archive also contains Markell's thin file folder labeled "Important Papers," which includes Markell's birth certificate, her marriage certificate, and love letters to her husband written on his birthdays in 1935, 1939, 1941, 1947, and 1954.

KAREN FULTS KALER has written two children's books about Eastcliff, *Rusty Goes Swimming* and *Weenie Meets Helen Keller*, as well as *What Should I Be When I Grow Up by Goldy Gopher* and *Born on Groundhog Day*. She coauthored "The Lives of Presidential Partners in Higher Education Institutions" and is now writing a novel of historical fiction. She had a career in communication design for thirty years before focusing on writing. She lived in Eastcliff from 2011 to 2019, while her husband, Dr. Eric W. Kaler, was president of the University of Minnesota.